The New York Times

PARENT'S GUIDE TO

THE BEST

B·O·O·K·S

FOR CHILDREN

EDEN ROSS LIPSON

Times
BOOKS

LIBRARY OF CONGRESS CATALOGING-IN-PUBLICATION DATA
Lipson, Eden Ross.
  The New York Times Parent's Guide to the Best Books for Children.
  Includes index.
    1. Bibliography—Best Books—Children's literature.   2. Children's
literature—Bibliography.   3. Reading—Parent participation.
I. New York Times.   II. Title.
Z1037.L724   1988   [PN1009.A1]   011'.62   87-40587
ISBN 0-8129-1649-2
ISBN 0-8129-1688-3 (pbk.)

Art Direction: Naomi Osnos
Design: Beth Tondreau Design
Designers: Beth Tondreau and Anne Scatto

Manufactured in the United States of America
9 8 7 6 5 4 3 2
First Edition

ERRATUM
The entry for *Mrs. Piggle-Wiggle* should appear within the
Early Reading section.

BECAUSE THE COPYRIGHT PAGE CANNOT ACCOMMODATE ALL
THE NECESSARY PERMISSIONS, THEY BEGIN HERE AND ARE
CONTINUED ON PAGE 419.

Grateful acknowledgment is made to the following for permission
to reprint previously published artwork:

Atheneum Publishers: Illustrations from *Alexander and the Terrible,
Horrible, No Good, Very Bad Day* by Judith Viorst, illustrated by Ray
Cruz. Illustrations copyright © 1972 Ray Cruz; illustration from
Cloudy with a Chance of Meatballs by Judi Barrett, illustrated by Ron
Barrett. Illustrations copyright © 1978 Ron Barrett; illustration

from *Nothing Ever Happens on My Block* by Ellen Raskin. Copyright
© 1966 Ellen Raskin.

Bradbury Press: Illustration from *Bea and Mr. Jones* by Amy
Schwartz. Copyright © 1982 by Amy Schwartz; illustrations from
The Girl Who Loved Wild Horses by Paul Goble. Copyright © 1978
by Paul Goble. Reprinted by permission of Bradbury Press, an
Affiliate of Macmillan, Inc.

This book is for
Delari, Tara, Margo, and Garth Johnston
and
for Neal, who made it possible.

ACKNOWLEDGMENTS

This would have been an impossible book to write alone.

My thanks go first to the children's publishing industry. From writers through editors, publishers, booksellers and librarians and parent buyers, it is an enclave completely dominated for generations by women. Scholars interested in the implications of gender might do well to observe the courtesy and collegiality that characterize it. I have received unfailingly generous support in preparing this book and I especially appreciate the last round of checking for bibliographic accuracy and the generous permission to use the wonderful illustrations on these pages. They speak for themselves.

Within the large and fascinating institution that is *The New York Times*, the *Book Review* is a tiny, rather protected enclave. It is also a rare catbird seat from which to watch the changing currents and themes in American life, which I have enjoyed enormously. I owe thanks to the three editors I have worked with: my friend John Leonard, who hired me; Harvey Shapiro, who twice feared I would have a baby in the office; and Mike Levitas, who thought, correctly, that I would have fun handling children's books. In addition I am grateful to the three remarkable deputy editors who have guided me through and over the years: Richard Locke, LeAnne Schreiber and especially Rebecca Pepper Sinkler. I will always miss Seymour Peck. I thank Andrea Stevens for her attention to the children's page, which goes far beyond copy editing.

[435]

If "friendship is a sheltering tree," as a little sampler says, then I am blessed to live in a lush and verdant glade. I feel the strength and support of many genuinely close friends, yet hardly see them. Fleeting phone calls, postcards, letters, a lunch. Life is rushing by and we are all over scheduled with work and families. But the bonds are strong and the support runs back and forth, and I am grateful for and thank each of them. We have helped each other over time, made life not just bearable, but fun.

Moving closer to home, I salute my father, Judge Milton Lipson, for his splendid taste in life's companions. Jean James keeps our household together. The bus gang families have been especially thoughtful about weekend play dates that allowed me to work at home.

Paul and Iris Brest gave us Notebook II, their nifty software before there was a book to think about. It served very well indeed. Alice Miller Bregman reviewed most of these entries in an earlier form, helped define categories, and made me laugh. The staff of Times Books coped with a much more complicated book than they imagined, and have made it look lovely. The errors, of course, are mine.

I can't thank Neal Johnston properly. He understood me, the project and the technology. He gave enormous amounts of his time, even when he realized I wasn't going to list Tarzan and the Hardy Boys. He says he only made my vision possible, but I know this book is as much his as mine.

[565]

CONTENTS

INTRODUCTION

This book is for the converted. It is for people who know and love particular children and want to help them to grow up loving to read. It is for adults who understand absolutely that reading is the key to the future, and also to the preservation of civilization, but who read for their own interests and entertainment as well, and fervently hope their children will, too.

One of the pleasures of being a parent, grandparent, godparent, or just an attentive adult to a child is helping to choose books. They make such wonderful gifts. Books cost more or less the same as toys, last much longer, and give endless pleasure. It is also true that "children can possess a book in a way they can never possess a video game, a TV show or a Darth Vader doll," as the artist-writer Chris Van Allsburg said in his 1982 Caldecott Medal speech. "A book comes alive when they read it. They give it life themselves by understanding it." And bring it back to life by remembering it. Just think of your own favorites. How many chills and terrors, tears and joys remain fresh? How many passages can you remember without hesitation?

Of course, as Katherine Paterson, a Newbery Medal winner and the author *The Bridge to Teribithia* and *The Great Gilly Hopkins* among other novels, has noted, "If we prescribe books as medicine, our children have a perfect right to refuse the nasty-tasting spoon."

So do choose books for birthdays, books for holidays, books for spring, books for school, books for Saturday, books for laughter,

[166]

books for tears, books to find out what happened next, or what if....
But in choosing or giving books, remember to try to find titles that
children can embrace, not suffer; seize, not shove away for the deferred
or postponed gratification of something to "grow into," like a winter
coat. Beverly Cleary, the author of the beloved Ramona series, remembers "When I was a child, a relative gave me *Ivanhoe* to grow into. I was
so disappointed that I still have not grown into it."

This selective guide to nearly a thousand of the best books for children published in the United States is organized to help you fend off
such disappointments and find books that will intrigue and delight
now. It is a mixture of classic, standard and distinguished new titles.
There are lots of books for lap-listening babies and toddlers, books to
read aloud with preschoolers, books for beginning readers to read to
themselves, books for middle school children to devour or dabble in as
they begin to sort out their lives, and, finally, a few books for teenagers
struggling toward maturity. Some are noble classics, some are just fun;
others may be helpful directly or indirectly as they address real issues
children face.

The purpose of the guide is to help you look for the next book to give
to your favorite child. But there are truths and tricks to choosing, and
as the sign in Manhattan's Argosy Book Store says, "So many books,
so little time." If we met, say, on a street corner, and you asked me to
help you find a book for your child, just the way people really do ask
me, I would quickly, like a teacher or librarian or a clerk in a good
bookstore, turn the question back to you. How old a child? A boy or a
girl? Where does he or she live? Siblings? Intact family? Special interests? A book to read aloud, or a book for a child to read to herself? I
would go on asking questions until I could make an educated guess of
an appropriate next title.

In the same way, I have organized the guide with its dozens of special
indexes so that you can tailor your choices in many different ways to
suit the tastes and interests of your child, and yours as well. The same
title may appear in many indexes because the ways we see and understand books changes as we ourselves grow. Karla Kuskin, the artist-
illustrator, said about a picture in one of her books showing a large
number of sleeping animals but "over there on the right, one cat with
one eye open...looking at a mouse. A two-and-a-half- or three-year-
old will spot that cat immediately, a six-year-old will take longer, a
twelve-year-old may miss it." And, she added, "At thirty-seven you
hardly have a chance."

As you browse through the listings and the indexes, or as illustrations catch your eye, I hope you will find many books you know, or
vaguely remember, especially if you are a "baby boomer" and came of
age since World War II, because more than 150 of them were published
before 1966. Once, on a summer holiday in Greece, my family took a
day trip by boat from Crete to the island of Santorini. Settled on deck at
sunset on the return trip, tired and relaxed, the youngest children were
"reading" their well-loved copy of *D'Aulaire's Book of Greek Myths*. A man
passed by and saw the book. He returned a few minutes later with one
of his friends and pointed excitedly, saying, "There, that's the book I
was telling you about, that's the one I had," and then turned to me,
saying with real urgency, "Where did you get it?"

For the purpose of this guide I have included only a few young adult
titles. Teenagers have many independent paths to finding their own
books. Young children are much more dependent on adult assistance.
Similarly, I have not included books published for adults that are now
considered children's titles and found on standard reading lists. It's
sometimes a very fine judgment, and today it is often a marketing, or
business, decision whether a book is published for adults or children.
But *Catcher in the Rye* and *To Kill a Mockingbird* were originally adult titles
and have become identified as children's books. (Indeed, the only
adults who read them today, it seems, are parents.) I have also confined
the guide to titles issued by children's trade book publishers because I
wanted them to be accessible to ordinary readers like your family and
mine who browse in ordinary bookstores and libraries.

THE GUIDE

Main titles are numbered consecutively and divided into groups
according to text level from wordless through picture books, story
books, early readers, middle and advanced readers. Remember
that wordless books are not necessarily for babies, and children can
pleasurably listen to stories that are much too hard for them to read
independently.

Within each section, books are listed alphabetically by title. Each
main title carries important bibliographic information—the author,
illustrator, publisher in hardcover and paperback, date of original
publication, and a notation of certain important prizes.

The John Newbery and Randolph Caldecott Medals, endowed by
Frederic G. Melcher and his family and administered by the Associa-

tion for Library Service to Children, are the best-known children's book prizes in the United States. Each year a changing committee of children's librarians gives a medal to the author of "the most distinguished contribution to American literature" (Newbery) and to the artist of the "most distinguished American picture book for children" (Caldecott) as well as a variable number of Honor Books. In bookstores and libraries you can recognize the winners because they usually have gold and silver stickers on the jackets.

Since 1952, *The New York Times* has annually asked a changing panel of judges to choose what they consider to be the best illustrated books of the year. They usually pick around ten, but the number varies. In recent years *The Times* has given each of the artists a certificate, and made sticker labels available to the publishers. Cheering for the home team, I have included mention of the New York Times Best Illustrated winners where appropriate.

I have tried to describe each book as succinctly as possible, in one paragraph that also refers to other books in the series, or related titles. The voice in the entries is mine. While there are no negative reviews, my tone, of course, reflects my own taste and enthusiasms. Since you need to establish a baseline of familiarity with any critic, and that is what I am here, why don't you begin by look up a half-dozen of your own favorite children's book titles. If you find the descriptions gibe with your memory and affection, then this is a book you can use to find other books, and I'll explain how. If the descriptions don't seem appropriate to you for any reason, this may not be the guide for you.

AVAILABILITY

Publishing in the United States, including the children's publishing industry, is in a state of flux, with titles going in and out of print at a great and unpredictable rate. Publishing houses are constantly being bought, sold, combined and recombined. In selecting the main titles in the guide I had the help of members of the Children's Book Council, the nonprofit trade organization of the children's publishing industry. I wrote and asked editors at each house to annotate their catalogues to show me which titles on their back list—i.e., previously published books—sold steadily and best, and which favorite titles I might have otherwise overlooked. I also talked to editors, writers, teachers, librarians, journalists. The selections reflect my judgment and opinions.

As I worked on the book, the titles I describe were all in print, which

[761]

means available for bookstores and libraries to order for you if they don't have them in stock. But it took me more than a year and a half to put the guide together, and I knew, just watching paperback editions cross my desk, that there had been substantial changes in who published what even in that short period of time. So, just before press time, we sent the final list of titles (not the comments) back to the publishers and asked them to help make sure the bibliographic information was as accurate as possible.

Paperback publishers change with some frequency and a few hardcover titles are now technically out of print, but they still should be available in libraries. The list is as sound as we could make it. Errors of omission, of course, are entirely my fault, and I would hope to correct them in subsequent editions.

THE INDEXES

The key to the indexes lies in the fact that each main title book (each title with its own entry) has a permanent record number. Every reference to the book carries the record number, and you can use it to go back into the guide and get bibliographic information for ordering, or refresh your memory of the book's description.

The first index includes every book mentioned in the guide, main titles, series titles, and related titles, using the record number of the main title as the reference number. The related titles are indicated by an asterisk. Then follow indexes by author and illustrator, which will help you find another book by someone whose work you have enjoyed. The books in the guide are listed by reading level, but a special set of indexes suggests listening levels and suitability for books for younger children. Some books almost ask to be read aloud, so there is also an index of those pleasurable titles.

The subject indexes cover a wide range of special interests. But a word of warning. Bibliotherapy—looking to a book to solve a problem—is a little like over-the-counter cold remedies: it may help, but it isn't likely to solve the problem alone. I have included some fine books about sibling rivalry, death, divorce, health issues; loving families working with children to address those problems integrate such books into their lives. The books just help. It's the family attention that really counts.

There are indexes of familiar categories—fairy tales, folk tales, bedtime tales—and some more specialized ones as well: books about minorities, science, music. In truth I don't think the indexes of boys' and girls' books are particularly controversial or troublesome in this day and age; if I had, I wouldn't have included them. Children are different. There are many books directed specifically to boy readers or girl readers, and my simple purpose is to encourage reading by appealing to children's enthusiasms. Those two categories are suggestions, not rules or orders. In the same spirit of pursuing or following up on expressed interests, I have included an index of titles included in the first five seasons of Reading Rainbow, the popular public television program about children's books.

Please take some time to play with the guide and the indexes. A reference book can be full of serendipitous surprises if you let it fall open to random pages. If you are working your way, book by book, through a special index, flip occasionally to another, or scout around for a new book by a writer you admire.

DESIGN AND ILLUSTRATIONS

The illustrations scattered throughout the guide are from the books I review in it. Each one carries the record number to the book it is from. The record numbers run consecutively through the book, and will lead you back to the entry in the main text where you will find the full bibliographic information.

The guide has unusually wide margins. We always tell children not to write in books, and generally speaking, that's right. But if you are really using this guide, and you buy and borrow books for more than one child, take a pencil and make notes in the margin about which books you give to those children, at what age and for what occasion and how they were received. That way the guide goes forward with your family, and also becomes a meaningful reading record.

I end where I began, hoping for our future that your children will learn to enjoy reading books as much as you and I do. Have fun.

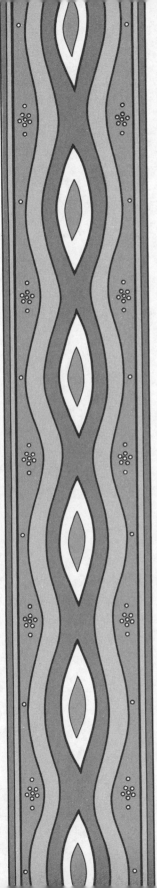

Wordless Books

The reader supplies the language to accompany these all-picture books. But please do not assume that because there are no words, the titles in this section are for very young children. Some are extremely sophisticated and are meant for older readers.

AIRPLANE RIDE [1]

WRITTEN AND ILLUSTRATED BY DOUGLAS FLORIAN

Cloth: Crowell

Published: 1984

A bright, cartoon-style adventure as a perky little biplane goes soaring over the variegated landscape including plains and canyons.

ANIMAL ALPHABET [2]

WRITTEN AND ILLUSTRATED BY BERT KITCHEN

Cloth: Dial

Paper: Dial

Published: 1984   PRIZES: NEW YORK TIMES BEST ILLUSTRATED BOOK

This large-format alphabet book features stern roman letters adorned by exotic animals meticulously painted in somber colors. Younger children may peer at it, but older children are more likely to be taken by the intensity of the art and the power of the illustrations. In *Animal Numbers*, various creatures and their offspring illustrate numerals.

ANNO'S COUNTING BOOK [3]

WRITTEN AND ILLUSTRATED BY MITSUMASA ANNO

Cloth: Crowell

Paper: Harper

Published: 1977

The great Japanese artist sets his rich and complex counting book in a countryside that looks like New England. Each full-color picture represents a succeeding month, as well as time of day, and the growth and development of a small town, with houses, roads, plantings, all sorts of things to count in number sequence. While preschoolers can look at and talk about it, this is a picture book to return to with children in the early grades for more discussion and inventing games.

ANNO'S FLEA MARKET [4]

WRITTEN AND ILLUSTRATED BY MITSUMASA ANNO

Cloth: Philomel

Published: 1984

One of the remarkable wordless narratives by the distinguished Japanese artist, this book could easily be a scroll, it unrolls so fluidly. The

[18]

3

eye moves across a landscape into a town where an amazingly rich flea market takes place. The market itself combines objects and people from many times and cultures, and proceeds with a kind of majestic serenity and then ends. Older children and adults will find numerous detailed items to study and ponder.

ANNO'S JOURNEY [5]

WRITTEN AND ILLUSTRATED BY MITSUMASA ANNO
Cloth: Philomel
Paper: Philomel
Published: 1978

One man in a small boat arrives at an unknown shore. The reader has a kind of bird's-eye view of the wordless pages as the traveler sets off, and the shore gives way to meadows, forest, farmlands, and a European city. This is a good book to begin with if you are not familiar with the remarkably complex picture books by the great Japanese children's book artist. With their extraordinary detail and complex construction, yet simple narrative movement, they are for all ages. Indeed, children tend to accept a richness of detail and cross-cultural complexity in his work that adults often find awesome. If this book intrigues you, then look for the brilliant "guidebooks" *Anno's Britain*, *Anno's Italy*, and *Anno's Medieval World*.

THE BEAR AND THE FLY [6]

WRITTEN AND ILLUSTRATED BY PAULA WINTER
Cloth: Crown
Paper: Crown
Published: 1987   PRIZES: NEW YORK TIMES BEST ILLUSTRATED BOOK

Three bears at dinner. Enter one fly. Chaos ensues. Hilarious, ridiculous, undignified, amusing chaos. No need for words.

A BOY, A DOG AND A FROG [7]

WRITTEN AND ILLUSTRATED BY MERCER MAYER
Cloth: Dial
Paper: Dial
Published: 1967

The first of four droll and appealing books for preschoolers. The boy's discoveries and amusing adventures are spelled out in simple illustra-

[4]

tions. The other titles include *A Boy, a Dog, a Frog and a Friend, One Frog Too Many, Frog on His Own,* and *Frog, Where Are You?*

[7]

BUILDING THE SNOWMAN [8]

WRITTEN AND ILLUSTRATED BY RAYMOND BRIGGS
Cloth: Little, Brown
Published: 1985

One of four small books for very young children. A boy builds a snowman and has magical adventures with him. The other titles are *Dressing the Snowman, Walking in the Air,* and *The Party.*

CHANGES, CHANGES [9]

WRITTEN AND ILLUSTRATED BY PAT HUTCHINS
Cloth: Macmillan
Paper: Aladdin
Published: 1971   PRIZES: NEW YORK TIMES BEST ILLUSTRATED BOOK

A delightful romp involving the transformation and reconfiguration of two wooden figures, a man and a woman, and brightly colored blocks that turn into a boat, a wagon, eventually even a home.

A DAY ON THE AVENUE [10]

WRITTEN AND ILLUSTRATED BY ROBERT ROENNFELT
Cloth: Viking
Published: 1984

This book, with its stylized illustrations, captures the mood and details of an ordinary sort of day on a street in a provincial town. It is from Australia, and speaks to adult nostalgia and to the interest in the past of some preschool and school-age children.

THE GREY LADY AND THE STRAWBERRY SNATCHER [11]

WRITTEN AND ILLUSTRATED BY MOLLY BANG
Cloth: Four Winds
Published: 1980

This eerie book adventure involves a basket of strawberries, a skateboard, and more. The full-color illustrations of the grey lady and the

5

green creature with a purple hat who follows her through swamp and wood are lush and startling.

HAPPY BIRTHDAY, MAX! [12]

WRITTEN AND ILLUSTRATED BY HANNE TURK
Cloth: Picture Book
Published: 1984

One of a number of stories about Max, a dapper and imaginative mouse. Here he stages an elaborate birthday picnic for himself alone on a hill. Some of the other titles include *Good Night, Max*, *Max the Art Lover*, and *Rainy Day Max*.

IS IT RED? IS IT YELLOW? IS IT BLUE? [13]

WRITTEN AND ILLUSTRATED BY TANA HOBAN
Cloth: Greenwillow
Paper: Mulberry
Published: 1978

This handsome book illustrates the primary colors with clarity and wit using simple, handsomely reproduced photographs of everyday objects. Tana Hoban sets a standard for photojournalism and concept books for the very young. Her work is remarkably handsome to look at. Each new idea is demonstrated so clearly that even the youngest child can understand. Some of the other titles for preschoolers are *I Read Signs*, *I Walk and Read*, *Shapes, Shapes, Shapes*, *Children's Zoo*, *Is It Rough? Is It Smooth? Is It Shiny?*, and *26 Letters and 99 Cents*. There are also chunky board books for toddlers, including *What Is It?*, *Red, Blue, Yellow Shoe*, *1, 2, 3*, and *Panda, Panda*.

MOONLIGHT [14]

WRITTEN AND ILLUSTRATED BY JAN ORMEROD
Cloth: Lothrop
Paper: Puffin
Published: 1982

The bedtime rituals in one little girl's family on an evening when, in fact, her parents fall asleep before she does are described in this quiet and appealing book. Closely observed, and illustrated with delicacy and intimate detail in soft colors. The companion book is *Sunshine*,

[9]

about morning ritual in the same family. These are delightful to read with toddlers and preschoolers.

THE OTHER BONE [15]

WRITTEN AND ILLUSTRATED BY ED YOUNG

Cloth: Harper
Published: 1984

A hound dog loses his bone to his watery reflection in this handsome book drawn in pencil—but in a soft, blurred style reminiscent of Chinese watercolors. Companion to *Up a Tree*.

PADDY'S EVENING OUT [16]

WRITTEN AND ILLUSTRATED BY JOHN S. GOODALL

Cloth: McElderry
Published: 1973

Paddy Pork is the pig-hero of a series of adventure books told in lavish, full-color, full-page and half-page illustrations. The ingeniously conceived half pages speed the action. Paddy, who appeals to grown-ups almost as much as children of school age and under, lives in a bucolic world earlier in this century. He is lovable and accident prone, and also appears in *Paddy Goes Traveling*, *Paddy Pork—Odd Jobs*, *Paddy Pork's Holiday*, *Paddy's Evening Out* and *Paddy Under Water*. There are also several books about the charming mice Shrewbettina and Naughty Nancy that use the same format, and are equally appealing.

PETER SPIER'S RAIN [17]

WRITTEN AND ILLUSTRATED BY PETER SPIER

Cloth: Doubleday
Published: 1981

It is a clear, fair summer's day as a young girl and her younger brother go out to play in the yard. Soon the sky darkens and it begins to rain. The storm lasts all day, and the children and their dog are in and out of the house. They explore in the garden, splash out to the park, and study their neighborhood. A delightful book of closely observed details of daily life and the magic of rain. The full-color illustrations are affectionately drawn and appeal to preschoolers as well as their older siblings.

[15]

PICNIC [18]

WRITTEN AND ILLUSTRATED BY EMILY ARNOLD McCULLY
Cloth: Harper
Published: 1984

It's a perfect summer day, so the mouse family sets off in a red pickup truck to have a picnic by a lake. One child falls out, and the family doesn't notice that she's missing till late afternoon. No real damage is done and there is a happy ending. A wordless charmer. The companion books are *First Snow* and *School*.

THE SNOWMAN [19]

WRITTEN AND ILLUSTRATED BY RAYMOND BRIGGS
Cloth: Random House
Paper: Random House
Published: 1978

A boy builds a snowman that comes to life in his dreams. This book has unusual, almost haunting power. Perhaps it comes from the snowman's wise expression throughout the full-color cartoon format.

THE YELLOW UMBRELLA [20]

WRITTEN AND ILLUSTRATED BY HENRIK DRESCHER
Cloth: Bradbury
Published: 1987   PRIZES: NEW YORK TIMES BEST ILLUSTRATED BOOK

In this giddy little book two monkeys, a parent and child, open one yellow umbrella and simply take off. The umbrella carries them high into the sky, away from the city and over mountains, then turns into a boat to cross seas. It is a wonderful trip. Perfect for reading with a toddler, but older children will pore over it for the pleasures of the quirky details.

[18]

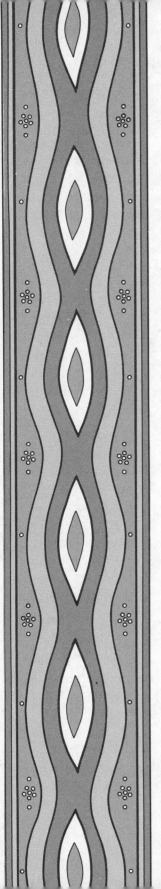

Picture Books

These books have simple texts, and for the most part, a very young child can read and understand what they are about. Some picture books can be understood at a glance, others will continue to reveal detail and nuance as a child studies them, and perhaps take on personal meaning as treasured favorites. Picture books are principally for preschool children, but school-age children often continue to enjoy them.

Picture Books

A APPLE PIE [21]

WRITTEN AND ILLUSTRATED BY TRACEY CAMPBELL PEARSON
Cloth: Dial
Published: 1986

An alphabet book based on the nursery rhyme. In this version that folds out to become an eighteen-foot-long poster, twenty-six children sit at a very long table and attack that tasty baked dish. The full-color illustrations look delicious.

A-APPLE PIE [22]

WRITTEN AND ILLUSTRATED BY KATE GREENAWAY
Cloth: Warne
Published: 1886

A fine Victorian version of the alphabet rhyme about what happened to the apple pie. The pictures show dainty children at play.

ABC [23]

WRITTEN AND ILLUSTRATED BY ELIZABETH CLEAVER
Cloth: Atheneum
Published: 1985

A cheerful and exciting alphabet book using collages of objects and animals familiar and less so. Brilliant color.

ABIYOYO [24]

WRITTEN BY PETE SEEGER
ILLUSTRATED BY MICHAEL HAYS
Cloth: Macmillan
Published: 1986

The full-color illustrations capture the exuberant words of Pete Seeger's beloved song story about the magician and his son who played the ukulele and vanquished the monster Abiyoyo. The music is included at the end.

ALL BY MYSELF   [25]

WRITTEN AND ILLUSTRATED BY ANNA GROSSNICKLE HINES

Cloth: Clarion

Published: 1984

Here is gentle bibliotherapy for preschoolers—one night Josie goes to the bathroom in the dark all by herself. Hooray!

ALL SMALL   [26]

WRITTEN BY DAVID McCORD

ILLUSTRATED BY MADELAINE GILL LINDEN

Cloth: Little, Brown

Paper: Little, Brown

Published: 1986

A fine collection of twenty-five short poems by a modern master.

ALL WET! ALL WET!   [27]

WRITTEN BY JAMES SKOFIELD

ILLUSTRATED BY DIANE STANLEY

Cloth: Harper

Published: 1984

A little boy in a raincoat and boots, with a big umbrella, spends a day outside in the summer rain, where he sees a great deal of animal and insect life. The illustrations are soft and misty.

ALPHABATICS   [28]

WRITTEN AND ILLUSTRATED BY SUSE MacDONALD

Cloth: Bradbury

Published: 1986   PRIZES: CALDECOTT HONOR BOOK

The letters of the brilliantly colored alphabet roll over and turn into appropriate things — *a* becomes an ark, *f* becomes a fish, *g* a giraffe— and the single word appears on the page with the illustration.

ALPHABEARS: AN ABC BOOK [29]

WRITTEN BY KATHLEEN HAGUE
ILLUSTRATED BY MICHAEL HAGUE
Cloth: Holt
Published: 1984

This alphabet book stars cute bears with a 1920s quality to the illustrations. There is a companion volume called *Numbears: A Counting Book.*

AMOS & BORIS [30]

WRITTEN AND ILLUSTRATED BY WILLIAM STEIG
Cloth: Farrar, Straus
Paper: Penguin
Published: 1971   PRIZES: NEW YORK TIMES BEST ILLUSTRATED BOOK

This splendid and affecting story of the true friendship between a whale and a mouse shows, rather than announces, the real merits of cooperation and helpfulness. It is also, of course, funny, and the illustrations are playful.

ANANSI THE SPIDER:
A TALE FROM THE ASHANTI [31]

WRITTEN AND ILLUSTRATED BY GERALD McDERMOTT
Cloth: Holt
Paper: Holt
Published: 1972

In this wittily illustrated story about Anansi, the West African spider-hero, he has six sons who combine their talents to save their father.

[30]

Picture Books

AND MY MEAN OLD MOTHER WILL BE SORRY, BLACKBOARD BEAR   [32]

WRITTEN AND ILLUSTRATED BY MARTHA ALEXANDER
Cloth: Dial
Paper: Dial
Published: 1972

A little boy has an argument with his mother and runs away to live in the woods with his friend Blackboard Bear. *Blackboard Bear* and *I Sure Am Glad To See You, Blackboard Bear* are other stories about Anthony and his imaginary friend (who is always pictured in black outlined in white as if he'd just stepped off a blackboard).

ANGELINA BALLERINA   [33]

WRITTEN BY KATHARINE HOLABIRD
ILLUSTRATED BY HELEN CRAIG
Cloth: Crown
Published: 1983

The first in a series of books about a little mouse who wants to be a ballerina and gets her heart's desire. The rather English, full-color illustrations are particularly whimsical and appealing, and include wonderful bits of backstage detail. Other titles in the series feature Angelina's Cousin Henry and include *Angelina on Stage*, *Angelina's Christmas*, and *Angelina at the Fair.*

ANIMALS SHOULD DEFINITELY NOT ACT LIKE PEOPLE   [34]

WRITTEN BY JUDI BARRETT
ILLUSTRATED BY RON BARRETT
Cloth: Atheneum
Paper: Aladdin
Published: 1980

A book for preschoolers about some funny things that might happen if animals did try to act like people. Illustrated in bold colors.

ANIMALS SHOULD DEFINITELY NOT WEAR CLOTHING   [35]

WRITTEN BY JUDI BARRETT
ILLUSTRATED BY RON BARRETT
Cloth: Atheneum
Paper: Aladdin
Published: 1970

Some things are just silly to think about — a walrus in a tie and jacket, and many other possibilities are included in this book. The illustrations are, as it were, suitable.

ANNO'S ALPHABET: AN ADVENTURE IN IMAGINATION   [36]

WRITTEN AND ILLUSTRATED BY MITSUMASA ANNO
Cloth: Crowell
Paper: Harper
Published: 1975   PRIZES: NEW YORK TIMES BEST ILLUSTRATED BOOK

This alphabet book, by the Japanese artist relatively early in his career, indicates the richness of his imagination. Look carefully as the wooden letters and tools are shaped and transformed. The *j* yields a juggler.

APE IN A CAPE: AN ALPHABET OF ODD ANIMALS   [37]

WRITTEN AND ILLUSTRATED BY FRITZ EICHENBERG
Cloth: Harcourt Brace
Paper: Voyager/HBJ
Published: 1952   PRIZES: CALDECOTT HONOR BOOK

An alphabet book of unusual animals and original rhymes—dove in love, goat in a boat. The illustrations may seem old-fashioned to adult eyes, but their large size and simplicity remain appealing to the very young.

[33]

Picture Books

APPLEBET: AN ABC [38]

WRITTEN BY CLYDE WATSON
ILLUSTRATED BY WENDY WATSON
Cloth: Farrar, Straus
Paper: Farrar, Straus
Published: 1982

The organizing principle of this cheerful, rhyming alphabet book is that a farmer and her daughter are taking apples to a country fair.

AN ARTIST [39]

WRITTEN AND ILLUSTRATED BY M. B. GOFFSTEIN
Cloth: Harper
Published: 1980   PRIZES: NEW YORK TIMES BEST ILLUSTRATED BOOK

A small book, with tiny, precise pen-and-ink illustrations with dabs of color, that shows what it means to be an artist in a way young children can absorb. The artist pictured here has a beard and a hat. There are similar books called *A Writer* and *An Actor.*

AS I WAS GOING UP AND DOWN [40]

WRITTEN AND ILLUSTRATED BY NICOLA BAYLEY
Cloth: Macmillan
Published: 1986

A happy little book of nonsense rhymes.

THE BABY'S BEDTIME BOOK [41]

WRITTEN AND ILLUSTRATED BY KAY CHORAO
Cloth: Dutton
Published: 1984

A pretty collection of classic poems and songs, with gentle, pretty illustrations. The two companion volumes are *The Baby's Lap Book* and *The Baby's Story Book.*

[183]

16

A BEAR'S BICYCLE [42]

WRITTEN BY EMILIE WARREN McLEOD
ILLUSTRATED BY DAVID McPHAIL
Cloth: Atlantic-Little, Brown
Paper: Atlantic-Little, Brown
Published: 1975

A book about bicycle safety couched in comic terms. The little boy rider follows all the rules; it is his gigantic teddy bear who's the terror on the road. The full-color bears are a special attraction.

THE BERENSTAIN BEARS AND THE SPOOKY OLD TREE [43]

WRITTEN AND ILLUSTRATED BY STAN AND JAN BERENSTAIN
Cloth: Beginner Books
Published: 1978

By thoroughly exploring an old tree, inside and out, three little bears work through spatial concepts—into, up, through, etc. This is for infant to toddler readers and different from the Berenstains' other popular books that deal with issues and behavior for slightly older children.

BIG SISTER AND LITTLE SISTER [44]

WRITTEN BY CHARLOTTE ZOLOTOW
ILLUSTRATED BY MARTHA ALEXANDER
Cloth: Harper
Published: 1966

Sometimes you just have to run away from your bossy big sister to find out how she really feels about you.

BLUEBERRIES FOR SAL [45]

WRITTEN AND ILLUSTRATED BY ROBERT McCLOSKEY
Cloth: Viking
Paper: Puffin
Published: 1948

The parallel adventures of a little girl and a baby bear, both of whom go hunting blueberries with their mothers one summer morning in

Picture Books

Maine. They each lose track of time and follow the wrong mothers. Suffice it to say they end up with the right ones. The story is as appealing to contemporary blueberry pickers as it was to their parents.

BRINGING THE RAIN TO KAPITI PLAIN: A NANDI TALE [46]

WRITTEN BY VERNA AARDEMA
ILLUSTRATED BY BEATRIZ VIDAL
Cloth: Dial
Paper: Dial
Published: 1981

A cumulative story (like *The House That Jack Built*) from East Africa, about how Ki-pat brought the rain to the "dry, oh so dry, Kapiti Plain." The rhythms and repetitions in the text are so engaging that the story almost asks to be read out loud, and the full-color pictures evoke the widest and driest of plains.

BUNCHES AND BUNCHES OF BUNNIES [47]

WRITTEN BY LOUISE MATHEWS
ILLUSTRATED BY JENI BASSETT
Cloth: Dodd
Paper: Scholastic
Published: 1978

The bunches of bunnies, lots and lots of them, are arranged across these pages to help teach the principles of addition.

CAN I KEEP HIM? [48]

WRITTEN AND ILLUSTRATED BY STEVEN KELLOG
Cloth: Dial
Paper: Dial
Published: 1971

The narrator, a little boy, is so desperate for a pet that he tries to persuade his mother to let him keep a succession of creatures—a dog, a bear cub, a tiger, and even another little boy. The full-color, cartoon-style illustrations capture his longing perfectly.

CAPS FOR SALE [49]

WRITTEN AND ILLUSTRATED BY ESPHYR SLOBODKINA
Cloth: Harper
Paper: Harper
Published: 1947

A peddler dozes under a tree, and the naughty monkeys snatch his wares, the pile of caps, right off his head. A wonderful, plausibly funny picture book, endlessly entertaining, for generation upon generation.

CAT & CANARY [50]

WRITTEN AND ILLUSTRATED BY MICHAEL FOREMAN
Cloth: Dial
Paper: Dial
Published: 1985

Cat wishes he could fly like Canary, and one day he does. The dazzling full-color illustrations by a distinguished British illustrator are a lyric paean to Manhattan.

CATCH ME & KISS ME & SAY IT AGAIN [51]

WRITTEN BY CLYDE WATSON
ILLUSTRATED BY WENDY WATSON
Cloth: Philomel
Paper: Philomel
Published: 1978

A bubbling collection of short rhymes and verses with cheerful, chunky, three-color illustrations of children and a winsome cat.

CAT GOES FIDDLE-I-FEE [52]

WRITTEN AND ILLUSTRATED BY PAUL GALDONE
Cloth: Clarion
Paper: Clarion
Published: 1985

A bright resetting of the English folk song that is a cumulative rhyme, introducing favorite farm animals and their sounds.

[64]

CLOUDY WITH A CHANCE OF MEATBALLS [53]

WRITTEN BY JUDI BARRETT
ILLUSTRATED BY RON BARRETT
Cloth: Atheneum
Paper: Aladdin
Published: 1978   PRIZES: NEW YORK TIMES BEST ILLUSTRATED BOOK

It's a wild story Grandpa makes up. He says that in the magical land of Chewandswallow meals come from the sky, but what happens when the weather changes? Silly to even think about. The illustrations are both sophisticated and outrageously funny, and appeal to most school-age children.

CORDUROY [54]

WRITTEN AND ILLUSTRATED BY DON FREEMAN
Cloth: Viking
Paper: Puffin
Published: 1968

Corduroy is a small stuffed bear, waiting in a department store, who eventually goes home with a little black girl named Lisa. His adventures continue in *A Pocket for Corduroy*. Although the story is complete and understood by young children, there are some appealing abridgments of *Corduroy* available for even younger children in a chunky board format.

[53]

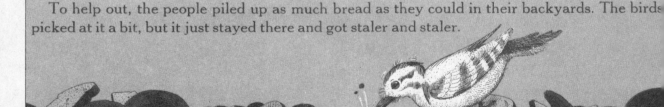

To help out, the people piled up as much bread as they could in their backyards. The birds picked at it a bit, but it just stayed there and got staler and staler.

CRASH! BANG! BOOM! [55]

WRITTEN AND ILLUSTRATED BY PETER SPIER

Cloth: Doubleday
Published: 1972

A book of inspired imagination, filled with detailed illustrations of things, from soldiers in a marching band with their instruments, to zoo animals and birds. The text, such as it is, consists of approximations of the sounds each and every creature and thing makes.

CURIOUS GEORGE [56]

WRITTEN AND ILLUSTRATED BY H. A. REY

Cloth: Houghton Mifflin
Paper: Houghton Mifflin
Published: 1941

The first of a series of books about a small monkey captured in Africa by a man wearing a yellow hat and brought back to live in a city. George's curiosity leads him to wreak havoc everywhere he goes. But he is always well-meaning, rather like many of his most devoted pre-school readers. Other original titles include *Curious George Gets a Medal*, *Curious George Rides a Bike*. Eight other titles have illustrations taken from the animated television series, which are less vibrant.

DANCING IN THE MOON: COUNTING RHYMES [57]

WRITTEN AND ILLUSTRATED BY FRITZ EICHENBERG

Cloth: Harcourt Brace
Paper: Voyager/HBJ
Published: 1955

Verses with ridiculous premises for counting from 1 to 20. Distinctive, eccentric illustrations.

DANIEL O'ROURKE [58]

WRITTEN AND ILLUSTRATED BY GERALD McDERMOTT

Cloth: Viking
Paper: Puffin
Published: 1986

A bright, and very green, version of a classic Irish folktale. Perfect for St. Patrick's Day, and top o' the day to you.

A DARK DARK TALE [59]

WRITTEN AND ILLUSTRATED BY RUTH BROWN

Cloth: Dial
Paper: Dial
Published: 1981

A mysterious night, a moor, a cat, a search, a very simple vocabulary, heightened suspense, and a surprise comic ending to a darkly colorful adventure. Even very young children get the joke.

DAWN [60]

WRITTEN AND ILLUSTRATED BY MOLLY BANG

Cloth: Morrow
Published: 1983

A shipbuilder tells his daughter how he once rescued a wounded goose and later met a mysterious woman who wove sails. A beautiful version of a traditional tale from the Orient. The illustrations are haunting.

DAWN [61]

WRITTEN AND ILLUSTRATED BY URI SHULEVITZ

Cloth: Farrar, Straus
Paper: Farrar, Straus
Published: 1974

The text of this lovely picture book comes from a Chinese poem about an old man and his grandson. They are asleep by the shore of a mountain lake, and dawn approaches. The full-color illustrations capture the subtle changes of light in the early morning.

DON'T TOUCH MY ROOM [62]

WRITTEN BY PATRICIA LAKIN
ILLUSTRATED BY PATIENCE BREWSTER

Cloth: Little, Brown
Paper: Little, Brown
Published: 1985

Aaron is determined not to share his very special bedroom with anyone, especially not his baby brother. Time passes, however, and things get predictably better. A sequel of sorts, set years later, is *Oh, Brother.*

DRUMMER HOFF   [63]

WRITTEN BY BARBARA EMBERLEY
ILLUSTRATED BY ED EMBERLEY

Cloth: Prentice-Hall
Paper: Simon and Schuster Books for Young Readers
Published: 1967   PRIZES: CALDECOTT MEDAL

The simplest cumulative rhyme and precise funny illustrations
describe the firing of a cannon by a gaggle of soldiers dressed in the
style of the American Revolution.

EACH PEACH PEAR PLUM: AN "I SPY" STORY   [64]

WRITTEN AND ILLUSTRATED BY JANET AND ALLEN AHLBERG

Cloth: Viking
Paper: Puffin
Published: 1979

An enchanting picture book set on a summery afternoon in the countryside in which nursery rhyme characters such as Goldilocks, the
Three Bears, Bo Peep, and Jack and Jill can be spotted by sharp-eyed
readers before they can be fully seen.

THE EGG TREE   [65]

WRITTEN AND ILLUSTRATED BY KATHERINE MILHOUS

Cloth: Scribners
Paper: Aladdin
Published: 1950   PRIZES: CALDECOTT MEDAL

The egg tree is made with special eggs found in the Easter egg hunt.
This prize-winning book may seem old-fashioned to older children,
but it retains its charm for younger readers.

[64]

23

Picture Books

THE ELEPHANT AND THE BAD BABY [66]

WRITTEN BY ELFRIDA VIPONT
ILLUSTRATED BY RAYMOND BRIGGS
Cloth: Coward
Paper: Coward
Published: 1969

It's never clear just why the baby is "bad," but in this jolly, cumulative tale, the elephant and the infant go "rumpeta, rumpeta, rumpeta" down the road, and are followed by half the town before it's time for pancakes. The illustrations are amusing and somehow plausible.

THE EMERGENCY ROOM [67]

WRITTEN AND ILLUSTRATED BY HARLOW ROCKWELL
Cloth: Macmillan
Published: 1985

An elementary and straightforward introduction to that place most families somehow end up visiting at least once. This is for very young children, and the author has done *My Dentist* and *My Doctor* for them as well.

THE EMPEROR'S NEW CLOTHES [68]

WRITTEN BY HANS CHRISTIAN ANDERSEN
ILLUSTRATED BY ANNE ROCKWELL
Cloth: Harper
Paper: Harper
Published: 1982

In this version of the story of the vain, silly emperor and the wicked and clever thieves, the illustrations are particularly airy and light and amusing. The emperor is very pink and silly in only his crown and curly, pointed beard.

THE ENCHANTED CARIBOU [69]

WRITTEN AND ILLUSTRATED BY ELIZABETH CLEAVER
Cloth: Atheneum
Published: 1985

A haunting folktale from Canada about an Indian maiden who is changed into a white caribou by the old woman she allows into the tent of the hunters she is caring for. The evocative illustrations are made of cut-paper collage.

ERNEST AND CELESTINE [70]

WRITTEN AND ILLUSTRATED BY GABRIELLE VINCENT
Cloth: Greenwillow
Paper: Mulberry
Published: 1982

[70]

The first in a series of books from a Belgian author about Ernest the bear and Celestine the little mouse. The affection between them, the delicacy of the illustrations, and the plausibility of their adventures are all endearing. In this story, Celestine loses her duck-doll in the snow and Ernest tries to solve the problem. Other titles include *Bravo, Ernest and Celestine*, the wordless *Breakfast Time, Ernest and Celestine*, and *Ernest and Celestine's Patchwork Quilt*. There are more, all charming and evocative.

EYES OF THE DRAGON [71]

WRITTEN BY MARGARET LEAF
ILLUSTRATED BY ED YOUNG
Cloth: Lothrop
Published: 1987

A deftly written and dramatically illustrated cautionary tale based on the wise Chinese principle that one should not paint the eyes of the dragon. A great artist paints a dragon on the wall of little Li's village, and Li's grandfather, the magistrate, won't pay till the artist puts in the dragon's eyes.

FAMILY [72]

WRITTEN AND ILLUSTRATED BY HELEN OXENBURY
Cloth: Little Simon
Published: 1981

This chunky little board book, along with *Dressing, Friends, Playing*, and *Working*, comprises one of the first of the contemporary toddler books and remains outstanding. The simple ideas are conveyed in illustrations that seem very simple and appealing to adults, but babies seem to find them enthralling. Perhaps because the babies look so...so babyish.

A FARMER'S ALPHABET [73]

WRITTEN AND ILLUSTRATED BY MARY AZARIAN

Cloth: Godine
Paper: Godine
Published: 1981

A rugged, rural alphabet book of handsome woodcuts depicting farm life.

FATHER FOX'S PENNYRHYMES [74]

WRITTEN BY CLYDE WATSON
ILLUSTRATED BY WENDY WATSON

Cloth: Crowell
Paper: Harper
Published: 1971

A cheerful collection of fine nonsense verses, with delicate cartoon panels of illustrations that include details and conversational commentary on the verses. *Father Fox's Feast of Songs* is by the same author and illustrator.

FEELINGS [75]

WRITTEN AND ILLUSTRATED BY ALIKI

Cloth: Greenwillow
Paper: Mulberry
Published: 1984

A catalog of emotions—witty illustrations of faces showing sorrow, joy, love, hate, pride, fear, frustration, and more. Since some children have difficulty explaining their emotions, often because they don't have the words for them, this is useful as well as entertaining, and excellent for shared reading.

[51]

FINDERS KEEPERS [76]

WRITTEN AND ILLUSTRATED BY
  WILL AND NICHOLAS MORDVINOFF

Cloth: Harcourt Brace
Paper: Voyager/HBJ
Published: 1951   PRIZES: CALDECOTT MEDAL

Who owns the bone two dogs have found? A funny story with funny
pictures just right for lap listeners and small children, although adults
will see the illustrations as old-fashioned.

FINGER RHYMES [77]

WRITTEN AND ILLUSTRATED BY MARC BROWN

Cloth: Dutton
Published: 1980

Finger rhymes are those rhymes and games your fingers play with
babies and very young children in which everyone ends up laughing.
The animal-filled illustrations in this pleasing collection are encouraging for older readers who may have to follow the instructions. The companion volume is *Hand Rhymes*.

FIRST FLIGHT [78]

WRITTEN AND ILLUSTRATED BY DAVID McPHAIL

Cloth: Joy Street/Little, Brown
Published: 1987

A little boy goes on his first airplane trip to visit his grandmother. His
teddy bear turns into the traveling companion who acts out every
behavioral fantasy and neurosis. Stylishly done with both humor
and sympathy.

FIRST THERE WAS FRANCES [79]

WRITTEN AND ILLUSTRATED BY BOB GRAHAM

Cloth: Bradbury
Published: 1986

An ebullient book about the growth of a household, starting with
Frances, adding Graham, then more and more people and animals.
The full-color illustrations have a giddy quality that adds to the general
merriment.

FIVE LITTLE FOXES AND THE SNOW [80]

WRITTEN BY TONY JOHNSTON
ILLUSTRATED BY CYNDY SZEKERES
Paper: Harper
Published: 1977

It starts to snow the week before Christmas, and in the cozy den, Gramma Fox has her hands full trying to manage the five little foxes as well as her knitting project. All is revealed on Christmas morning. A delightful story of anticipation, with funny full-color illustrations. The text has a nice cadence for reading aloud.

FIVE MINUTES PEACE [81]

WRITTEN AND ILLUSTRATED BY JILL MURPHY
Cloth: Putnam
Published: 1986

In this, a slice-of-life-for-mommies book, Mrs. Large's elephant children follow her everywhere. She finally retreats to the bathtub. They follow her. She slips away, leaving them to play in the tub while she catches a cup of coffee in peace in the kitchen. The Larges reappear in *All in One Piece*.

FIX-IT [82]

WRITTEN AND ILLUSTRATED BY DAVID McPHAIL
Cloth: Dutton
Paper: Dutton
Published: 1984

The television won't work, and Emma Bear is in despair. Her parents try to distract her, even read to her, and when the infernal machine is finally back in order, she is busy reading to her doll. Her adventures continue in *Emma's Pet* and *Emma's Vacation*.

[90]

THE FOOLISH FROG [83]

WRITTEN BY PETE AND CHARLES SEEGER
ILLUSTRATED BY MIROSLAV JAGR
Cloth: Macmillan
Published: 1973
The bubbling nonsense folk song about the merry bullfrog who sets off a chain of improbable, silly events "because he'd nothing better for to do" is illustrated with zest.

FOOLISH RABBIT'S BIG MISTAKE [84]

WRITTEN BY RAFE MARTIN
ILLUSTRATED BY ED YOUNG
Cloth: Putnam
Published: 1985
A retelling of an African version of a story adults might recognize as "Chicken Little" in which the foolish rabbit dreams under an apple tree. The illustrations take on a gleaming intensity as the chaos builds.

FORGET-ME-NOT [85]

WRITTEN BY PAUL ROGERS
ILLUSTRATED BY CELIA BERRIDGE
Cloth: Viking
Paper: Puffin
Published: 1984
Sidney is a very absentminded lion, and on the way to a day at the seaside he manages to lose something on every page. Sharp young eyes love finding missing objects in these whimsical illustrations.

FOUR BRAVE SAILORS [86]

WRITTEN BY MIRRA GINSBURG
ILLUSTRATED BY NANCY TAFURI
Cloth: Green
Published: 1987
The four sailors are fearless mice, brave and true, and their white ship sails over waves of wondrous blues. The pictures fill the page, and very little children are caught up in the exciting voyage.

Picture Books

FOX'S DREAM [87]

WRITTEN AND ILLUSTRATED BY TEJIMA

Cloth: Philomel

Published: 1987   PRIZES: NEW YORK TIMES BEST ILLUSTRATED BOOK

This large-format book follows a solitary fox on a snowy winter's night, capturing his dreams and an exciting chase of a snow rabbit in thrilling and technically dazzling woodcuts.

FREDERICK [88]

WRITTEN AND ILLUSTRATED BY LEO LIONNI

Cloth: Pantheon

Paper: Knopf   PRIZES: CALDECOTT HONOR BOOK

Published: 1967   NEW YORK TIMES BEST ILLUSTRATED BOOK

[88]

The first of the wonderful books about Frederick the mouse, a daydreamer and a poet, who, when winter comes, is also an entertainer. (There is a one-volume collection of six Frederick books—*Frederick's Fables: A Leo Lionni Treasury of Favorite Stories*—available from Pantheon, as well as individual picture books.) The artist works in a distinctive, full-color collage style.

FREIGHT TRAIN [89]

WRITTEN AND ILLUSTRATED BY DONALD CREWS

Cloth: Greenwillow

Paper: Puffin

Published: 1978

A freight train hurtles across the pages, through day and night from the city into the countryside, with a sense of speed that is quite magical, as the train becomes almost an abstraction of color. A wonderful book to read with young children.

FRIENDS [90]

WRITTEN AND ILLUSTRATED BY HELME HEINE

Cloth: McElderry

Paper: Aladdin

Published: 1982

A rooster, a mouse and a pig are best friends and have a fine time together. The witty and lighthearted full-color illustrations are ebul-

lient. The companions also appear in the small-sized, charming Three
Friends Series—*The Alarm Clock*, *The Visitor*, and *The Racing Cart*.

FROG WENT A-COURTIN'   [91]

WRITTEN BY JOHN LANGSTAFF
ILLUSTRATED BY FEODOR ROJANKOVSKY
Cloth: Harcourt Brace
Paper: Voyager/HBJ
Published: 1955   PRIZES: CALDECOTT MEDAL

A charming, old-fashioned fancy-dress version of a familiar song. Miss
Mouse is quite coy. The large format works very well with very young
children.

GEORGE SHRINKS   [92]

WRITTEN AND ILLUSTRATED BY WILLIAM JOYCE
Cloth: Harper
Paper: Harper
Published: 1985

A beautifully realized dream fantasy in which George wakes up to find
that his parents are out, that he has shrunk to tiny size, and that he
must nevertheless deal with a whole list of chores. The illustrations
capture the problems of scale perfectly—the toothbrush, the cat, the
garbage, and a tiny George.

[89]

Picture Books

GERALDINE'S BLANKET [93]

WRITTEN AND ILLUSTRATED BY HOLLY KELLER
Cloth: Greenwillow
Paper: Mulberry
Published: 1984

Geraldine's pink blanket was a baby present from Aunt Bessie. It's worn now and patched, and when Aunt Bessie sends her a doll, Geraldine preserves and transfers her affections simultaneously by using the scraps for a doll dress. Gentle story, gentle illustrations.

GILA MONSTERS MEET YOU AT THE AIRPORT [94]

WRITTEN BY MARJORIE WEINMAN SHARMAT
ILLUSTRATED BY BYRON BARTON
Cloth: Macmillan
Paper: Puffin
Published: 1980

[109]

Moving is bad enough, but what if you are from the big city, and when the airplane lands, giant lizards meet you? The little boy whose worries these are meets a boy out west who has similarly outlandish fantasies about life in New York.

GOING TO THE POTTY [95]

WRITTEN BY FRED ROGERS
ILLUSTRATED BY JIM JUDKIS
Cloth: Putnam
Paper: Putnam
Published: 1986

Television's Mr. Rogers's First Experience Series books are as low-key and reassuring as his faithful audience might expect. This photo essay, with its familiar, plausible families, deals with one of life's great transitions. The text is direct and encouraging. Other titles in the series include *Going to Day Care*, *Going to the Doctor*, and *The New Baby*.

GONE FISHING [96]

WRITTEN BY EARLENE LONG
ILLUSTRATED BY RICHARD BROWN
Cloth: Houghton Mifflin
Paper: Houghton Mifflin
Published: 1984

An understated little tale of a boy and his father who get up before
dawn, see all sorts of creatures on their expedition, catch two fish, and
experience both delight and genuine satisfaction. Nicely illustrated,
and underscores the concept of large and small.

GOODBYE HOUSE [97]

WRITTEN AND ILLUSTRATED BY FRANK ASCH
Cloth: Prentice-Hall
Published: 1986

A father helps his child bid farewell to the house after the moving men
have emptied it. A problematic and upsetting situation handled in a
thoughtful and soothing way.

GOOD MORNING, CHICK [98]

WRITTEN BY MIRRA GINSBURG
ILLUSTRATED BY BYRON BARTON
Cloth: Greenwillow
Paper: Scholastic
Published: 1980

A barnyard story for young children—in bright, simple, full-color
illustrations, a little chick comes out of its little white house and goes
exploring the new world.

[109]

Picture Books

GOODNIGHT MOON [99]

WRITTEN BY MARGARET WISE BROWN
ILLUSTRATED BY CLEMENT HURD
Cloth: Harper
Paper: Harper
Published: 1947

One of the most popular of all ritual bedtime books. A small rabbit settles down for the night in that familiar but fantastic place, "the great green room," and says good-night to all the things and creatures there. The illustrations, subtle and complex as well as droll, are perhaps even more soothing than the text.

GRANDFATHER TWILIGHT [100]

WRITTEN AND ILLUSTRATED BY BARBARA HELEN BERGER
Cloth: Philomel
Paper: Philomel
Published: 1984

A peaceful bedtime book with some gentle magic. Grandfather Twilight spreads dusk and mysterious shadow with his magic pearl, which, as darkness comes and he reaches the shore, is transformed into the rising moon. The full-color illustrations have a luminous quality.

GRANDMA AND GRANDPA [101]

WRITTEN AND ILLUSTRATED BY HELEN OXENBURY
Cloth: Dial
Published: 1983

One of a fine series of "out and about" board books for toddlers and preschoolers, about daily experiences and relationships. Other titles include *The Dancing Class*, *The Important Visitor*, and *The Car Trip*.

GRANPA [102]

WRITTEN AND ILLUSTRATED BY JOHN BURNINGHAM
Cloth: Crown
Published: 1985

Captured in an airy, light style of illustration suggesting memory rather than immediate experience, these vignettes about the relationship between a little girl and her grandfather are winsome and appealing.

THE GROWING-UP FEET [103]

WRITTEN BY BEVERLY CLEARY
ILLUSTRATED BY DYANNE DiSALVO RYAN

Cloth: Morrow
Paper: Dell
Published: 1987

Jimmy and Janet are four-year-old twins whose adventures are recounted in a bright series of books including *Janet's Thingamajigs* and *Two Dog Biscuits*. This story is about red boots that stretch to fit growing feet.

THE GUINEA PIG ABC [104]

WRITTEN AND ILLUSTRATED BY KATE DUKE

Cloth: Dutton
Paper: Dutton
Published: 1983

The letters in this sunny ABC are made by a troupe of winning guinea pigs with unusual acrobatic skills. *Guinea Pigs Far and Near* features the same cast illustrating concepts such as behind, beside, and between.

Prickly

[104]

HAPPY BIRTHDAY, MOON [105]

WRITTEN AND ILLUSTRATED BY FRANK ASCH

Cloth: Prentice-Hall
Paper: Simon and Schuster Books for Young Readers
Published: 1982

This is one of a series of bright stories illustrated in a particularly appealing and rather childlike fashion that young children find very pleasing. Other favorites include: *Good-Night, Horsey, Bear's Bargain*, and *Bread & Honey*.

HAROLD AND THE PURPLE CRAYON [106]

WRITTEN AND ILLUSTRATED BY CROCKETT JOHNSON

Cloth: Harper
Paper: Harper
Published: 1955

One night when Harold cannot sleep, he takes his purple crayon and draws himself a walk. He follows the moon, goes to a desert isle, climbs

Picture Books

a stair, and ends up home and in bed. Simple and glorious, this book is especially loved by very young children. The related titles are *Harold's ABC*, *Harold's Circus*, and *Harold's Trip to the Sky*.

HARRY AND THE TERRIBLE WHATZIT [107]

WRITTEN AND ILLUSTRATED BY DICK GACKENBACH

Cloth: Clarion
Paper: Clarion
Published: 1978

Harry follows his mother down into the dark cellar to save her from the terrible two-headed Whatzit that shrinks when confronted by Harry's courage. Emboldened, Harry even sends it away. Reassuring to youngsters passing through a monster phase. There is also a Spanish-language paperback edition.

THE HATING BOOK [108]

WRITTEN BY CHARLOTTE ZOLOTOW
ILLUSTRATED BY BEN SHECTER

Cloth: Harper
Published: 1969

A small, classic story about the vicissitudes of being best friends.

HAVE YOU SEEN MY DUCKLING? [109]

WRITTEN AND ILLUSTRATED BY NANCY TAFURI

Cloth: Greenwillow
Paper: Penguin
Published: 1984   PRIZES: CALDECOTT HONOR BOOK

In a series of stunning double-page illustrations executed in a bold and vaguely Oriental style, the mother duck looks for her eighth duckling, who the reader can see in some visible, but cleverly camouflaged, corner. Great fun with very young children.

[106]

HECTOR PROTECTOR AND AS I WENT OVER THE WATER: TWO NURSERY RHYMES [110]

WRITTEN AND ILLUSTRATED BY MAURICE SENDAK

Cloth: Harper
Paper: Harper
Published: 1965

Knowing the text of these familiar nursery rhymes is no preparation for the exuberant interpretation in this witty edition. In particular, Hector's protestations about hating green are memorable.

HERE I AM, AN ONLY CHILD [111]

WRITTEN BY MARLENE FANTA SHYER
ILLUSTRATED BY DONALD CARRICK

Cloth: Scribners
Paper: Aladdin
Published: 1985

The pros and cons of being an only child are affectionately stated and illustrated with charm and in full color: you always get the wishbone, you always get the blame.

HIPPOS GO BERSERK [112]

WRITTEN AND ILLUSTRATED BY SANDRA BOYNTON

Paper: Little, Brown
Published: 1979

In this counting book, one hippo invites two friends over, and then three more drop by, and, well, it gets crowded and funny.

[107]

Picture
Books

A HOLE IS TO DIG: A FIRST BOOK OF DEFINITIONS [113]

WRITTEN BY RUTH KRAUSS
ILLUSTRATED BY MAURICE SENDAK
Cloth: Harper
Paper: Harper
Published: 1952   PRIZES: NEW YORK TIMES BEST ILLUSTRATED BOOK

This little book fits perfectly into preschool- and kindergarten-size hands and is full of wonderful things to think about. The small line drawing illustrations capture chunky, wistful, funny, ordinary children in motion. The text sets out fine child-evolved definitions—arms are to hug. A favorite for decades.

HOLES AND PEEKS [114]

WRITTEN AND ILLUSTRATED BY ANN JONAS
Cloth: Greenwillow
Published: 1984

This is a reassuring book for toddlers who worry about holes (such as toilets) that are sometimes scary and find things they can peek at (say through a buttonhole) less frightening. The illustrations have a bright, appealing simplicity.

HONEY, I LOVE AND OTHER LOVE POEMS [115]

WRITTEN BY ELOISE GREENFIELD
ILLUSTRATED BY DIANE AND LEO DILLON
Cloth: Crowell
Paper: Harper
Published: 1978

A collection of short poems about emotions and ordinary childhood experiences. The illustrations of black children are winsome.

[116]

HOORAY FOR SNAIL   [116]

WRITTEN AND ILLUSTRATED BY JOHN STADLER
Cloth: Crowell
Paper: Harper
Published: 1984

The idea of Snail hitting a home run, which means that Snail must circle the bases, is a joke everyone, even the youngest sports fan, can see coming and enjoy all the way around. *Snail Saves the Day* shifts the action to the football field.

HOW DO I PUT IT ON?   [117]

WRITTEN BY SHIEGO WATANABE
ILLUSTRATED BY YASUO OHTOMO
Cloth: Philomel
Paper: Philomel
Published: 1979

One of a series of concept books for very young children that deals with the issues of "doing it all by myself." The illustrations show a cheerful little bear, but the reader understands who the series is really about. Other titles include *I Can Take a Walk*, *I Can Build a House!* and *I'm the King of the Castle*.

HUMPHREY'S BEAR   [118]

WRITTEN BY JAN WAHL
ILLUSTRATED BY WILLIAM JOYCE
Cloth: Holt
Published: 1987

His father thinks Humphrey is too old to sleep with his bear, so in his dream Humphrey goes off to sea with the stuffed animal. The illustrations are quite magical.

Picture Books

HURRY HOME, GRANDMA!   [119]

WRITTEN BY ARIELLE NORTH OLSON
ILLUSTRATED BY LYDIA DABCOVICH
Cloth: Dutton
Published: 1984

Grandma is an explorer, and Timothy and Melinda are very anxious that she get home in time for Christmas.

HUSH LITTLE BABY   [120]

WRITTEN AND ILLUSTRATED BY JEANETTE WINTER
Cloth: Pantheon
Published: 1984

The traditional lullaby, featuring a sturdy father and son, as well as the familiar mockingbird, horse and cart, billy goat, and, of course, the dog named Rover, is put in a gentle contemporary setting.

I AM A BUNNY   [121]

WRITTEN BY OLE RISOM
ILLUSTRATED BY RICHARD SCARRY
Cloth: Golden Books/Western
Published: 1963

"I am a bunny. I live in a hollow tree." This tall, sturdy book, with its very simple text and illustrations that capture the seasons in the life of a little rabbit wearing red overalls, is a timeless favorite, especially with toddlers. There are companion stories: *I Am a Kitten*, *I Am a Puppy*, and, for those old enough to get the Sesame Street joke, *I Am a Monster.*

IF THERE WERE DREAMS TO SELL   [122]

WRITTEN BY BARBARA LALICKI
ILLUSTRATED BY MARGOT TOMES
Cloth: Lothrop
Published: 1984   PRIZES: NEW YORK TIMES BEST ILLUSTRATED BOOK

An unusual alphabet book with droll text and muted illustrations of an elfin world that are distinctive.

I GO WITH MY FAMILY
TO GRANDMA'S [123]

WRITTEN BY RIKI LEVINSON
ILLUSTRATED BY DIANE GOODE
Cloth: Dutton
Published: 1986

Five cousins and their families from the five boroughs of New York City assemble at their grandparents' home in Manhattan on a summery day around the turn of the century. The text is straightforward, and the detailed illustrations showing the different families and different children are rich and intriguing, as well as fun to count.

I KNOW AN OLD LADY
WHO SWALLOWED A FLY [124]

WRITTEN AND ILLUSTRATED BY NADINE BERNARD WESCOTT
Cloth: Atlantic-Little, Brown
Paper: Atlantic-Little, Brown
Published: 1981

A brightly illustrated version of the folk song about that silly old woman who kept on swallowing larger and larger things until eventually she swallowed a horse. She died, of course.

I LOVE MY BABY SISTER
(MOST OF THE TIME) [125]

WRITTEN BY ELAINE EDELMAN
ILLUSTRATED BY WENDY WATSON
Cloth: Lothrop
Paper: Penguin
Published: 1984

As this little girl describes life with her baby sister, she is very honest about the initial disadvantages of the situation. Nevertheless, she hopes that as the baby gets older, they will play together.

Picture Books

I'M TELLING YOU NOW [126]

WRITTEN BY JUDY DELTON
ILLUSTRATED BY LILLIAN HOBAN
Cloth: Dutton
Paper: Dutton
Published: 1983

Every time Artie gets out of an improbable but plausible scrape he tells his mother, "You never told me I couldn't," and like mothers everywhere, she replies predictably. This is all too real, but also endearing and funny.

THE INSIDE-OUTSIDE BOOK OF NEW YORK CITY [127]

WRITTEN AND ILLUSTRATED BY ROXIE MUNRO
Cloth: Dodd
Published: 1985   PRIZES: NEW YORK TIMES BEST ILLUSTRATED BOOK

Views of famous sights and buildings in New York City, including the Statue of Liberty, the spire of the Chrysler Building, the front car of a subway train, and many more, are seen from the outside and the inside in witty colored drawings. A wonderful idea, handsomely executed and full of details. A companion book of sorts is *Christmas in New York*.

IT DOES NOT SAY MEOW AND OTHER ANIMAL RIDDLE RHYMES [128]

WRITTEN BY BEATRICE SCHENK de REGNIERS
ILLUSTRATED BY PAUL GALDONE
Cloth: Clarion
Paper: Clarion
Published: 1972

Rhymed riddles about nine familiar animals, from ant to elephant. The verse is on the right side of the page, the illustrated answer follows on the next double page. Preschoolers revel in such questions.

IT'S RAINING SAID JOHN TWAINING: DANISH NURSERY RHYMES [129]

WRITTEN AND ILLUSTRATED BY N. M. BRODECKER

Cloth: McElderry

Paper: Aladdin

Published: 1973

The distinguished translator/illustrator offers a delightful collection of Danish nursery rhymes that American children find enchanting.

I WON'T GO TO BED! [130]

WRITTEN BY HARRIET ZIEFERT

ILLUSTRATED BY ANDREA BARUFFI

Cloth: Little, Brown

Published: 1987

Harry won't. So his father leaves him downstairs. And as the hours grow later, things seem larger and stranger than they do in the daytime, until the little boy falls asleep on the floor. The illustrations capture the way a child feels smaller as the night grows darker.

JAMBO MEANS HELLO: SWAHILI ALPHABET BOOK [131]

WRITTEN BY MURIEL FEELINGS

ILLUSTRATED BY TOM FEELINGS

Cloth: Dial

Paper: Dial

Published: 1974   AWARDS: CALDECOTT HONOR BOOK

A fine anthropological alphabet book that conveys a vision of tribal life in East Africa. A companion volume, *Moja Means One*, is a counting book. This is really for school-age children and interested adults.

Picture Books

JAMES MARSHALL'S MOTHER GOOSE [132]

SELECTED AND ILLUSTRATED BY JAMES MARSHALL

Cloth: Farrar, Straus
Paper: Sunburst/Farrar, Straus
Published: 1979

This Mother Goose collection is illustrated in a distinctively manic style by the artist who created *George and Martha* and *The Stupids*. The pictures are broad and cartoonish, the selection of verses all bright and cheery as well as familiar.

JESSE BEAR, WHAT WILL YOU WEAR? [133]

WRITTEN BY NANCY WHITE CARLSTROM
ILLUSTRATED BY BRUCE DEGEN

Cloth: Macmillan
Published: 1986

A lilting rhyme that begins as Jesse Bear wakes up and makes some decisions about his day. A happy book, with happy illustrations, for preschoolers who enjoy making the same kinds of decisions. The bears are wonderful.

THE LADY AND THE SPIDER [134]

WRITTEN BY FAITH McNULTY
ILLUSTRATED BY BOB MARSTALL

Cloth: Harper
Paper: Harper
Published: 1986

A spider lives quietly in a vegetable garden. One day the lady who tends the garden picks the head of lettuce in which he lives, but stops short of destroying him. This is fine science writing for very young children, accessible to preschoolers and of interest to school-age children.

[133]

LET'S GO SWIMMING WITH MR. SILLYPANTS [135]

WRITTEN AND ILLUSTRATED BY M. K. BROWN
Cloth: Crown
Published: 1986

Mr. Sillypants, whose name doesn't nearly convey what a ridiculous-looking fellow he is, signs up for swimming lessons and immediately becomes terrified of water. He has an explicit dream about his fears and then goes to try to learn how to swim. The illustrations are witty and, well, silly.

A LION FOR LEWIS [136]

WRITTEN AND ILLUSTRATED BY ROSEMARY WELLS
Cloth: Dial
Paper: Dial
Published: 1982

Tag-along Lewis is always just a beat behind his older siblings, either too late for their games or the brunt of them. Then one day he finds a stuffed lion suit in the attic. The full-color illustrations are apt, especially when Lewis gets into that lion. A special favorite of preschool younger siblings.

THE LITTLE DUCK [137]

WRITTEN BY JUDY DUNN
ILLUSTRATED BY PHOEBE DUNN
Paper: Random House
Published: 1976

One of a fine series of paperback photo-essays about small creatures. The simple story is about a year in the life of a duck, lovingly hatched and raised by a small boy. The photography, particularly of the hatching egg, is very clear and uncluttered. Other titles in the series include *The Little Goat*, *The Little Kitten*, *The Little Lamb*, *The Little Puppy*, and *The Little Rabbit*.

[147]

45

Picture Books

THE LITTLE ENGINE THAT COULD   [138]

WRITTEN BY WATTY PIPER
ILLUSTRATED BY GEORGE AND DORIS HAUMAN
Cloth: Platt & Munk
Published: 1930

One of the basic books of American childhood, this is the saga of the little engine that thought it could help deliver toys and fruits to the children living over the mountain. Avoid the gussied-up editions. The little engine need not pop up or go fast; it is, after all, just a little engine, like the very young child who is listening to the chant "I think I can, I think I can..."

THE LITTLE FIR TREE   [139]

WRITTEN BY MARGARET WISE BROWN
ILLUSTRATED BY BARBARA COONEY
Cloth: Crowell
Paper: Harper
Published: 1954, reprinted 1979

A Christmas story about a lame boy and a little fir tree that is brought to him. The small, delicately illustrated format is appealing.

THE LITTLE FUR FAMILY   [140]

WRITTEN BY MARGARET WISE BROWN
ILLUSTRATED BY GARTH WILLIAMS
Cloth: Harper
Paper: Harper
Published: 1951

A day in the life of a little fur child that ends with a bedtime song. The little fur family is "warm as toast, smaller than most." The cover is fuzzy fake fur.

LITTLE GORILLA [141]

WRITTEN AND ILLUSTRATED BY RUTH BORNSTEIN
Cloth: Clarion
Paper: Clarion
Published: 1976

This is the story of a wide-eyed Little Gorilla who grows and grows and grows and is still loved, even when he is a great big gorilla. Very young children find it soothing, perhaps because the gorilla is so winsome.

THE LITTLE ISLAND [142]

WRITTEN BY GOLDEN MacDONALD
ILLUSTRATED BY LEONARD WEISGARD
Cloth: Doubleday
Paper: Scholastic
Published: 1946   PRIZES: CALDECOTT MEDAL

The little island itself is the hero of a low-key illustrated fantasy. It communes with visiting creatures, including lobsters, seals, and a kitten, and muses about life. If the quiet anthropomorphizing seems vaguely familiar somehow, it is because the author of this old-fashioned charmer is Margaret Wise Brown using a pseudonym.

LOUANNE PIG IN THE TALENT SHOW [143]

WRITTEN AND ILLUSTRATED BY NANCY CARLSON
Cloth: Carolrhoda
Paper: Penguin
Published: 1986

[90]

One of a series of believable little adventures of a very nice pig who might be just like someone in your neighborhood. Both the text and the illustrations are uncluttered and bright. Other titles include *The Mysterious Valentine, The Perfect Family, Making the Team,* and *Witch Lady.* The author also writes and illustrates comparable series about Loudmouth George, a rabbit, and Harriet, a charming golden retriever.

Picture Books

LUCY & TOM'S 1 2 3 [144]

WRITTEN AND ILLUSTRATED BY SHIRLEY HUGHES

Cloth: Viking
Paper: Penguin
Published: 1987

One of a series of concept books for toddlers and preschoolers about two engaging young children, Lucy and Tom, who deal with the alphabet, a busy day, counting, and Christmas. Though the books were first published in Britain in the 1970s, they have only recently been widely available here. *Lucy & Tom's Day*, *Lucy & Tom's Christmas*, and *Lucy & Tom's a.b.c.* are available in paperback.

MADELINE [145]

WRITTEN AND ILLUSTRATED BY LUDWIG BEMELMANS

Cloth: Viking
Paper: Puffin
Published: 1939

"In an old house in Paris that was covered with vines" the story begins, and the sing-song text carries the twelve little girls and their headmistress, dear Miss Clavel, through a series of madcap adventures. The brilliant, busy, Gallic illustrations capture, and indeed encapsulate, a sense of Paris as so many people, children and adults, believe it once was. Other titles include *Madeline and the Bad Hat*, *Madeline and the Gypsies*, *Madeline in London*, and *Madeline's Rescue*.

THE MAGGIE B [146]

WRITTEN AND ILLUSTRATED BY IRENE HAAS

Cloth: McElderry
Paper: Aladdin
Published: 1975

Margaret Barnstable has a very simple fantasy—she dreams of spending a perfect day aboard the sturdy little ship the *Maggie B* with only her baby brother James for company. But because it is a fantasy, the enchanting little ship comes equipped with a top deck that holds a farm and a peach tree, among other unusual amenities. It is very easy to substitute names of real siblings when reading the nicely cadenced text aloud.

[145]

MAKE WAY FOR DUCKLINGS [147]

WRITTEN AND ILLUSTRATED BY ROBERT McCLOSKEY

Cloth: Viking
Paper: Puffin
Published: 1941   PRIZES: CALDECOTT MEDAL

[147]

In Boston, where there is a higher order to things, a family of ducklings on their way to the Public Gardens can stop traffic. It doesn't matter a whit if these illustrations seem old-fashioned—they are endearing and firmly establish the Public Gardens as an estimable place to raise a family.

MAMA DON'T ALLOW [148]

WRITTEN AND ILLUSTRATED BY THACHER HURD

Cloth: Harper
Paper: Harper
Published: 1984

Noise, noise, noise! The Swamp Band plays loudly all night for the Alligator Ball. Lush, funny illustrations and a new setting of a familiar folk song.

MAMA'S SECRET [149]

WRITTEN BY MARIA POLUSHKIN
ILLUSTRATED BY FELICIA BOND

Cloth: Four Winds
Published: 1984

Mama slips out of the house while the children are napping and picks enough blueberries for lots of sweet treats. The pastel illustrations have the clear quality of a summer afternoon.

THE MAN WHO KEPT HOUSE [150]

WRITTEN BY KATHLEEN AND MICHAEL HAGUE
ILLUSTRATED BY MICHAEL HAGUE

Cloth: Harcourt Brace
Paper: Voyager/HBJ
Published: 1981

The farmer decides to switch roles with his wife and makes a colossal botch of things. Based on a Scandinavian folktale, this is an ever-perti-

nent lesson for all ages. The old-fashioned full-color illustrations are fun, especially those involving the pig.

MARMALADE'S NAP   [151]

WRITTEN AND ILLUSTRATED BY CINDY WHEELER
Cloth: Knopf
Published: 1983

One of a series of small books about a smug and sassy orange cat. In this one, Marmalade is looking for a place to nap out of doors on a spring day. Other titles include *Marmalade's Picnic*, *Marmalade's Snowy Day*, and *Marmalade's Yellow Leaf*.

MARTIN'S HATS   [152]

WRITTEN BY JOAN W. BLOS
ILLUSTRATED BY MARC SIMONT
Cloth: Morrow
Paper: Mulberry
Published: 1984

With his wardrobe of hats to fit every fantasy, Martin is a kind of pre-school Walter Mitty. The illustrations are properly fanciful.

[150]

MARY HAD A LITTLE LAMB   [153]

WRITTEN BY MARY JOSEPHA HALE
ILLUSTRATED BY TOMIE de PAOLA
Cloth: Holiday
Paper: Holiday
Published: 1984

A bright and stylized version of one of the best-known songs of early childhood. A musical arrangement is included.

MARY WORE HER RED DRESS, AND HENRY WORE HIS GREEN SNEAKERS [154]

WRITTEN AND ILLUSTRATED BY MERLE PEEK

Cloth: Clarion
Paper: Clarion
Published: 1985

Katie's animal friends wear different-colored clothing to her birthday-party. The music to this folk song is included, and the verses can be adapted to your family and your preschool birthday parties.

MAX'S FIRST WORD [155]

WRITTEN AND ILLUSTRATED BY ROSEMARY WELLS

Cloth: Dial
Published: 1979

Max, the lovable rabbit toddler who has a bossy and talkative older sister named Ruby, stars in an outstanding series of board books for very young children. Max is curious, and quite independent. In addition to *Max's New Suit*, *Max's Ride*, and *Max's Toys: A Counting Book*, there is a series of four "very first" titles covering bath, bedtime, birthday, and breakfast, and *Max's Christmas*.

MAY I BRING A FRIEND? [156]

WRITTEN BY BEATRICE SCHENK de REGNIERS
ILLUSTRATED BY BENI MONTRESOR

Cloth: Atheneum
Paper: Aladdin
Published: 1964   PRIZES: CALDECOTT MEDAL

The King and Queen keep inviting the little boy to visit, and each time he comes, he brings along a growing entourage of remarkable animal friends whose manners are not what they should be.

[155]

MICE TWICE [157]

WRITTEN AND ILLUSTRATED BY JOSEPH LOW

Cloth: McElderry

Paper: Aladdin

Published: 1980   PRIZES: CALDECOTT HONOR BOOK

Cat invites Mouse to dinner, planning to eat him; Mouse brings an unexpected companion, and a frenzy of competitiveness and surprises ensues, all illustrated with great wit.

THE MILK MAKERS [158]

WRITTEN AND ILLUSTRATED BY GAIL GIBBONS

Cloth: Macmillan

Paper: Aladdin

Published: 1985

Just how does milk get from cow to cup? The answers are given here in clear, accurate illustrations and spare, precise text.

MILLIONS OF CATS [159]

WRITTEN AND ILLUSTRATED BY WANDA GAG

Cloth: Coward

Paper: Coward

Published: 1928   PRIZES: NEWBURY HONOR BOOK

This is the story of the little old man who went to find a cat to please the little old woman, and brought home hundreds of cats, thousands of cats, millions of cats. Eventually the cats fight, and only one scrawny, shy kitten is left to keep the old couple company. A classic picture book whose text can be recited by hundreds of people, thousands of people, millions and millions and millions of people. Timeless. Ageless.

[159]

MITCHELL IS MOVING [160]

WRITTEN BY MARJORIE WEINMAN SHARMAT
ILLUSTRATED BY JOSE ARUEGO AND ARIANE DEWEY
Cloth: Macmillan
Paper: Aladdin
Published: 1978

Moving can be a real problem. Mitchell the dinosaur has decided to move after sixty years in the same place. His friend Margo decides to stop him.

THE MIXED-UP CHAMELEON [161]

WRITTEN AND ILLUSTRATED BY ERIC CARLE
Cloth: Crowell
Paper: Harper
Published: 1975

A chameleon goes to the zoo and imagines becoming a variety of other creatures. The illustrations—finger-painted collages—are distinctive and in the winning style of Carle's best-loved *The Very Hungry Caterpillar.*

MOTHER, MOTHER, I WANT ANOTHER [162]

WRITTEN BY MARIA POLUSKIN
ILLUSTRATED BY DIANE DAWSON
Cloth: Crown
Paper: Crown
Published: 1978

It's bedtime and the little mouse should be settled down, but suddenly she wants another...so Mama scurries about trying to figure out what it is she wants. The answer will please. (It's a kiss!)

MR. AND MRS. PIG'S EVENING OUT [163]

WRITTEN AND ILLUSTRATED BY MARY RAYNER
Cloth: Atheneum
Paper: Aladdin
Published: 1976

Mr. and Mrs. Pig don't take careful notice of the baby-sitter before they leave Mrs. Wolf in charge of their ten piglets. Her true nature

[159]

Picture Books

emerges late in the evening, and she is about to make a meal of the youngest when she is routed and vanquished, only to reappear in *Garth Pig and the Ice-Cream Lady.* In *Mrs. Pig's Bulk Buy* there is no wolf, but a lightly told moral about what happens when the piglets have all they want of catsup, their favorite food, and more. There is also a collection of family stories, *Mrs. Pig Gets Cross.*

MR. GUMPY'S OUTING   [164]

WRITTEN AND ILLUSTRATED BY JOHN BURNINGHAM
Cloth: Holt
Paper: Puffin Books
Published: 1971   PRIZES: NEW YORK TIMES BEST ILLUSTRATED BOOK
On a hot summer afternoon an ungainly assortment of children and animals pile into Mr. Gumpy's little boat, but of course they don't all fit —with predictable results. Another delightful book about Mr. Gumpy is *Mr. Gumpy's Motor Car.*

MR. RABBIT AND
THE LOVELY PRESENT   [165]

WRITTEN BY CHARLOTTE ZOLOTOW
ILLUSTRATED BY MAURICE SENDAK
Cloth: Harper
Paper: Harper
Published: 1962   PRIZES: CALDECOTT HONOR BOOK
Mr. Rabbit helps a gentle little girl gather the components of a truly lovely present for her mother.

MRS. PIGGLE-WIGGLE   [166]

WRITTEN BY BETTY MacDONALD
ILLUSTRATED BY HILARY KNIGHT
Cloth: Lippincott
Paper: Harper
Published: 1957
These well-loved and easy-to-read books are a kind of catalogue of childhood misbehavior and pranks, all cured by the delightful Mrs.

Piggle-Wiggle. She is not a witch but a rare and perceptive old lady who never scolds but has some very clever ideas about how to handle children who aren't really naughty but are, for example, Never-Want-to-Go-to-Bedders, or Tattle-Tales, or Fraidy-Cats. The series includes *Hello, Mrs. Piggle-Wiggle, Mrs. Piggle-Wiggle's Farm,* and *Mrs. Piggle-Wiggle's Magic.* There is a boxed set of four titles.

MY BOOK [167]

WRITTEN AND ILLUSTRATED BY RON MARIS
Paper: Puffin
Published: 1983

The first in a series of cleverly illustrated books using alternating full pages and cut half pages that reveal details of the illustration. Here the reader follows a child home to bed where he reads this very book. Other titles include *My Room* and *Is Anyone Home?*

MY GRANDSON LEW [168]

WRITTEN BY CHARLOTTE ZOLOTOW
ILLUSTRATED BY WILLIAM PÈNE DU BOIS
Cloth: Harper
Paper: Harper
Published: 1974

Lew's grandfather died when Lew was quite small, but it turns out that Lew remembers him in vivid fragments when he and his mother talk about remembering him one night.

MY MAMA NEEDS ME [169]

WRITTEN BY MILDRED PITTS WALKER
ILLUSTRATED BY PAT CUMMINGS
Cloth: Lothrop
Published: 1983

Jason wants to be a good big brother, but he is both excited and scared about the new baby coming home. Then it turns out she sleeps all the time, and Jason is relieved.

[161]

Picture Books

MY MOM TRAVELS A LOT [170]

WRITTEN BY CAROLINE FELLER BAUER
ILLUSTRATED BY NANCY WINSLOW PARKER
Cloth: Warne
Paper: Puffin
Published: 1981   PRIZES: NEW YORK TIMES BEST ILLUSTRATED BOOK

This is a good-news/bad-news story familiar to all children with parents whose work requires them to travel. It is told in a bright, breezy way, because after all, travel is a fact of life.

MY RED UMBRELLA [171]

WRITTEN AND ILLUSTRATED BY ROBERT BRIGHT
Cloth: Morrow
Paper: Morrow, Jr.
Published: 1959, reissued 1985

A small-hand-size, endearing book about a perky little girl whose red umbrella expands during a shower to shelter a whole menagerie of animals.

NANA UPSTAIRS & NANA DOWNSTAIRS [172]

WRITTEN AND ILLUSTRATED BY TOMIE de PAOLA
Cloth: Putnam
Paper: Puffin
Published: 1973

As a grown-up, Tommy remembers the rituals of his visits to the house his active grandmother (Nana Downstairs) shared with his bedridden, 94-year-old great-grandmother (Nana Upstairs), both of whom he loved dearly. Death is a fact, presented and accepted. Even now Tommy sees the Nanas' spirits in shooting stars. A very fine book.

[177]

THE NAPPING HOUSE [173]

WRITTEN BY AUDREY WOOD
ILLUSTRATED BY DON WOOD
Cloth: Harcourt Brace
Published: 1984   PRIZES: NEW YORK TIMES BEST ILLUSTRATED BOOK

A silly, sleepy tale set in a blue house in a blue world in which all the
sleeping creatures in the house—child, cat, dog, and more—drift into
granny's bed in a great cuddly heap.

THE NIGHT BEFORE CHRISTMAS [174]

WRITTEN BY CLEMENT C. MOORE
ILLUSTRATED BY ANITA LOBEL
Cloth: Knopf
Paper: Knopf
Published: 1984

The ultimate New York (or rather, Brooklyn) edition of the Christmas
verse, with illustrations set in a cozy Victorian brownstone house in
Brooklyn with the Brooklyn Bridge in the background. There are
many other editions available, from the 1912 version with illustrations
by Jessie W. Smith to James Marshall's (cartoonish) and Cyndy
Szekeres's (cuddly). All are appealing.

NOAH'S ARK [175]

WRITTEN AND ILLUSTRATED BY NONNY HOGROGIAN
Cloth: Knopf
Published: 1986

This version of the story of Noah actually begins with the Creation.
The prize-winning illustrator uses a pale palette and text from the
King James version.

[233]

Picture Books

NOTHING EVER HAPPENS ON MY BLOCK [176]

WRITTEN AND ILLUSTRATED BY ELLEN RASKIN
Cloth: Atheneum
Paper: Aladdin
Published: 1966   PRIZES: NEW YORK TIMES BEST ILLUSTRATED BOOK

A jewel-like example of ironic story telling and droll illustration. Chester Filbert sits on his stoop, complaining that nothing ever happens on his block, while all around him there is mystery, excitement, and adventure—witches, fires, robbery, mayhem. All ages find it fresh and funny. The trick in reading it aloud is "reading" everything that is happening as well as the text.

NOT SO FAST, SONGOLOLO [177]

WRITTEN AND ILLUSTRATED BY NIKI DALY
Cloth: McElderry
Paper: Puffin
Published: 1986

Cheerful, detailed watercolor illustrations accompany the story of little Malusi and his trip to the city with his granny to buy what in South Africa are called tackies and what American children know as sneakers. The ordinary everyday quality of the expedition is part of the book's charm.

NUTSHELL LIBRARY [178]

WRITTEN AND ILLUSTRATED BY MAURICE SENDAK
Cloth: Harper
Published: 1962

These four little books—*Alligators All Around: An Alphabet, Chicken Soup with Rice: A Book of Months, One Was Johnny: A Counting Book,* and *Pierre: A Cautionary Tale in Five Chapters and a Prologue*—come in a small box, fit in small hands, and are memorable both separately and together. In addition, they are the source of the lyrics to many of the best and catchiest songs in "Really Rosie," the TV special/video/play with music by Carole King. The whole family may well end up singing the words from memory.

OH, A-HUNTING WE WILL GO   [179]

WRITTEN BY JOHN LANGSTAFF
ILLUSTRATED BY NANCY WINSLOW PARKER
Cloth: McElderry
Published: 1974
A very jolly version of the familiar folk song with piano and guitar accompaniment.

ONCE A MOUSE...   [180]

WRITTEN AND ILLUSTRATED BY MARCIA BROWN
Cloth: Scribners
Paper: Aladdin   PRIZES: CALDECOTT MEDAL,
Published: 1961   NEW YORK TIMES BEST ILLUSTRATED BOOK
A reconsideration of magic in a successful picture book. A hermit transforms a mouse successively into a car, a dog, a tiger. But the tiger is so proud the hermit pauses.

ONE FINE DAY   [181]

WRITTEN AND ILLUSTRATED BY NONNY HOGROGIAN
Cloth: Macmillan
Paper: Aladdin
Published: 1971   PRIZES: CALDECOTT MEDAL
In this wittily illustrated Armenian folktale, a sly fox steals milk from an old woman. She gets her revenge and his tail.

ONE FISH, TWO FISH, RED FISH, BLUE FISH   [182]

WRITTEN AND ILLUSTRATED BY DR. SEUSS
Cloth: Beginner Books
Published: 1960
Designed as an early reader using rhyme and a very limited vocabulary, this collection of verses about Seussian creatures at play and rest is wildly successful with toddlers and younger children, and remains endurable to the reading adult.

[182]

Picture Books

101 THINGS TO DO WITH A BABY [183]

WRITTEN AND ILLUSTRATED BY JAN ORMEROD

Cloth: Lothrop
Paper: Puffin
Published: 1984

A catalog of activities, this is also a record of a day in the life of a family with a father, an active older sister, a dear baby, and a black cat. Mother is the loving artist. The three-color illustrations and gentle domestic ideas are both enchanting and encouraging. A book for siblings of many ages.

1 HUNTER [184]

WRITTEN AND ILLUSTRATED BY PAT HUTCHINS

Cloth: Greenwillow
Paper: Mulberry
Published: 1982

A counting book that is both comic and suspenseful, because one hunter going through the jungle does not see two elephants or three giraffes, but they see him. And so on.

ONE MONDAY MORNING [185]

WRITTEN AND ILLUSTRATED BY URI SHULEVITZ

Cloth: Scribners
Paper: Aladdin
Published: 1967

In this fine urban fantasy, a little boy who lives in an old apartment building in a downtown somewhere imagines that the King and Queen are coming to visit him. But since he's very busy, he misses them on each return visit as their retinue grows so that while the text remains disarmingly simple, the illustrations grow increasingly complex.

[200]

ON MARKET STREET   [186]

WRITTEN BY ARNOLD LOBEL AND ANITA LOBEL
ILLUSTRATED BY ANITA LOBEL

Cloth: Greenwillow
Paper: Scholastic
Published: 1981   PRIZES: NEW YORK TIMES BEST ILLUSTRATED BOOK

An unusual and lavish alphabet book in which a boy goes down Market Street, buying presents beginning with each letter of the alphabet for a friend. The letters are figures made of apples, quilts, wigs, and such.

OUR ANIMAL FRIENDS AT MAPLE HILL FARM   [187]

WRITTEN AND ILLUSTRATED BY ALICE AND MARTIN
  PROVENSEN

Cloth: Random House
Published: 1974

The creatures who live at the authors' Maple Hill Farm in New York State—the cats, dogs, sheep, goats, horses, children, and others—have whimsical names (the cats are Eggnog, Willow, and Gooseberry), but the owners are matter-of-fact about their behavior and witty about their foibles.

OVER AND OVER   [188]

WRITTEN BY CHARLOTTE ZOLOTOW
ILLUSTRATED BY GARTH WILLIAMS

Cloth: Harper
Paper: Harper
Published: 1957

Very little children don't understand the passage of time very well. The little girl in this story makes a birthday wish for things to happen again, and, day by day, then week by week and month by month. The charming illustrations capture the passing seasons in her year.

[185]

Picture Books

OWLY [189]

WRITTEN BY MIKE THALER
ILLUSTRATED BY DAVID WIESNER
Cloth: Harper
Published: 1982

Owly keeps asking his mother questions about the nature and shape of the world, and she wisely suggests that he seek answers for himself. This is a very quiet bedtime story. The illustrations are in the pale colors of predawn (Owly's bedtime). Parental love is enabling, not possessive.

PAT THE BUNNY [190]

WRITTEN AND ILLUSTRATED BY DOROTHY KUNHARDT
Cloth: Golden Books/Western
Published: 1940

The original baby's activity book—pat the bunny, feel Daddy's scratchy face, look in the mirror, put your finger through Mummy's ring. Some babies love it, eat several copies before they have even learned to walk; others could care less. It is not a litmus test of future literary taste either way.

PEABODY [191]

WRITTEN AND ILLUSTRATED BY ROSEMARY WELLS
Cloth: Dial
Paper: Dial
Published: 1983

Peabody is Annie's teddy bear, and everything is just fine till Annie gets a walking, talking doll. This plays nicely on a story familiar to grown-ups. Like the plain brown nightingale, the familiar teddy proves best.

THE PEARL [192]

WRITTEN AND ILLUSTRATED BY HELME HEINE
Cloth: McElderry
Paper: Aladdin
Published: 1985

Playing by the pond one day, Beaver finds a mussel and is sure it contains a pearl. In his dream, the pearl causes nothing but dissension and strife among his friends. This cautionary tale by the German artist is illustrated with his usual wit and charm.

PETUNIA [193]

WRITTEN AND ILLUSTRATED BY ROGER DUVOISIN
Cloth: Knopf
Published: 1950

Some creatures never to do seem to learn, but Petunia, a very silly goose, thinks if she carries a book around the barnyard she will be wise. There are five stories about her collected in *Petunia the Silly Goose Stories*.

PIGGYBOOK [194]

WRITTEN AND ILLUSTRATED BY ANTHONY BROWNE
Cloth: Knopf
Published: 1986

Mr. Piggott and the boys are, as the note Mrs. Piggott leaves them says, pigs, and she is tired of doing all the "unimportant" household maintenance jobs without any help. And lo, they turn into real pigs. Clever illustrations underscore the basic feminist/humanist/real life point about cooperation at home.

THE PIGS' WEDDING [195]

WRITTEN AND ILLUSTRATED BY HELME HEINE
Cloth: McElderry
Published: 1979

What do you think would happen at the pigs' wedding? In fact, the answers given in the full-color, whimsical illustrations are full of surprises.

POOKINS GETS HER WAY [196]

WRITTEN BY HELEN LESTER
ILLUSTRATED BY LYNN MUNSINGER
Cloth: Houghton Mifflin
Published: 1987

[196]

Pookins is spoiled rotten, and by golly she wants to be a flower. She gets her way but learns a lesson about cooperation. The author and illustra-

Picture Books

tor have produced a group of funny/wise picture books that make small, important lessons lightly. Other titles include *A Porcupine Named Fluffy* and *It Wasn't My Fault*.

POPPY THE PANDA   [197]

WRITTEN AND ILLUSTRATED BY DICK GACKENBACH
Cloth: Clarion
Paper: Clarion
Published: 1984

Poppy the Panda, who belongs to Katie O'Keefe, wants a special costume, and Katie does her best, but nothing satisfies Poppy until Katie's mother tries her idea. A nice book for preschoolers with strong notions about getting dressed.

POTATOES, POTATOES   [198]

WRITTEN AND ILLUSTRATED BY ANITA LOBEL
Cloth: Harper
Published: 1967

Two generals are reconciled after a battle over their mother's only remaining potato field. In other words, a fable about war and peace in picture book form, with illustrations that are suggestive, not preachy.

THE RAFFI SINGABLE SONGBOOK   [199]

WRITTEN BY RAFFI
Cloth: Crown
Published: 1987

Sing along with your records and tapes, boys and girls, mothers and dads. This spiral-bound collection of the Canadian singer's song arrangements is pleasing. There is *The Second Raffi Songbook* as well, and two favorites have been illustrated amusingly in separate editions— *Shake My Sillies Out* and *Down by the Bay*.

READ-ALOUD RHYMES
FOR THE VERY YOUNG   [200]

SELECTED BY JACK PRELUTSKY
ILLUSTRATED BY MARC BROWN
Cloth: Knopf
Published: 1986

A fine, brightly illustrated collection of more than 200 rhymes, mostly
familiar, ideal for reading aloud to young children. An introduction by
Jim Trelease emphasizes the importance of reading aloud.

THE REAL MOTHER GOOSE   [201]

SELECTED AND ILLUSTRATED BY BLANCHE FISHER WRIGHT
Cloth: Checkerboard
Published: 1916

This selection from the Mother Goose canon comes in a distinctive
checkerboard binding and has delightful, old-fashioned illustrations. It
is, indeed, one that great-grandparents and grandparents first read. It
has also been adapted, cut up into smaller selections of verses about
animals, children, playtime, and so on.

THE RELATIVES CAME   [202]

WRITTEN BY CYNTHIA RYLANT
ILLUSTRATED BY STEPHEN GAMMELL
Cloth: Bradbury   PRIZES: CALDECOTT HONOR BOOK,
Published: 1985   NEW YORK TIMES BEST ILLUSTRATED BOOK

One summer a whole slew of relatives gets up before dawn to come and
visit. They crowd the house, create the happiest kind of chaos and com-
motion, but eventually have to leave. The spikey illustrations capture
a homey confusion and delight that memory does not blur. A real
charmer.

Picture Books

RICHARD SCARRY'S BEST WORD BOOK EVER [203]

WRITTEN AND ILLUSTRATED BY RICHARD SCARRY

Cloth: Golden Books/Western

Published: 1963 (revised 1980)

Most adults find this book unappealing—the pages are crowded with details, jumbles of jokes, and anthropomorphized creatures such as Lowly Worm who are involved in running jokes. But they are adults. Children, especially toddlers and preschoolers, consider it almost endlessly interesting, full of things to label, activities to imagine, and jokes to savor again and again. If you remember it from your own childhood and think this edition is slimmer, you are right, it has been abridged, but the dental hygienist is still a walrus. There is also *Richard Scarry's Best Mother Goose Ever. Lowly Worm's Word Book* is a small chunky book published by Random House.

ROSIE'S WALK [204]

WRITTEN AND ILLUSTRATED BY PAT HUTCHINS

Cloth: Macmillan

Paper: Aladdin

Published: 1968

Rosie the hen goes for a stroll around the barnyard, oblivious to the fox who keeps botching his attempts to catch her. If the jokes are all telegraphed to the adult eye, that doesn't make them a whit less funny to toddlers and preschoolers.

ROTTEN RALPH [205]

WRITTEN BY JACK GANTOS

ILLUSTRATED BY NICOLE RUBEL

Cloth: Houghton Mifflin

Paper: Houghton Mifflin

Published: 1976

The first of a series of books about a very naughty cat named Ralph. Sarah, his owner, can never believe how badly he behaves, but oh, the reader can. The illustrations are distinctive and offbeat. Other titles are *Rotten Ralph's Rotten Christmas* and *Worse than Rotten Ralph*.

THE RUNAWAY BUNNY   [206]

WRITTEN BY MARGARET WISE BROWN
ILLUSTRATED BY CLEMENT HURD
Cloth: Harper
Paper: Harper
Published: 1972

The little bunny plays a pretend game of hide and seek and is comforted to realize that his mother will always know how to find him wherever he hides. The illustrations are wonderful—very young children love spotting the bunny in the garden, on the mountain, at the circus. Some grownups think the mother's absolute authority is smothering and prefer other ways to tell how much a mother loves her child.

17 KINGS AND 42 ELEPHANTS   [207]

WRITTEN BY MARGARET MAHY
ILLUSTRATED BY PATRICIA McCARTHY
Cloth: Dial
Published: 1987   PRIZES: NEW YORK TIMES BEST ILLUSTRATED BOOK

A glorious nonsense verse about royalty and pachyderms trundling through the jungle one mysterious night. Handsomely illustrated by batik fabric designs. Watch that tiger!

SHEEP IN A JEEP   [208]

WRITTEN BY NANCY SHAW
ILLUSTRATED BY MARGOT APPLE
Cloth: Houghton Mifflin
Published: 1986

What a ride! On a bright, sunny day a flock of sheep set off for a ride in a Jeep. The short (83 words), chantable text is great fun for toddlers and preschoolers in particular.

[204]

Picture Books

SING A SONG OF PEOPLE [209]

WRITTEN BY LOIS LENSKI
ILLUSTRATED BY GILES LAROCHE
Cloth: Little, Brown
Published: 1987

Lois Lenski's poem was set to extraordinary illustrations composed of three-dimensional paper figures depicting downtown Boston in the 1980s. The effect is enchanting even to non–New Englanders.

THE SKY IS FULL OF SONG [210]

WRITTEN BY LEE BENNETT HOPKINS
ILLUSTRATED BY DIRK ZIMMER
Cloth: Harper
Paper: Harper
Published: 1983

A very small book for small hands to hold—an anthology of short, seasonal poems, from fall to fall, perfect for children who know the year begins when school starts. Light and airy wood block illustrations complement the verses.

SLEEPY PEOPLE [211]

WRITTEN AND ILLUSTRATED BY M. B. GOFFSTEIN
Cloth: Farrar, Straus
Published: 1966, revised edition 1979

Streeeetch, yawn, relax. This bedtime story is about a family of very small folks, who possibly are living in one of "your old bedroom slippers" and are getting ready for bed, too. Delicate pen-and-ink drawings portray the sleepy people as soft, cuddly dolls.

[212]

THE SNOWY DAY [212]

WRITTEN AND ILLUSTRATED BY EZRA JACK KEATS
Cloth: Viking
Paper: Puffin
Published: 1962   PRIZES: CALDECOTT MEDAL

One snowy day, a little black boy named Peter puts on his red snowsuit and explores his city neighborhood. The brightly colored collage illustrations have an undiminished freshness...like new-fallen snow itself. Peter also appears in *Goggles*, *A Letter to Amy*, *Peter's Chair*, and the delightful *Whistle for Willie*.

SNUGGLE PIGGY AND THE MAGIC BLANKET [213]

WRITTEN BY MICHELE STEPTO
ILLUSTRATED BY JOHN HIMMELMAN
Cloth: Dutton
Published: 1987

One day Snuggle Piggy's magically beautiful security blanket is left on the line when it begins to rain. He has a satisfying dream adventure to rationalize the situation.

SONG OF THE SWALLOWS [214]

WRITTEN AND ILLUSTRATED BY LEO POLITI
Cloth: Scribners
Paper: Aladdin
Published: 1949   PRIZES: CALDECOTT MEDAL

The story of the swallows who come each year to Capistrano is told here through young Juan and old Julian who lived in the town a long time ago. Although the story remains fresh and interesting to adult eyes, the prize-winning art may seem cartoonish and dated.

SPECTACLES [215]

WRITTEN AND ILLUSTRATED BY ELLEN RASKIN
Cloth: Atheneum
Paper: Aladdin
Published: 1968   PRIZES: NEW YORK TIMES BEST ILLUSTRATED BOOK

What is ordinary? Iris Fogel sees remarkable things such as couches that look like hippos until her mother figures out that she is myopic and needs glasses. This book manages to be funny and helpful at the same time.

Picture Books

THE STONECUTTER: A JAPANESE FOLKTALE   [216]

WRITTEN AND ILLUSTRATED BY GERALD McDERMOTT

Cloth: Viking
Paper: Puffin
Published: 1975

A handsomely told version of a traditional Japanese folktale about a foolish man's grandiose longings and greed. The illustrations are dramatic and somewhat austere.

STONE SOUP   [217]

WRITTEN AND ILLUSTRATED BY MARCIA BROWN

Cloth: Scribners
Paper: Aladdin
Published: 1947   PRIZES: CALDECOTT HONOR BOOK

This is a large-format, old-fashioned, and very charming version of the familiar story featuring distinctively French peasants and soldiers. No one in the village will offer hospitality to three hungry soldiers—the stone soup they prepare teaches the virtue of cooperation.

A STORY, A STORY   [218]

WRITTEN AND ILLUSTRATED BY GAIL E. HALEY

Cloth: Atheneum
Paper: Aladdin
Published: 1970   PRIZES: CALDECOTT MEDAL

One of the African tales of Anansi the Spider. In this episode, dramatically illustrated in full color in a style that evokes African images, he brings to earth all the stories owned by the Sky God.

[219]

THE STORY OF FERDINAND [219]

WRITTEN BY MUNRO LEAF
ILLUSTRATED BY ROBERT LAWSON
Cloth: Viking
Paper: Puffin
Published: 1936   PRIZES: CALDECOTT HONOR BOOK

Ferdinand the bull does not want to go into the ring and fight; he really
wants to sit under the cork tree and smell the flowers. A funny, wise
story more than half a century old, and fresh as the daisy Ferdinand
loves so well. (Some things change, but adults will be pleased to see that
corks still grow on the cork trees here.)

THE STORY OF JUMPING MOUSE [220]

WRITTEN AND ILLUSTRATED BY JOHN STEPTOE
Cloth: Lothrop
Paper: Mulberry
Published: 1984

A Great Plains Indian legend about how the mouse was transformed
and finally found the far-off land, retold in a handsome edition with
large, mysterious black-and-white illustrations.

SWIMMY [221]

WRITTEN AND ILLUSTRATED BY LEO LIONNI
Cloth: Pantheon
Paper: Knopf   PRIZES: NEW YORK TIMES BEST ILLUSTRATED BOOK,
Published: 1963   CALDECOTT HONOR BOOK

Little Swimmy is alone in the sea. The rest of his school was swallowed
by a tuna, but he figures out a camouflage plan for survival. It is a
delightful tale told with minimal text and elegant collage illustrations.

[219]

Picture Books

THE TALE OF PETER RABBIT [222]

WRITTEN AND ILLUSTRATED BY BEATRIX POTTER
Cloth: Warne
Paper: Warne
Published: 1902

Flopsy, Mopsy, and Cottontail are good little bunnies, but Peter disobeys and goes to Mr. MacGregor's garden with nearly disastrous consequences. One of the best-known and best-loved stories for children, *Peter Rabbit* is dramatic, exciting, and complete all on a very small scale. The watercolor illustrations are exquisite. The original Warne editions, with their smooth paper and trim green binding, small to hold in the hand, were rephotographed and reissued in 1987 and are as readily available and inexpensive as, and far nicer than, any others. But others abound. There are all sorts of auxiliary books and merchandise as well: coloring, cut-out, and pop-up books, for example. Some are well done, others sloppy and exploitative; choose carefully among them. Peter's immediate relative is, of course, *The Tale of Benjamin Bunny*, but some of the other books in the canon include *The Tale of Squirrel Nutkin*, *The Tale of Mrs. Tiggy-Winkle*, *The Tale of Tom Kitten*, and *The Tale of Jemima Puddle-Duck*.

TATTIE'S RIVER JOURNEY [223]

WRITTEN BY SHIRLEY ROUSSEAU MURPHY
ILLUSTRATED BY TOMIE de PAOLA
Cloth: Dial
Paper: Dial
Published: 1983

Kind Tattie gives refuge to the animals as rain swells and floods the river.

[222]

TEDDY BEARS CURE A COLD [224]

WRITTEN AND ILLUSTRATED BY SUZANNA GRETZ
Cloth: Four Winds
Paper: Scholastic
Published: 1985

His friends take care of William the teddy bear when he first catches the cold, but he gets so cranky that they leave him mostly alone to let nature take its course. The illustrations are wonderful. Never has a head cold been personified so well as in William's half-lidded, red-nosed face. The same crew of bears (who look like children in teddy bear costumes) also appear in *Teddy Bears Go Shopping*, *Teddy Bears' Moving Day*, and *Teddy Bears ABC*, and in board books for toddlers, *I'm Not Sleepy*, *Ready for Bed*, *Hide and Seek*.

THE TEENY-TINY WOMAN [225]

WRITTEN AND ILLUSTRATED BY PAUL GALDONE

Cloth: Clarion
Paper: Clarion
Published: 1984

The teeny-tiny woman hides the teeny-tiny bone she finds in the teeny-tiny churchyard. A slightly scary and mostly funny old English ghost story, retold with enthusiasm. Other versions have been illustrated by Tomie de Paola and Jane O'Conner, and there is one called *The Funny Little Woman* by Arlene Mosel, illustrated by Blair Lent.

TEN, NINE, EIGHT [226]

WRITTEN AND ILLUSTRATED BY MOLLY BANG

Cloth: Greenwillow
Paper: Puffin
Published: 1983   PRIZES: CALDECOTT HONOR BOOK

This is both a bedtime and a counting book. The story, told in lush and soothing illustrations, is about the bedtime rituals of one little girl and her father.

THIS IS BETSY [227]

WRITTEN AND ILLUSTRATED BY GUNILLA WOLDE

Cloth: Random House
Paper: Random House
Published: 1975

Small, bright books about an engaging preschooler's ordinary experiences. Titles in the series include *Betsy's Baby Brother*, *Betsy's First Day at Nursery School*, *Betsy and the Doctor*. The illustrations are simple and appealing.

[227]

THE THREE BILLY GOATS GRUFF [228]

WRITTEN AND ILLUSTRATED BY PAUL GALDONE

Cloth: Clarion
Paper: Clarion
Published: 1973

The troll in this large-format version of the familiar folktale is truly loathsome. Happily, the billy goats are quite fearless as they trit trot over that bridge to the meadow full of sweet grass and bright daisies.

THREE JOVIAL HUNTSMEN: A MOTHER GOOSE RHYME [229]

WRITTEN AND ILLUSTRATED BY SUSAN JEFFERS

Cloth: Bradbury
Published: 1973   PRIZES: CALDECOTT HONOR BOOK

Three gentlemen hunters just cannot see the camouflaged animals all around them in the forest and the open field. The lushness of the illustrations is part of the joke.

THE THREE LITTLE PIGS [230]

WRITTEN AND ILLUSTRATED BY ERIK BLEGVAD

Cloth: McElderry
Paper: Aladdin
Published: 1980

This thoughtful version of the familiar story extends the wise pig's experiences with the wolf beyond the brick house. It is handsomely illustrated and small, convenient for small hands to hold as young readers study the illustrations. There are, of course, many other editions, including an exuberant one by Paul Galdone.

[230]

THE THREE ROBBERS [231]

WRITTEN AND ILLUSTRATED BY TOMI UNGERER

Cloth: Atheneum
Paper: Aladdin
Published: 1962

This eternally modern, alarming, funny-scary tale has been reissued in the original large format. The three fierce black robbers gallop across the pages unchecked until the girl named Tiffany changes their lives. The natural audience for the story is made up of school-age children and adults.

[232]

THY FRIEND OBADIAH   [232]

WRITTEN AND ILLUSTRATED BY BRINTON TURKLE

Cloth: Viking
Paper: Puffin
Published: 1969   PRIZES: CALDECOTT HONOR BOOK

One of a number of books about the Starbuck family of Nantucket, nineteenth-century Quakers, featuring Obadiah and his sister Rachel. The illustrations are full of period detail that are easy to discuss. The other books are *Rachel and Obadiah*, *Obadiah the Bold*, and *The Adventures of Obadiah*.

TIKKI TIKKI TEMBO   [233]

WRITTEN BY ARLENE MOSEL
ILLUSTRATED BY BLAIR LENT

Cloth: Holt
Paper: Scholastic
Published: 1968

A story about how Chinese children came to have short names, as chanted by generations of nursery school children. Help can be summoned for brother Chang, who falls down the well, but for Tikki Tikki Tembo it's more problematic. Teenagers and adults, too, remember, and find themselves absently mumbling that wonderful rolling name: Tikki Tikki Tembo No Sa Rembo Chari Bari Ruchi Piri Piri Bembo.

TOMIE de PAOLA'S MOTHER GOOSE   [234]

SELECTED AND ILLUSTRATED BY TOMIE de PAOLA

Cloth: Putnam
Published: 1985

A buoyant collection of some two hundred familiar verses and rhymes illustrated in de Paola's characteristic bright and stylized manner.

TORTILLITAS PARA MAMA AND OTHER NURSERY RHYMES, SPANISH AND ENGLISH [235]

WRITTEN BY MARGOT C. GRIEGO AND OTHERS
ILLUSTRATED BY BARBARA COONEY
Cloth: Holt
Paper: Holt
Published: 1981

Enchanting folkloric illustrations accompany a selection of delightful rhymes from Latin America. The words are given in both Spanish and English and are accompanied by suggestions for finger play.

TOUCH! TOUCH! [236]

WRITTEN BY RIKI LEVINSON
ILLUSTRATED BY TRUE KELLEY
Cloth: Dutton
Published: 1987

This enchanting person in overalls and sailor hat is a total terror as he lurches through the house with hands covered with cake batter. It's a funny, messy domestic adventure, the sort that will please toddlers and tickle their slightly older siblings as well.

TOWN AND COUNTRY [237]

WRITTEN AND ILLUSTRATED BY ALICE AND MARTIN PROVENSEN
Cloth: Crown
Published: 1985

A stunning, large-format picture book by the distinguished artists that shows, in two groups of richly detailed paintings, the differences between life in the city and country as seen from a child's perspective. The city resembles, but is not, New York; the countryside resembles, but perhaps is not quite, the Provensens' own Maple Hill Farm.

A TREE IS NICE [238]

WRITTEN BY JANICE MAY UDRY
ILLUSTRATED BY MARC SIMONT
Cloth: Harper
Paper: Harper
Published: 1956   PRIZES: CALDECOTT MEDAL

Some pleasing reasons for trees in all seasons. The simple text and
charming illustrations in this slim, tall book may seem old fashioned to
adult eyes, but the text reads aloud nicely for young children.

A TRIP TO THE DOCTOR [239]

WRITTEN BY MARGOT LINN
ILLUSTRATED BY CATHERINE SIRACUSA
Cloth: Harper
Published: 1988

Each double-page spread in this foldout-page book consists of a question about a visit to the doctor with three possible answers. There is at
least one laugh for even a very small child on each page. Who is going
to weigh and measure Joey? The nurse. What will he stand on? A
stool, a skateboard, or the scale? The doctor has a friendly puppy
hand puppet.

THE TWELVE DAYS OF CHRISTMAS [240]

ILLUSTRATED BY JAN BRETT
Cloth: Dodd
Published: 1986

This version of the traditional Christmas carol is bright and gay, with
jewel-like, detailed illustrations embellished with the artist's characteristic style of borders and embroiderylike patterns. There are other editions, including a mysteriously romantic one by Louise Brierley.

[226]

Picture
Books

UP GOES THE SKYSCRAPER [241]

WRITTEN AND ILLUSTRATED BY GAIL GIBBONS
Cloth: Four Winds
Published: 1986
A wonderfully clear account of how a skyscraper is built, from drawing up the plans and digging the foundation to moving the tenants into their offices. Recommended for adults who accompany small children on city walks and don't know the difference between an H beam and an I beam.

THE VERY BUSY SPIDER [242]

WRITTEN AND ILLUSTRATED BY ERIC CARLE
Cloth: Philomel
Published: 1985
The spider spins her web in raised lines, making this remarkable picture book accessible to both sighted and blind children.

THE VERY HUNGRY CATERPILLAR [243]

WRITTEN AND ILLUSTRATED BY ERIC CARLE
Cloth: Philomel
Published: 1969
The very hungry caterpillar eats his way through his life cycle and the cut-out pages of this classic picture book until he becomes a butterfly. If you are going to buy it, this is a book to have in the original hardback edition, with its large format and stiff pages, because little fingers need to poke through the holes in the apple, pear, strawberry, and other edibles.

WAITING FOR MAMA [244]

WRITTEN BY BEATRICE SCHENK de REGNIERS
ILLUSTRATED BY VICTORIA de LARREA
Cloth: Clarion
Published: 1984
A little girl sits under a tree, as she is told to, and imagines a whole lifetime passing by while she waits for her mother to finish an errand.

[241]

She might grow up, get married, have children, even grandchildren, before the shopping is finally done.

WAKE UP, BEAR...IT'S CHRISTMAS   [245]

WRITTEN AND ILLUSTRATED BY STEPHEN GAMMELL
Cloth: Lothrop
Paper: Penguin
Published: 1981

Bear manages to wake up for Christmas Eve, and even entertains an unusual guest who takes him for a fine ride. A nice variation on the usual Christmas themes. The full-color illustrations are relaxed and amusing.

WASHDAY ON NOAH'S ARK   [246]

WRITTEN AND ILLUSTRATED BY GLEN ROUNDS
Cloth: Holiday
Published: 1985

If you stop to think about it, the question of how they did the washing on Noah's ark is a reasonable and a difficult one. The answer propounded here, which involves a living laundry line, is hilarious, as are the illustrations.

THE WEDDING PROCESSION OF THE RAG DOLL AND THE BROOM HANDLE AND WHO WAS IN IT   [247]

WRITTEN BY CARL SANDBURG
ILLUSTRATED BY HARRIET PINCUS
Cloth: Harcourt Brace
Paper: Voyage/HBJ
Published: 1967

A glorious setting for an excerpt from the *Rootabaga Stories,* about a fine procession that included Spoon Lickers, Dirty Bibs, Musical Soup Eaters, and others. The funny illustrations are eccentric and angular. Perfect for bedtime reading aloud together.

[241]

WHAT DO YOU SAY, DEAR?/
WHAT DO YOU DO, DEAR? [248]

WRITTEN BY SESYLE JOSLIN
ILLUSTRATED BY MAURICE SENDAK
Cloth: Harper
Paper: Harper   PRIZES: CALDECOTT HONOR BOOK,
Published: 1958   NEW YORK TIMES BEST ILLUSTRATED BOOK

As Miss Manners has reminded us, good manners are a matter of constant practice. These two books, reissued after being out of print for many years, are wonderfully instructive. By placing those basic responses every child must learn in ludicrous, hilarious situations, the whole subject becomes positively palatable. "What do you say when you bump into a crocodile on a busy street?"

WHAT'S INSIDE?
THE ALPHABET BOOK [249]

WRITTEN AND ILLUSTRATED BY SATOSHI KITAMURA
Cloth: Farrar, Straus
Paper: Sunburst/Farrar, Straus
Published: 1985

This imaginative and handsomely illustrated alphabet book, set in what looks like a run-down district of London, involves clever puzzles and concealment, as each page not only contains two letters and words using them, but the next letters to come.

WHEN THE NEW BABY COMES
I'M MOVING OUT [250]

WRITTEN AND ILLUSTRATED BY MARTHA ALEXANDER
Cloth: Dial
Paper: Dial
Published: 1971

Oliver's problem is pretty clear, but he learns to cope. There is a related title, also low-key and comic: *Nobody Asked Me If I Wanted a Baby Sister.*

WHEN THE TIDE IS LOW   [251]

WRITTEN BY SHEILA COLE

ILLUSTRATED BY VIRGINIA WRIGHT-FRIERSON

Cloth: Lothrop

Published: 1985

A little girl is very anxious to get to the beach, but it's not time yet, and meanwhile, as she swings up and down on her swing, her mother answers her questions about what they will see "when the tide is low." The illustrations add to the spirit of this subtle and informative book.

WHEN YOU WERE A BABY   [252]

WRITTEN AND ILLUSTRATED BY ANN JONAS

Cloth: Greenwillow

Published: 1982

A book for toddlers and preschoolers who find great pleasure and also reassurance in being reminded of the times when they were little and helpless. All examples end with "but now you can…"

WHERE ARE YOU GOING, LITTLE MOUSE?   [253]

WRITTEN BY ROBERT KRAUS

ILLUSTRATED BY JOSE ARUEGO AND ARIANE DEWEY

Cloth: Greenwillow

Published: 1986

Having decided that no one loves him, there's nothing left for Little Mouse to do but run away from home. He gets to the nearest phone booth, and his parents come to the rescue. An earlier book is *Whose Mouse Are You? Come Out and Play, Little Mouse* completes the trilogy.

[33]

Picture Books

WHERE DOES THE SUN GO AT NIGHT? [254]

WRITTEN BY MIRRA GINSBERG

ILLUSTRATED BY JOSE ARUEGO AND ARIANE DEWEY

Cloth: Greenwillow

Paper: Mulberry

Published: 1980

A comical cast of characters gather to watch the sun set. The pictures are funny; the text is soothing.

WHERE IS MY FRIEND? A WORD CONCEPT BOOK [255]

WRITTEN AND ILLUSTRATED BY BETSY AND GIULIO MAESTRO

Cloth: Crown

Paper: Crown

Published: 1976

Two-year-olds adore Harriet the elephant and her bright, simple adventures. Here she looks for her friend and looks, for example, "up and down," "between and around." There are board books, *Around the Clock with Harriet* and *Harriet Goes to the Circus,* as well as *Through the Year with Harriet.*

WHERE'S SPOT? [256]

WRITTEN AND ILLUSTRATED BY ERIC HILL

Cloth: Putnam

Published: 1980

Sally cannot find her puppy Spot and goes searching, and behind the flap on each double-page illustration is something silly—there's a striped snake in the clock, a funny lion under the stairs. Perfectly wonderful nonsense, satisfying to children of most early ages. This is the first and the best in a large and generally successful series. Other good titles are *Spot's First Walk*, *Spot's First Christmas*, and *Spot Goes to School.*

[259]

WHERE'S THE BEAR? [257]

WRITTEN BY CHARLOTTE POMERANTZ
ILLUSTRATED BY BYRON BARTON
Cloth: Greenwillow
Paper: Penguin
Published: 1984

This story of how a bear is sighted in the forest and how the villagers respond is brilliantly told in just seven words of text. The bold illustrations capture a breathless, exciting chase. Great fun to read aloud with the very young.

WHERE THE RIVER BEGINS [258]

WRITTEN AND ILLUSTRATED BY THOMAS LOCKER
Cloth: Dial
Published: 1984   PRIZES: NEW YORK TIMES BEST ILLUSTRATED BOOK

The first of a series of stunning picture books featuring landscape paintings in the style of the Hudson River School of the nineteenth century. The story line, which is secondary to the spectacular illustrations, tells of two boys who hike with their grandfather to the river's source. Related titles include *The Mare on the Hill* and *Sailing with the Wind.*

WHERE THE WILD THINGS ARE [259]

WRITTEN AND ILLUSTRATED BY MAURICE SENDAK
Cloth: Harper
Paper: Harper   PRIZES: CALDECOTT MEDAL,
Published: 1962   NEW YORK TIMES BEST ILLUSTRATED BOOK

This is the story of the night Max wore his wolf suit and was sent to bed supperless only to dream a strange, wild, violent, and glorious dream and then return to where he is loved best of all. It is perhaps the greatest picture book of permission for young children, acknowledging and allowing the terrible temper and urge to independence that they feel but cannot fully act upon. The illustrations remain fresh and funny/scary; only time passes.

[259]

Picture Books

WHISKERS & RHYMES   [260]

WRITTEN AND ILLUSTRATED BY ARNOLD LOBEL

Cloth: Greenwillow
Paper: Scholastic
Published: 1985

The conceit of this collection of delightful nonsense verses is that they are all illustrated by cats—dandified cats in old-fashioned costumes, perhaps visiting from the eighteenth century.

WHO SANK THE BOAT?   [261]

WRITTEN AND ILLUSTRATED BY PAMELA ALLEN

Cloth: Coward
Paper: Coward
Published: 1983

A cow, a donkey, a sheep, a pig, and a mouse decide to go out rowing in a boat that is, however, too small. The joke is unmistakable, even to very small children.

WILLIAM'S DOLL   [262]

WRITTEN BY CHARLOTTE ZOLOTOW
ILLUSTRATED BY WILLIAM PENE du BOIS

Cloth: Harper
Paper: Harper
Published: 1972

It was shocking, years ago, that William wanted a doll to play with. Certainly his father and his brother objected. But William got his doll, and in playing with him imagined how he would one day be a father. Time has passed since this book was published, and what we read today seems modest and wry.

[256]

WILLIAM THE VEHICLE KING [263]

WRITTEN BY LAURA P. NEWTON
ILLUSTRATED BY JACQUELINE ROGERS
Cloth: Bradbury
Published: 1987

Vroom, vroom, rrrrhhhhhoar. This book is for and about every little
boy obsessed with his racing cars. William, who gets a demonic look in
his eye as he sees potential racecourses on the rug, has half a dozen
prize vehicles, and a wonderful time playing with them. The delightful
full-color illustrations look up at William from the floor.

THE WINTER BEAR [264]

WRITTEN BY RUTH CRAFT
ILLUSTRATED BY ERIK BLEGVAD
Cloth: McElderry
Paper: Aladdin
Published: 1975

Three children take a walk in the snow, and, of course, find a bear. A
delicately illustrated consideration of winter.

THE YEAR AT MAPLE HILL FARM [265]

WRITTEN AND ILLUSTRATED BY ALICE AND MARTIN PROVENSEN
Cloth: Atheneum
Paper: Aladdin
Published: 1978

The seasons go by on the old-fashioned farm in upstate New York
where the authors live. The illustrations are deceptively simple and
provide much to discuss with toddlers and older children.

YELLOW AND PINK [266]

WRITTEN AND ILLUSTRATED BY WILLIAM STEIG
Cloth: Farrar, Straus
Paper: Michael di Capua/Sunburst/Farrar, Straus
Published: 1984

Two small wooden figures lie on their backs on a sheet of newspaper in
a meadow and debate the origins of the universe. Their creator appears
at the end. This is one of Steig's most sophisticated books.

Picture Books

YOUR TURN, DOCTOR [267]

WRITTEN BY CARLA PEREZ AND DEBORAH ROBINSON
ILLUSTRATED BY DEBORAH ROBINSON

Cloth: Dial
Paper: Dial
Published: 1982

One joke here, but a fine one—role reversal on a visit to the pediatrician. The plump, mustachioed fellow (with funny underpants) doesn't like a brisk examination any more than youngsters do.

[267]

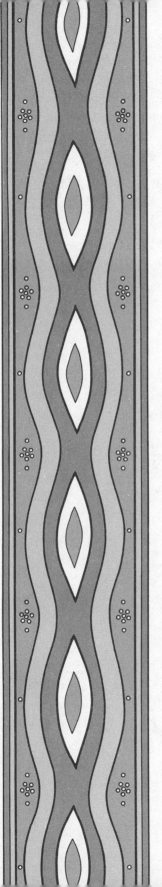

Story Books

Here are books with ample, sometimes lavish illustration, and strong stories as well. Younger children can often listen to the text and then read the books for themselves with pleasure, but they are best suited to children in the early grades. Precocious readers have not graduated from the pleasures of story books either, and find special satisfaction in the combination of pictures and text.

THE ACCIDENT [268]

WRITTEN BY CAROL CARRICK
ILLUSTRATED BY DONALD CARRICK
Cloth: Clarion
Paper: Clarion
Published: 1976

This is the pivotal book of three about a boy named Christopher and his dog, Bodger. In *Lost in the Storm*, the boy must wait out a storm before searching for his dog. In *The Accident*, his dog is hit by a truck and killed, and Christopher must grieve. In *The Foundling*, Christopher concludes his mourning. The stories are all sensitively and thoughtfully done, worthwhile if read separately or serially. The illustrations are low-key and unobtrusive.

ALEXANDER AND THE TERRIBLE, HORRIBLE, NO GOOD, VERY BAD DAY [269]

WRITTEN BY JUDITH VIORST
ILLUSTRATED BY RAY CRUZ
Cloth: Atheneum
Paper: Aladdin
Published: 1972

This story is about one of those truly rotten days when everything that can go wrong does. It is somehow soothing for readers of all ages to know that it happens to other people. The two-color illustrations fairly quiver with Alexander's mounting frustrations. Other books about Alexander and his brothers are *I'll Fix Anthony* and *Alexander, Who Used to Be Rich Last Sunday*.

ALFIE GIVES A HAND [270]

WRITTEN AND ILLUSTRATED BY SHIRLEY HUGHES
Cloth: Lothrop
Paper: Mulberry
Published: 1984

Alfie is the quintessential four-year-old—kind, well-meaning, not quite as brave as he would like to be. His adventures are small and perfectly told. In this episode, he takes his blanket to a birthday party,

[269]

but eventually puts it down in order to help care for a little girl even shyer than he. The deft full-color illustrations sweetly capture characters as well as the domestic settings. Other titles in the series include *Alfie Gets in First*, *Alfie's Feet*, and *An Evening at Alfie's*. Alfie's little sister, Annie Rose, stars in books for younger children: *Bathwater's Hot* and *All Sizes and Shapes*.

ALWAYS, ALWAYS   [271]

WRITTEN BY CRESCENT DRAGONWAGON
ILLUSTRATED BY ARICH ZELDICH
Cloth: Macmillan
Published: 1984

A low-key story about a little girl whose parents are divorced. She spends her summers with her father in Colorado, the school year with her mother in New York, and has learned to accept the situation and even find some merits in it.

ALWAYS ROOM FOR ONE MORE   [272]

WRITTEN BY SORCHE NIC LEODHAS
ILLUSTRATED BY NONNY HOGROGIAN
Cloth: Holt
Paper: Holt
Published: 1965   PRIZES: CALDECOTT MEDAL

A retelling of a Highlands tale about Lachie MacLachlan, whose hospitality extends to every traveler who passes by until the walls of his house burst. The three-color illustrations have a misty, mountain air quality.

AMAHL AND THE NIGHT VISITORS   [273]

WRITTEN BY GIAN CARLO MENOTTI
ILLUSTRATED BY MICHELE LEMIEUX
Cloth: Morrow
Published: 1986

The popular modern Christmas opera tells of the Three Kings stopping en route to Bethlehem at the home of a poor, crippled shepherd boy. Handsome, evocative full-color illustrations add an aura of mystery and reverence.

THE AMAZING BONE [274]

WRITTEN AND ILLUSTRATED BY WILLIAM STEIG

Cloth: Farrar, Straus
Paper: Penguin
Published: 1976   PRIZES: CALDECOTT HONOR BOOK

Steig stories are always different, always identifiable. Here Pearl, a heroine who happens to be a piglet, finds a talking bone that has fallen out of a witch's basket.

AMERICAN FOLK SONGS FOR CHILDREN [275]

WRITTEN BY RUTH CRAWFORD SEEGER
ILLUSTRATED BY BARBARA COONEY

Paper: Doubleday
Published: 1970

A collection of ninety songs you probably know but can't remember all the words to anymore. This standard collection has user-friendly suggestions for adapting songs for play and dancing, altering the words for your family.

ANIMAL FACT, ANIMAL FABLE [276]

WRITTEN BY SEYMOUR SIMON
ILLUSTRATED BY DIANE de GROAT

Cloth: Crown
Paper: Crown
Published: 1979

The illustrations are low-key, and the text in this nature book is clear. One page asserts a common myth about an animal; turn it over and find a truthful answer that may surprise a young reader.

[270]

ANNA BANANA AND ME [277]

WRITTEN BY LENORE BLEGVAD
ILLUSTRATED BY ERIK BLEGVAD
Cloth: McElderry
Paper: Aladdin
Published: 1985

The boy who tells this story is afraid of a lot of things, unlike his utterly brave friend Anna Banana. They are playing in New York's Central Park. The illustrations capture Anna's daring and the narrator's anxiety and eventual triumph.

ANNIE AND THE OLD ONE [278]

WRITTEN BY MISKA MILES
ILLUSTRATED BY PETER PARNELL
Paper: Little, Brown
Published: 1971   PRIZES: NEWBERY HONOR BOOK

A little Indian girl recognizes that her grandmother is going to die and learns to accept the cycle of life and death. The story is told with delicacy and caring, and the fine line illustrations are a perfect complement.

ANNIE AND THE WILD ANIMALS [279]

WRITTEN AND ILLUSTRATED BY JAN BRETT
Cloth: Houghton Mifflin
Published: 1985

It's midwinter somewhere in the north country when Annie's cat Taffy disappears. The story of what is really happening is told in the borders while on the center of the page, Annie tries to make friends with a series of wild animals. The illustrations are exquisitely detailed and have a folkloric and Scandinavian quality.

[279]

ARDIZZONE'S HANS ANDERSEN: FOURTEEN CLASSIC TALES   [280]

WRITTEN BY HANS CHRISTIAN ANDERSEN
ILLUSTRATED BY EDWARD ARDIZZONE
Cloth: Deutsch
Published: 1985

This English illustrator is best known in the United States today for the Little Tim books. The combination of his charmingly color-washed drawings and text scrupulously translated from the Danish is an engaging one. *Ardizzone's English Fairy Tales*, a collection of twelve traditional stories, is another handsome, easy-to-read-aloud collection.

ARNOLD OF THE DUCKS   [281]

WRITTEN AND ILLUSTRATED BY MORDICAI GERSTEIN
Cloth: Harper
Paper: Harper
Published: 1983

A grand fantasy about Arnold, who is living happily with Mrs. Leda Duck and her ducklings, dressing in feathers and learning to swim, even to fly. He is, however, a little boy, and eventually returns to his more conventional family.

ARTHUR'S NOSE   [282]

WRITTEN AND ILLUSTRATED BY MARC BROWN
Cloth: Atlantic-Little, Brown
Paper: Atlantic-Little, Brown
Published: 1976

The first of a popular series of gently comic books that appeal to children in the early grades, and their younger siblings as well, about a young aardvark who deals with life's issues in an appealing way. Here he learns to accept his most distinctive features. Other titles include *Arthur's Eyes* (about getting glasses), *Arthur's Tooth* (about losing the first one), and *Arthur's Halloween* (about not being so frightened). There are also books about Arthur's kid sister, D.W.

[279]

93

ASHANTI TO ZULU: AFRICAN TRADITIONS [283]

WRITTEN BY MARGARET MUSGROVE
ILLUSTRATED BY LEO AND DIANE DILLON
Cloth: Dial
Paper: Dial
Published: 1976

PRIZES: CALDECOTT MEDAL,
NEW YORK TIMES BEST ILLUSTRATED BOOK

This stunning alphabet book also describes and brilliantly illustrates aspects of African culture. The captions are small gems of anthropological reporting. Among the tribes described are the Dogon, the Fanta, and the Kung. This is an illustrated book for older children and adults. Libraries and bookstores may have it shelved with large-format and travel books, but keep looking, it's worth it.

AUNT NINA AND HER NEPHEWS AND NIECES [284]

WRITTEN BY FRANZ BRANDENBERG
ILLUSTRATED BY ALIKI
Cloth: Greenwillow
Published: 1983

Aunt Nina invites her six nephews and nieces to celebrate her cat Fluffy's birthday. It turns out to be the birthday of Fluffy's six kittens as well. *Aunt Nina's Visit* is another book about the same large family.

BABUSHKA: AN OLD RUSSIAN FOLKTALE [285]

WRITTEN AND ILLUSTRATED BY CHARLES MIKOLAYCAK
Cloth: Holiday
Paper: Holiday
Published: 1984

PRIZES: NEW YORK TIMES BEST ILLUSTRATED BOOK

An affecting retelling of a traditional Russian tale about an old woman who was too busy to go when she was invited to visit the baby Jesus and now searches endlessly for him.

A BABY FOR MAX [286]

WRITTEN BY KATHRYN LASKY
ILLUSTRATED BY CHRISTOPHER G. KNIGHT
Cloth: Scribners
Paper: Aladdin
Published: 1984

The true story of the Knights and how they and their five-year-old son, Max, prepared for the arrival of a new baby. It is for preschoolers and early-grade readers, with black-and-white photographs.

THE BALANCING GIRL [287]

WRITTEN BY BERNICE RABE
ILLUSTRATED BY LILLIAN HOBAN
Cloth: Dutton
Paper: Dutton
Published: 1981

This remarkable book is about Margaret, who is confined to a wheel-chair and has developed her own special skill in balancing things. She uses her talent to benefit her whole school in an imaginative way. It is a book about a physically disabled child and social tolerance that is accessible to a preschool child. *Margaret's Moves*, for older readers, takes up the story a few years later as Margaret deals with new problems and especially her brother Rusty. Margaret is a determined, optimistic, and yet believable character.

BÁ-NĂM [288]

WRITTEN AND ILLUSTRATED BY JEANNE M. LEE
Cloth: Holt
Published: 1987

A story about the special day on which the Vietnamese honor their ancestors, and the day Nan is finally old enough to go to the graveyard with her family. The full-color illustrations convey great poignance. For school-age children.

[287]

BEA AND MR. JONES [289]

WRITTEN AND ILLUSTRATED BY AMY SCHWARTZ

Cloth: Bradbury
Paper: Puffin
Published: 1982

Bea is tired of kindergarten, and Mr. Jones is tired of being an advertising executive, so they swap jobs. The results are very satisfying. The distinctive line drawings, old-fashioned and almost cartoonish, are amusing, especially Bea and Mr. Jones with their smug, fat faces.

THE BEACHCOMBER'S BOOK [290]

WRITTEN BY BERNICE KOHN

Paper: Puffin
Published: 1976, reissued 1987

This compendium of information and projects is the perfect take-along paperback for a beach vacation or beach house. Although aimed at grade-school children, it includes a lot of information a browsing parent might find fascinating.

THE BEAST OF MONSIEUR RACINE [291]

WRITTEN AND ILLUSTRATED BY TOMI UNGERER

Cloth: Farrar, Straus
Paper: Sunburst/Farrar, Straus
Published: 1971   PRIZES: NEW YORK TIMES BEST ILLUSTRATED BOOK

A retired tax collector finds a strange, friendly, rather squooshy creature in his garden. Approaching it scientifically, Monsieur Racine takes it to the Academy of Sciences in Paris, where it breaks apart, revealing the two children from next door. This quirky fable suggests a Gallic worldliness in inimitable style.

[289]

BEAUTY AND THE BEAST   [292]

WRITTEN BY MARIANNA MAYER
ILLUSTRATED BY MERCER MAYER
Cloth: Four Winds
Paper: Aladdin
Published: 1979

A lushly illustrated version of the familiar fairy tale. Other editions, illustrated by Michael Hague and Warrick Hutton, among others, follow the traditional text with different visual emphasis.

BEDTIME FOR FRANCES   [293]

WRITTEN BY RUSSELL HOBAN
ILLUSTRATED BY GARTH WILLIAMS
Cloth: Harper
Paper: Harper
Published: 1960

Frances is a bright, willful, whimsical little badger who often makes up song fragments about aspects of her days—bedtime, sibling rivalry, friendship, candy. Her adventures in this and the other books in the series (the others are illustrated by Lillian Hoban) reflect the small and specific concerns of children in preschool and the early grades but transcend bibliotherapy. *A Baby Sister for Frances*, *Best Friends for Frances*, *A Birthday for Frances*, and *Bread and Jam for Frances* and *Egg Thoughts and Other Frances Songs*, are all delightful. Whenever you hear someone talk about a Chompo bar, they have been reading Frances. The Frances books have more text than pictures but because they read aloud so well they appeal to children of a wide age range—from toddlers to third grade, roughly.

THE BERENSTAIN BEARS' TROUBLE WITH MONEY   [294]

WRITTEN AND ILLUSTRATED BY STAN AND JAN BERENSTAIN
Paper: Random House
Published: 1983

The popular bears are featured in a series of "first time" books that address issues of family life. In this case, the young bears must work to earn money to play video games, and the story provides reasonable guidance on a familiar problem. While parents may feel that the writing is both pedantic and didactic, children accept moral instruction from the bears they would reject if it came directly from the real authority figures in their lives. Other titles in the series that may already be familiar from Saturday morning cartoon adaptations include *The Berenstain Bears* and *Too Much Junk Food*, *Too Much TV*, *Mama's New Job*, and *The Messy Room*.

BEST FRIENDS [295]

WRITTEN AND ILLUSTRATED BY STEVEN KELLOGG
Cloth: Dial
Published: 1985

Kathy and Louise are best friends. While Louise is away for the summer, Kathy meets a new neighbor whose dog is expecting puppies, with some unforeseen and poignant results. Detailed and imaginative full-color illustrations add depth and humor.

THE BEST TOWN IN THE WORLD [296]

WRITTEN BY BYRD BAYLOR
ILLUSTRATED BY RONALD HIMLER
Cloth: Scribners
Paper: Aladdin
Published: 1983

A prose poem that celebrates a place in the American Southwest where all the wildflowers had "butterflies to match" and "of course you knew everyone's name and everyone knew yours." The full-color illustrations are romantic and sun dappled.

THE BFG [297]

WRITTEN BY ROALD DAHL
ILLUSTRATED BY QUENTIN BLAKE
Cloth: Farrar, Straus
Paper: Penguin
Published: 1982

The Roald Dahl fantasies all share a special mixture of hilarious and macabre characters and plot turns. Here the BFG is the Big Friendly Giant who kidnaps Sophie, an eight-year-old orphan, and takes her to Giantland. There they encounter nine giants who, regrettably, eat children. It all works out (of course) with the help of the Queen of England.

THE BIG GREEN BOOK   [298]

WRITTEN BY ROBERT GRAVES
ILLUSTRATED BY MAURICE SENDAK
Cloth: Macmillan
Published: 1962

Jack is an orphan who finds the Big Green Book full of magic spells in the attic. He promptly turns himself into a little old man, then tricks his tedious aunt and uncle, terrifies the dog, and puts away the book before further mischief can be done. A distinguished collaboration of author and illustrator. The black-and-white drawings, especially the full-page of the dog running from a rabbit, are dandy.

THE BIONIC BUNNY SHOW   [299]

WRITTEN BY MARC AND LAURENE BROWN
ILLUSTRATED BY MARC BROWN
Cloth: Atlantic-Little, Brown
Paper: Atlantic-Little, Brown
Published: 1984

In the story of the making of an episode of the "Bionic Bunny Show" this witty picture book debunks the myth of the effortless superhero and also shows how television programs are made. A glossary of television terms is included, and the illustrations are funny and detailed.

THE BOOK OF PIGERICKS:
PIG LIMERICKS   [300]

WRITTEN AND ILLUSTRATED BY ARNOLD LOBEL
Cloth: Harper
Paper: Harper
Published: 1983

A piggy feast: thirty-eight original limericks (very hard to accomplish—try writing some) illustrated in glowing good humor and lavish costumes with a splendid cast of Lobelian porkers.

THE BOY WHO WAS FOLLOWED HOME [301]

WRITTEN BY MARGARET MAHY
ILLUSTRATED BY STEVEN KELLOGG
Cloth: Dial
Paper: Dial
Published: 1975

An inspired (kind of) shaggy hippopotamus story. One day an amiable hippo follows a proper little boy home from school. The hippo multiply daily until there are forty-three of them. The story has a compelling logic, a ridiculous witch, some magic, and an unexpected and funny final twist. The manic illustrations are hilarious. This is the only Mahy picture book currently available in the United States in which the illustrations are the equal of the text.

THE BRAMBLY HEDGE BOOKS [302]

WRITTEN AND ILLUSTRATED BY JILL BARKLEM
Cloth: Philomel
Published: 1980

There are four small books in this endearing series about some very English mice who dress in nineteenth-century period costumes and live in an elaborately detailed world—*Autumn Story, Spring Story, Summer Story,* and *Winter Story.*

BRATS [303]

WRITTEN BY X. J. KENNEDY
ILLUSTRATED BY JAMES WATTS
Cloth: McElderry
Published: 1986

A bright collection of forty-two short original poems about an assortment of brats—obnoxious, rude, noisy, and various other combinations of familiar and unpleasant. The illustrations are apt and amusing.

BRAVE IRENE [304]

WRITTEN AND ILLUSTRATED BY WILLIAM STEIG
Cloth: Farrar, Straus
Paper: Michael di Capua/Sunburst/Farrar, Straus
Published: 1986   PRIZES: NEW YORK TIMES BEST ILLUSTRATED BOOK

Irene Bobbin, the dressmaker's daughter, volunteers to deliver the duchess's new ball gown and sets off in a fierce snowstorm. The wicked wind blows the dress out of the box, Irene musters on, and there is a happy ending. This is vintage Steig. As with his other picture books, lap listeners are almost as interested as children who can read the story for themselves.

BUFFALO WOMAN [305]

WRITTEN AND ILLUSTRATED BY PAUL GOBLE
Cloth: Bradbury
Paper: Aladdin
Published: 1984

The young hunter's bride, scorned by his people, returns to her own— the Buffalo Nation. He follows and proves his love for her and their son with the son's help. The hunter is then transformed into a buffalo, too, and honor is given to all. Dramatic, eloquent, and beautifully illustrated in highly stylized full-color illustrations, this is a profound love story. Children in the early grades find it particularly thrilling.

BUGS [306]

WRITTEN BY NANCY WINSLOW PARKER
  AND JOAN RICHARDS WRIGHT
ILLUSTRATED BY NANCY WINSLOW PARKER
Cloth: Greenwillow
Paper: Mulberry
Published: 1987

[301]

Humorous verses introduce sixteen common insects—including fleas, flies, and mosquitoes—and make a handsomely illustrated first book of entomology into an engaging browsing book. A good early independent-reading book for young scientists.

CALEB AND KATE   [307]

WRITTEN AND ILLUSTRATED BY WILLIAM STEIG
Cloth: Farrar, Straus
Paper: Sunburst/Farrar, Straus
Published: 1978

After yet another spat, Caleb goes into the forest to get away from Kate, a witch casts a spell, and he's turned into a dog. He returns to Kate, who accepts him as a pet, until the day when thieves arrive. Impossible, of course. Wonderful, too, especially for children in the early grades.

CELEBRATIONS   [308]

WRITTEN BY MYRA COHN LIVINGSTON
ILLUSTRATED BY LEONARD EVERETT FISHER
Cloth: Holiday
Paper: Holiday
Published: 1985

Simple, appealing poems to mark the traditions, symbols, and memories of an assortment of days throughout the year. The author and illustrator have collaborated on other special collections, including *A Circle of Seasons*, *Earth Songs*, and *Sea Songs*.

A CHAIR FOR MY MOTHER   [309]

WRITTEN AND ILLUSTRATED BY VERA B. WILLIAMS
Cloth: Greenwillow
Paper: Mulberry
Published: 1982   PRIZES: CALDECOTT HONOR BOOK

[309]

The first of three stories about Rosa, her mother, who works in the Blue Tile Diner, and her grandmother. Burned out of their home, they relocate and start saving for a comfortable chair. The chair, lush and pink and covered with roses, is, like the book, unusual and fine. The illustrations, with their distinctive borders and themes, are wry rather than whimsical. The two other equally enchanting titles are *Something Special for Me* and *Music, Music Everywhere*.

THE CHANGING CITY [310]

WRITTEN AND ILLUSTRATED BY JORG MULLER
Cloth: McElderry
Published: 1977

In a series of delicately detailed paintings, the Swiss artist shows the changes over a twenty-three-year period in a European city. This is a case of a picture book whose most appropriate audience is older children, who can consider the implications of the changes the artist presents and then make value judgments about them. The companion volume is *The Changing Countryside*. There is a similarly illustrated study of an American town called *New Providence*.

A CHILD IS BORN: THE CHRISTMAS STORY [311]

WRITTEN BY ELIZABETH WINTHROP
ILLUSTRATED BY CHARLES MIKOLAYCAK
Cloth: Holiday
Published: 1983

This is the story of the birth of Christ, told in simple language. The strong, lush illustrations show very believable people. The author and illustrator have used the same techniques effectively in *He Is Risen*, about Easter.

THE CHILDREN WE REMEMBER [312]

WRITTEN BY CHANA BYERS ABELLS
Cloth: Greenwillow
Published: 1986

Taken from the archives of Yad Vashem, the Holocaust memorial in Israel, this is a collection of photographs with text about the lives and fate of Jewish children in Eastern Europe before and during World War II. The text is spare and low-key; the photographs are haunting. If you are searching for a way to begin a discussion of the Holocaust with a middle-grade child, use this book, but do not suggest it for independent reading: adult commentary and emotional guidance are necessary.

A CHILD'S GARDEN OF VERSES [313]

WRITTEN BY ROBERT LOUIS STEVENSON
ILLUSTRATED BY TASHA TUDOR
Cloth: Checkerboard
Published: 1981

This edition of sixty-six of the verses from one of the most famous collections of poems for children is illustrated in a sweet and rosy way. Artists who have taken different approaches include Michael Foreman, Erik Blegvad, Jesse W. Smith, and Brian Wildsmith.

A CHILD'S TREASURY OF POEMS [314]

COMPILED BY MARK DANIEL
Cloth: Dial
Published: 1986

A charming collection of familiar English poems mostly by nineteenth-century authors—Tennyson, Stevenson, Wordsworth, Rossetti. The lavish period illustrations of appropriate paintings and engravings are reproductions from museums and private collections. Many of the illustrations are unfamiliar but seem especially apt. This is a presentation gift/read-aloud collection for all ages.

THE CHOSEN BABY [315]

WRITTEN BY VALENTINE P. WASSON
ILLUSTRATED BY GLO COALSON
Cloth: Lippincott
Published: 1939, reprinted 1977

A gentle book about adoption for very young children that has been in print for decades.

[298]

CHRISTINA KATERINA AND THE TIME SHE QUIT THE FAMILY   [316]

WRITTEN BY PATRICIA LEE GAUCH
ILLUSTRATED BY ELSIE PRIMAVERA
Cloth: Putnam
Published: 1987

Family life sometimes gets to be too much. One morning when it did, Christina Katerina just up and quit the family. "Call me Agnes," she said, and spent the next days doing just what she wanted. Her savvy mother handles the situation neatly.

CHRISTMAS IN THE BARN   [317]

WRITTEN BY MARGARET WISE BROWN
ILLUSTRATED BY BARBARA COONEY
Cloth: Crowell
Paper: Harper
Published: 1949

A gentle and careful collaboration between author and artist makes this version of the Nativity particularly pleasing for very young children.

THE CHURCH MOUSE   [318]

WRITTEN AND ILLUSTRATED BY GRAHAM OAKLEY
Cloth: Atheneum
Paper: Aladdin
Published: 1972

Arthur, a rather intelligent mouse, arranges to have all the other mice in an English market town move into the church he shares with Sampson, the benign marmalade church cat. Their adventures, all illustrated in droll detail, continue in *The Church Mice and the Moon*, *The Church Mice Adrift*, *The Church Mice in Action*, *The Church Mice at Christmas*, and *The Church Mice Spread Their Wings*. In addition to youngsters, many adults admire the church mice as a group.

CINDERELLA [319]

WRITTEN BY CHARLES PERRAULT
ILLUSTRATED BY MARCIA BROWN
Cloth: Scribners
Paper: Aladdin
Published: 1954   PRIZES: CALDECOTT HONOR BOOK

A fine translation in a handsomely illustrated edition of the familiar story about the dutiful daughter and the glass slipper. There are also handsome or unusual editions illustrated by Susan Jeffers, Roberto Innocenti, and Errol Le Cain, among others.

THE CLOWN OF GOD [320]

WRITTEN AND ILLUSTRATED BY TOMIE de PAOLA
Cloth: Harcourt Brace
Paper: Voyager/HBJ
Published: 1978

A lovely retelling of a French folktale about a juggler's gift to the Christ Child.

THE CRACK OF DAWN WALKERS [321]

WRITTEN BY AMY HEST
ILLUSTRATED BY AMY SCHWARTZ
Cloth: Macmillan
Paper: Puffin
Published: 1984

A little girl explains how she and her brother take turns accompanying their grandfather on his early morning walks. The setting is winter in a city, the time is not so long ago, the affection between the characters, in the text and the black-and-white illustrations, is palpable.

[298]

THE CRANE WIFE [322]

WRITTEN BY SUMIKO YAGAWA
ILLUSTRATED BY SUEKICHI AKABA
Cloth: Morrow
Paper: Mulberry
Published: 1981   PRIZES: NEW YORK TIMES BEST ILLUSTRATED BOOK

Translated by Katherine Paterson, the prize-winning American writer, this is a beautiful version of a favorite, heartbreaking Japanese folktale. It tells about the farmer who marries a beautiful and mysterious stranger. She weaves fine cloth and warns him never to watch her, and for good reason: she is really the crane he once rescued from death, and if he sees her she must leave him.

CROCODARLING [323]

WRITTEN AND ILLUSTRATED BY MARY RAYNER
Cloth: Bradbury
Published: 1985

Sam says it is Crocodarling, his toy crocodile, who is having a hard time adjusting to nursery school. A perceptive story dealing with famil-iar problems of adjustment and transference.

DAKOTA DUGOUT [324]

WRITTEN BY ANN TURNER
ILLUSTRATED BY RONALD HIMLER
Cloth: Macmillan
Published: 1985

A memoir of the life of a young bride living in a sod house on the Dakota prairie in the late nineteenth century. The black-and-white illustrations set off the text with distinction.

[298]

THE DANCING GRANNY [325]

WRITTEN AND ILLUSTRATED BY ASHLEY BRYAN

Cloth: Atheneum
Paper: Aladdin
Published: 1977

A bright and engaging retelling of an African folktale about the Spider Ananse, who in this story lures Granny Anika into a dance so he can steal her crops. But she outwits Ananse.

D'AULAIRE'S BOOK OF GREEK MYTHS [326]

WRITTEN AND ILLUSTRATED BY INGRI AND
  EDGAR PARIN d'AULAIRE

Cloth: Doubleday
Paper: Doubleday
Published: 1962

The best-known modern book of the Greek myths adapted for children. The stories are organized around Zeus and his family, minor gods, and mortal descendants. The complex illustrations, full of symbols and evoking the classical tradition, are distinguished. The prose is straightforward and easy to read aloud. The stories are, of course, thrilling. The *Macmillan Book of Greek Myths*, a handsome compilation, has fewer stories but is also very readable.

[326]

D'AULAIRE'S NORSE GODS AND GIANTS   [327]

WRITTEN AND ILLUSTRATED BY INGRI AND
  EDGAR PARIN d'AULAIRE

Cloth: Doubleday
Paper: Doubleday
Published: 1967

This generous collection of the ancient Norse myths, including those describing creation and daily life, is set out in a lavishly illustrated, large-format volume. Wonderful to read aloud.

THE DAY JIMMY'S BOA ATE THE WASH   [328]

WRITTEN BY TRINKA HAKES NOBLE
ILLUSTRATED BY STEVEN KELLOGG

Cloth: Dial
Paper: Dial
Published: 1980

The day Jimmy's pet snake goes along on the class trip to the farm makes a memorable story told in a terse, offhand way. The full extent of the mayhem is revealed in the dizzy, funny illustrations. *Jimmy's Boa Bounces Back* tells about what happens when the boa goes to a proper tea party.

THE DESERT IS THEIRS   [329]

WRITTEN BY BYRD BAYLOR
ILLUSTRATED BY PETER PARNALL

Cloth: Scribners
Paper: Aladdin
Published: 1975   PRIZES: CALDECOTT HONOR BOOK

For readers who live near the desert (or in other parts of the world) this is a lyrical introduction to many of the creatures who live there. There is an ecological message about species adaptation to climate. The illustrations are fine line drawings.

THE DEVIL AND MOTHER CRUMP [330]

WRITTEN BY VALERIE SCHO CAREY
ILLUSTRATED BY ARNOLD LOBEL
Cloth: Harper
Published: 1987

Mother Crump was so mean and so stingy—but also so smart—that she even tricked the devil himself. She is something like the "mean old lady" everyone knows and tells stories about. A folkloric fable with thoughtful illustrations that young readers and listeners both enjoy.

THE DEVIL WITH THE THREE GOLDEN HAIRS [331]

RETOLD AND ILLUSTRATED BY NONNY HOGROGIAN
Cloth: Knopf
Published: 1983

A magical retelling of one of the lesser-known tales from Grimm about a boy who marries a princess and outwits both the king and a devil. The illustrations are delicate and sophisticated.

DINOSAURS, BEWARE! [332]

WRITTEN BY MARC BROWN AND STEPHEN KRENSKY
ILLUSTRATED BY MARC BROWN
Cloth: Atlantic-Little, Brown
Paper: Atlantic-Little, Brown
Published: 1982

A basic guide to household safety—everything from playing with fire to telephone manners—but the households pictured are those of ridiculously entertaining dinosaurs who set some truly bad examples.

Spending time with friends can help you feel less lonely.

DINOSAURS DIVORCE: A GUIDE FOR CHANGING FAMILIES [333]

WRITTEN BY MARC BROWN AND LAURENE KRASNY
ILLUSTRATED BY MARC BROWN

Cloth: Joy Street/Little, Brown
Published: 1986

Set in a cartoon world with a cast of dinosaurs, this picture book is for children of all ages, and deals with the trauma of divorce. The text is straightforward, and although silly and funny, the illustrations are also sophisticated enough to allow older children to return to the book for its sound and reassuring advice without feeling embarrassed.

DOCTOR DE SOTO [334]

WRITTEN AND ILLUSTRATED BY WILLIAM STEIG

Cloth: Farrar, Straus
Paper: Scholastic
Published: 1982

Doctor De Soto, a mouse, has a dental practice on a busy city street. As a rule, he does not accept patients threatening to his species, but he makes an exception for a fox with an emergency, and outsmarts the predator, whose gratitude is ultimately questionable. A glorious book with matchlessly witty full-color illustrations.

THE DO-SOMETHING DAY [335]

WRITTEN AND ILLUSTRATED BY JOE LASKER

Cloth: Viking
Published: 1982

Bernie is burning to *do something* on this bright, nice day, but no one needs his help at home, so he sets off on a tour of the neighborhood, visiting shopkeepers and doing errands. The story is pleasantly familiar to every child, the neighborhood of the illustrations is friendly and cozy and calls forth a certain nostalgia for grown-ups who remember small urban neighborhoods before and just after World War II.

DUFFY AND THE DEVIL   [336]

WRITTEN BY HARVE ZEMACH

ILLUSTRATED BY MARGOT ZEMACH

Cloth: Farrar, Straus

Paper: Sunburst/Farrar, Straus

Published: 1973   PRIZES: CALDECOTT MEDAL

This is a wry Cornish version of Rumpelstiltskin. Duffy is the servant girl Squire Lovel believes can spin and knit so well. But then the devil takes back the garments he made, much to the squire's embarrassment. Bright, cheerful, full-color illustrations.

ELOISE   [337]

WRITTEN BY KAY THOMPSON

ILLUSTRATED BY HILARY KNIGHT

Cloth: Simon & Schuster

Published: 1955

You may remember Eloise. She's six and rather adorable, and lives in the Plaza Hotel in New York City. She has lots of fun there: orders from room service and rides the elevators and checks out what's happening all over the hotel. She's terribly clever, to say the least. A timeless favorite about a terrorizing child.

THE ENORMOUS CROCODILE   [338]

WRITTEN BY ROALD DAHL

ILLUSTRATED BY QUENTIN BLAKE

Cloth: Knopf

Paper: Bantam, Skylark

Published: 1978

[338]

A droll story about an enormous crocodile who dares to leave the river and go to the town to find little children to eat. He poses as a coconut tree, a merry-go-round, and a picnic bench, and is foiled each time by other animals. Witty illustrations.

EVERETT ANDERSON'S GOODBYE   [339]

WRITTEN BY LUCILLE CLIFTON
ILLUSTRATED BY ANN GRIFALCONI
Cloth: Holt
Paper: Holt
Published: 1983

Everett Anderson, a little black boy, must deal with his father's death. His feelings are eloquently evoked in simple poems and are underscored in gentle pencil illustrations. Two other Everett Anderson books have been reissued—*Some of the Days of Everett Anderson* and *Everett Anderson's Nine Month Long*.

EVERYBODY NEEDS A ROCK   [340]

WRITTEN BY BYRD BAYLOR
ILLUSTRATED BY PETER PARNALL
Cloth: Scribners
Paper: Aladdin
Published: 1974

A guide to finding your own special rock, a bit of the earth to have and hold. Incidentally, the search for a special talisman teaches a good deal about the universe. The dramatic line drawings are engrossing. A seamless and persuasive collaboration between author and illustrator.

EVERYONE KNOWS WHAT A DRAGON LOOKS LIKE   [341]

WRITTEN BY JAY WILLIAMS
ILLUSTRATED BY MERCER MAYER
Cloth: Four Winds
Paper: Aladdin
Published: 1976

PRIZES: CALDECOTT MEDAL,
NEW YORK TIMES BEST ILLUSTRATED BOOK

Of course the truth is that everyone *doesn't* know what a dragon looks like, even in the Chinese kingdom wittily portrayed in this traditional tale.

[341]

Story Books

EVOLUTION [342]

WRITTEN BY JOANNA COLE
ILLUSTRATED BY ALIKI
Cloth: Crowell
Published: 1987

A carefully distilled explanation for early-grade children of the idea of evolution of complex plants and animals from one-celled beings. Cheerful children romp through the illustrations.

FABLES [343]

WRITTEN AND ILLUSTRATED BY ARNOLD LOBEL
Cloth: Harper
Paper: Harper
Published: 1980   PRIZES: CALDECOTT MEDAL

Short, original fables with unexpected and definitely contemporary morals—pleasing to adult readers as well as children for their gentle wit and full-color illustrations.

FIREFLIES [344]

WRITTEN AND ILLUSTRATED BY JULIE BRINKLOE
Cloth: Macmillan
Paper: Aladdin
Published: 1985

A favorite summer memory is captured in soft, mysterious two-color illustrations. A boy finishes his supper, grabs a jar, and rushes out into the dusk to catch fireflies.

FLOSSIE & THE FOX [345]

WRITTEN BY PATRICIA C. McKISSACK
ILLUSTRATED BY RACHEL ISADORA
Cloth: Dial
Published: 1986

Based on a Tennessee folktale. L'il Flossie Finley carries a basket of eggs through the woods, and outwits a pesky, furry, red figure who insists he is a fox. Flossie is a purely spunky and delightful heroine. The full-color illustrations are pleasingly sun-dappled.

THE FOOL OF THE WORLD AND
THE FLYING SHIP [346]

WRITTEN BY ARTHUR RANSOME
ILLUSTRATED BY URI SHULEVITZ

Cloth: Farrar, Straus
Paper: Farrar, Straus
Published: 1968   PRIZES: CALDECOTT MEDAL

The Fool of the World is a peasant who wins the hand of the Czar's
daughter by paying close attention to good advice and taking advan-
tage of the skills of the Listener, the Swift-goer, the Drinker, and others.
The old folktale is illustrated with great charm and wit.

FOR I WILL CONSIDER MY CAT
JEOFFRY [347]

WRITTEN BY CHRISTOPHER SMART
ILLUSTRATED BY EMILY ARNOLD McCULLY

Cloth: Macmillan
Published: 1984

A charmingly illustrated edition of the well-known eighteenth-century
ecstatic poem in praise of the author's beloved pet, who whirls, twirls,
twists, and veritably purrs on the page. The nonfeline illustrations are
set in the historic period.

[345]

FRANCIS: THE POOR MAN OF ASSISI [348]

WRITTEN AND ILLUSTRATED BY TOMIE de PAOLA
Cloth: Holiday
Published: 1982

An episodic life of the well-loved saint, illustrated in a characteristic, stylized fashion by an artist with a folkloric touch.

FROM PATH TO HIGHWAY: THE STORY OF THE BOSTON POST ROAD [349]

WRITTEN AND ILLUSTRATED BY GAIL GIBBONS
Cloth: Crowell
Published: 1986

An illustrated history of one of the earliest and most important roadways on the east coast of the North American continent. This account begins with the Indian footpath that cut through deep woodlands and is now the four-lane highway that exists today.

FROM THE HILLS OF GEORGIA: AN AUTOBIOGRAPHY IN PAINTINGS [350]

WRITTEN AND ILLUSTRATED BY MATTIE LOU O'KELLEY
Cloth: Atlantic-Little, Brown
Paper: Atlantic-Little, Brown
Published: 1983

Primitive-style full-color paintings tell the story of the author's childhood in the early years of this century. This is a book to pore over conversationally, as each painting is filled with details that make the past more immediate and imaginable.

THE GARDEN OF ABDUL GASAZI [351]

WRITTEN AND ILLUSTRATED BY CHRIS VAN ALLSBURG
Cloth: Houghton Mifflin
Published: 1979

PRIZES: CALDECOTT HONOR BOOK,
NEW YORK TIMES BEST ILLUSTRATED BOOK

A cautionary tale about a boy who lets the dog he is supposed to be caring for wander into the garden of a magician who specifically warns strangers not to enter. The first of a dazzling series of sophisticated picture books by an artist whose drawings are technically unparalleled and whose vision is often chilly.

GEORGE AND MARTHA [352]

WRITTEN AND ILLUSTRATED BY JAMES MARSHALL
Cloth: Houghton Mifflin
Paper: Houghton Mifflin
Published: 1972   PRIZES: NEW YORK TIMES BEST ILLUSTRATED BOOK

The first in a hilarious series of stories about two dear friends (who happen to be large, awkward hippos) with prominent buck teeth and a knack for finding themselves in farcical situations. Other titles include *George and Martha Back in Town, George and Martha One Fine Day, George and Martha Tons of Fun*, and *George and Martha Rise and Shine*.

GEORGIA MUSIC [353]

WRITTEN BY HELEN GRIFFITH
ILLUSTRATED BY JAMES STEVENSON
Cloth: Greenwillow
Published: 1986

A little girl spends sweet, private summers in Georgia with her grandfather until he becomes ill and comes to live with her family. When others fail, the child is able to penetrate his depression with her memories. Thoughtful, not maudlin, with wonderfully complementary text and illustrations. *Grandaddy's Place* tells the story of their first meeting.

GIANTS OF LAND, SEA & AIR: PAST AND PRESENT [354]

WRITTEN AND ILLUSTRATED BY DAVID PETERS
Cloth: Knopf
Published: 1986

A huge and enthralling compilation of detailed illustrations of all sorts of giant creatures that have really lived—from sharks to whales, mammoths, and dinosaurs. They are shown in a scaled relationship with a pair of human beings who appear on each double-page spread either jogging or swimming. This is a book that younger children can enjoy, older children find engrossing, and adults think is irresistible.

Story Books

THE GIFT OF THE SACRED DOG   [355]

WRITTEN AND ILLUSTRATED BY PAUL GOBLE

Cloth: Bradbury
Paper: Aladdin
Published: 1978

The handsomely illustrated legend of the arrival of the sacred dog, the horse, which totally changed the buffalo hunting ways of the Plains Indians.

THE GINGERBREAD RABBIT   [356]

WRITTEN BY RANDALL JARRELL
ILLUSTRATED BY GARTH WILLIAMS

Cloth: Macmillan
Paper: Aladdin
Published: 1964

A distinguished American poet wrote this story about a gingerbread rabbit who escapes the oven only to meet a fox who would eat him raw. The illustrations capture the spirit of the chase.

THE GIRL WHO LOVED THE WIND   [357]

WRITTEN BY JANE YOLEN
ILLUSTRATED BY ED YOUNG

Cloth: Harper
Paper: Harper
Published: 1972

A wealthy merchant in a kingdom to the east thought he could protect his precious daughter, but Danina heard the wind. The illustrations to this haunting fable are in a style that evokes, but does not exactly copy, Persian miniatures.

[358]

THE GIRL WHO LOVED WILD HORSES [358]

[358]

WRITTEN AND ILLUSTRATED BY PAUL GOBLE

Cloth: Bradbury
Paper: Aladdin
Published: 1978   PRIZES: CALDECOTT MEDAL

The romantic and compelling Plains Indian legend of a girl who so identifies with the wild horses that eventually she goes and joins them is beautifully illustrated in this prize-winning book. The artist's style abstracts traditional Indian motifs.

THE GIVING TREE [359]

WRITTEN AND ILLUSTRATED BY SHEL SILVERSTEIN

Cloth: Harper
Published: 1964

A much-loved story about a boy and a tree, one growing, the other giving generously.

THE GLASS MOUNTAIN [360]

RETOLD AND ILLUSTRATED BY NONNY HOGROGIAN

Cloth: Knopf
Published: 1985

A prize-winning illustrator brings her distinctive style to the Grimm's fairy tale about a princess who is turned into a raven and held on a glass mountain until a clever young man is able to set her free.

THE GLORIOUS FLIGHT: ACROSS THE CHANNEL WITH LOUIS BLÉRIOT [361]

WRITTEN AND ILLUSTRATED BY ALICE AND MARTIN PROVENSEN

Cloth: Viking
Paper: Puffin
Published: 1978   PRIZES: CALDECOTT MEDAL

A spectacular book—history and art in winning combination. This is the story of Louis Blériot, a Frenchman, and the flying machine he built to cross the English Channel.

GO AWAY, BAD DREAMS! [362]

WRITTEN BY SUSAN HILL
ILLUSTRATED BY VANESSA JULIAN-OTTIE
Paper: Random House
Published: 1985

Tom's mother helps him figure out how his imagination works to create some of his bad dreams, and then he can chase them away. This British import has a slightly stiff-upper-lip quality, but may be helpful to a school-age child with some simple nightmare troubles.

GOLDIE THE DOLLMAKER [363]

WRITTEN AND ILLUSTRATED BY M. B. GOFFSTEIN
Cloth: Farrar, Straus
Paper: Sunburst/Farrar, Straus
Published: 1969

Goldie the dollmaker, who appears in delicate, careful drawings, is an artist who lives alone and makes dolls. She chooses the wood, carves them carefully, paints them with precision. This is an unusually satisfying story about love and work.

[363]

THE GOOD GIANTS AND THE BAD
PUKWUDGIES [364]

WRITTEN BY JEAN FRITZ
ILLUSTRATED BY TOMIE de PAOLA

Cloth: Putnam
Paper: Putnam
Published: 1982

A folkloric account, drawn from Indian legends, about the formation of Cape Cod; the giant Mauship and his wife, Quant; their five sons; and the creatures, who sometimes appear as mosquitoes or fireflies, called the pukwudgies. The author is a distinguished historian for children, the artist a prizewinner.

GORKY RISES [365]

WRITTEN AND ILLUSTRATED BY WILLIAM STEIG

Cloth: Farrar, Straus
Paper: Sunburst/Farrar, Straus
Published: 1980   PRIZES: NEW YORK TIMES BEST ILLUSTRATED BOOK

Another zany Steig fable, this one tells about Gorky, a young frog, who fools around in the kitchen one summer morning when his parents are out. He makes a potion that, wondrously, later causes him to rise and fly through the soft afternoon.

GO WEST [366]

WRITTEN BY MARTIN WADDELL
ILLUSTRATED BY PHILIPPE DUPASQUIER

Cloth: Harper
Published: 1984

This bleak diary of a nine-year-old girl named Kate describes her pioneer family's trip across the United States by covered wagon. The busy and detailed cartoon-style illustrations seem lighthearted, although they depict harsh events and much suffering. This is sophisticated history if you look carefully.

A GREAT BIG UGLY MAN CAME UP AND TIED HIS HORSE TO ME   [367]

WRITTEN AND ILLUSTRATED BY WALLACE TRIPP

Cloth: Little, Brown
Paper: Little, Brown
Published: 1973

A hilarious collection of poems and nonsense, illustrated in deadpan fashion by an artist who challenges the reader's attention by inserting famous people, past and present, in improbable settings. Great fun to read with children, but they happily read it alone.

THE GREAT WALL OF CHINA   [368]

WRITTEN AND ILLUSTRATED BY LEONARD EVERETT FISHER

Cloth: Four Winds
Published: 1986

The story of the Great Wall told in brief text and very dramatic black-and-white illustrations, decorated with Chinese characters.

HANDTALK: AN ABC OF FINGER SPELLING AND SIGN LANGUAGE   [369]

WRITTEN BY REMY CHARLIP AND MARY BETH MILLER
ILLUSTRATED BY GEORGE ANCONA

Cloth: Four Winds
Paper: Aladdin
Published: 1974

The photographs in this introductory guidebook to sign language are so clear—both the gestures and the exaggerated expressions of the models—that very young children as well as sophisticated adults can understand the finger spelling. The full-color companion volume, *Handtalk Birthday,* has a bubbly spirit and aura of goodwill that is as irresistible as it is unexpected.

HANSEL AND GRETEL   [370]

WRITTEN BY RIKA LESSER
ILLUSTRATED BY PAUL O. ZELINSKY

Cloth: Dodd
Published: 1984   PRIZES: CALDECOTT HONOR BOOK

This lush version of one of the most familiar of the Grimm stories is
based on the first transcription of the tale. The oil paintings that illustrate it are in the style of eighteenth-century European landscape
painting. There are, of course, many other editions of the story, among
them handsome ones illustrated by Susan Jeffers, who favors large,
wide-eyed faces, Lisbeth Zwerger, whose style is very delicate and subtle, Paul Galdone, who uses broad, cartoonish lines, and Margot
Tomes, whose quirky pen-and-ink characters have psychological
weight.

HAVE YOU EVER SEEN...?
AN ABC BOOK   [371]

WRITTEN AND ILLUSTRATED BY BEAU GARDNER

Cloth: Dodd
Published: 1986

An alphabet book of graphic tricks and optical illusions. Very bright
and angular and very clever. This is for children who can read and get
the jokes.

HAWK, I'M YOUR BROTHER   [372]

WRITTEN BY BYRD BAYLOR
ILLUSTRATED BY PETER PARNALL

Cloth: Scribners
Paper: Aladdin
Published: 1976   PRIZES: CALDECOTT HONOR BOOK

The setting is the Southwest, a bare land of mountains and wide
sky. The boy named Rudy dreams of flying like a hawk over Santos
Mountain. He captures a young hawk and eventually sets it free.
The adults are wise and understanding. A very affecting book that is
thrilling to read out loud. The spare illustrations are evocative.

THE HELEN OXENBURY NURSERY STORY BOOK   [373]

WRITTEN AND ILLUSTRATED BY HELEN OXENBURY
Cloth: Knopf
Published: 1985

A collection of ten nursery stories, including "Goldilocks," "The Three Pigs," "The Gingerbread Boy," and "Three Billy Goats Gruff," told and illustrated in a bright and accessible fashion by an illustrator beloved by toddlers in particular.

HENRY THE CASTAWAY   [374]

WRITTEN BY MARK TAYLOR
ILLUSTRATED BY GRAHAM BOOTH
Cloth: Atheneum
Paper: Aladdin
Published: 1972

The first of three adventures Henry shares with his dog, Angus. After spring rain they go looking for an ocean and find themselves on an island. Other titles are *Henry Explores the Mountains* and *Henry the Explorer.*

HER MAJESTY, AUNT ESSIE   [375]

WRITTEN AND ILLUSTRATED BY AMY SCHWARTZ
Cloth: Bradbury
Paper: Puffin
Published: 1984

The little girl who narrates this story can just tell that her Aunt Essie, who has moved into her family's apartment (located in an inner city neighborhood in perhaps the 1940s), used to be a queen. Aunt Essie's style, habits, and gentleman caller make it clear. And believable. This is an affectionate look at eccentricity in family life.

[373]

HEY, AL [376]

WRITTEN BY ARTHUR YORINKS
ILLUSTRATED BY RICHARD EGIELSKI

Cloth: Farrar, Straus
Published: 1986   PRIZES: CALDECOTT MEDAL

Al, a janitor, and Eddie, his dog, live together in a small room on the
West Side of Manhattan. When they are offered a chance to escape to a
paradisiacal island they discover that the life of luxury has too high a
price. They manage to escape and are grateful to return home. The
brilliant full-color illustrations—from the cramped apartment to the
lush island—are just right.

HIGHER ON THE DOOR [377]

WRITTEN AND ILLUSTRATED BY JAMES STEVENSON

Cloth: Greenwillow
Published: 1987

The companion volume to *When I Was Nine* is also a memory book of
the details of the author's childhood. Both the watercolor illustrations
and the text are evocative, lyrical, and spare. They poignantly recall
the period before World War II in a suburb of New York City. The
books can be read separately or together. Both are memorable.

HILDILID'S NIGHT [378]

WRITTEN BY CHELI DURAN RYAN
ILLUSTRATED BY ARNOLD LOBEL

Cloth: Macmillan
Published: 1971

Hildilid is an old woman who is determined to put off the night. She
tries, among other things, to sweep it out, tie it up, burn it. She fails, of
course, but a sleep-resisting child enjoys the effort.

HIROSHIMA NO PIKA [379]

WRITTEN AND ILLUSTRATED BY TOSHI MARUKI

Cloth: Lothrop
Published: 1982

This beautiful but disturbing story about the atomic bomb details a
family's experiences in Hiroshima at the time the bomb was dropped.

Though it is essentially a story book, it should not be offered to any child to read alone. It requires adult support and discussion. It is not for the very young, either, and is best read with children in the middle and upper grades.

HORTON HATCHES THE EGG [380]

WRITTEN AND ILLUSTRATED BY DR. SEUSS
Cloth: Random House
Published: 1940

To be truly successful, nonsense has to be unrelenting, and, by its own lights, logical, and in his early books Dr. Seuss was a master of the genre. Horton the elephant agrees to hatch an egg, and he sticks to his promise through a year of hilarious trials and outrageous tribulations. Then his kindness and devotion are truly rewarded. There is also an early reader, *Horton Hears a Who*.

HOW MUCH IS A MILLION? [381]

WRITTEN BY DAVID M. SCHWARTZ
ILLUSTRATED BY STEVEN KELLOGG
Cloth: Lothrop
Paper: Scholastic
Published: 1985

A series of lighthearted conceptualizations and visualizations of really big numbers—such as how big a bowl would you need to hold a million goldfish, say. The giddy full-color illustrations hold up under intense scrutiny.

HOW MY PARENTS LEARNED TO EAT [382]

WRITTEN BY INA FRIEDMAN
ILLUSTRATED BY ALLAN SAY
Cloth: Houghton Mifflin
Paper: Houghton Mifflin
Published: 1984

A little girl describes her parents' courtship ritual, which was caring and thoughtful, because her father was an American sailor stationed in Japan and her mother a proper young Japanese lady. The illustrations are subtly reminiscent of nineteenth-century Japanese woodcuts.

HOW THE GRINCH STOLE CHRISTMAS [383]

WRITTEN AND ILLUSTRATED BY DR. SEUSS
Cloth: Random House
Published: 1957

Dr. Seuss's sermon on the true meaning of Christmas, with one of the best Scrooges of the twentieth-century, that wretched, selfish Grinch. The animated version is shown on television regularly, but, like "The Night Before Christmas," it's more fun to read aloud than watch.

HOW THE SUN WAS BROUGHT BACK TO THE SKY [384]

WRITTEN BY MIRRA GINSBERG
ILLUSTRATED BY JOSÉ ARUEGO AND ARIANE DEWEY
Cloth: Macmillan
Published: 1975

An Eastern European folktale about five chicks and their animal friends who set off to find the missing sun, illustrated in blazing full color.

HOW YOU WERE BORN [385]

WRITTEN BY JOANNA COLE
Cloth: Morrow
Paper: Morrow, Jr.
Published: 1984

When the appropriate time comes, this is a fine book to read with young children who want to know how babies grow inside the mother and are born. The text is clear and accurate; the photographs are beautiful rather than alarming for readers from toddler to middle-grade level.

[383]

IF YOU ARE A HUNTER OF FOSSILS   [386]

WRITTEN BY BYRD BAYLOR
ILLUSTRATED BY PETER PARNALL
Cloth: Scribners
Paper: Aladdin
Published: 1980

A fine introduction for school-age children to paleontology with spare, poetic prose and pictures showing how rocks reveal secrets of past life.

I HAD A FRIEND NAMED PETER: TALKING TO CHILDREN ABOUT THE DEATH OF A FRIEND   [387]

WRITTEN BY JANICE COHN, D.S.W.
ILLUSTRATED BY GAIL OWENS
Cloth: Morrow
Published: 1987

This is bibliotherapy; there is no natural way for the subject to arise, and yet it does. Betsy's friend Peter was killed by an automobile. This story tells how her parents and nursery school helped Betsy to understand what had happened. Very young children find death, even death of a peer, unimaginable, and there is no correct approach; however, this book has an introduction by a social worker with some thoughtful suggestions.

I KNOW A LADY   [388]

WRITTEN BY CHARLOTTE ZOLOTOW
ILLUSTRATED BY JAMES STEVENSON
Cloth: Greenwillow
Paper: Viking
Published: 1984

In this flawless collaboration between author and artist, a little girl describes the old lady in her small-town neighborhood who offers perfect friendship to the children as well as small seasonal gifts like homemade cookies or lemonade. The illustrations evoke New England and a nostalgic sense of a social order—of the way things ought to be.

I LIKE THE MUSIC   [389]

WRITTEN BY LEAH KOMAIKO
ILLUSTRATED BY BARBARA WESTMAN

Cloth: Harper
Published: 1987

The little girl who tells this story likes street music; she's hip and cool. Her grandmother, who is pretty hip herself, takes the child to her first outdoor symphony concert with happy results. The full-color illustrations are festive.

I'LL FIX ANTHONY   [390]

WRITTEN BY JUDITH VIORST
ILLUSTRATED BY ARNOLD LOBEL

Cloth: Harper
Paper: Aladdin
Published: 1969

A tale of revenge intended—all the things the narrator wants to do to get even with his older brother, "when I am six" like Anthony.

I'LL MISS YOU, MR. HOOPER   [391]

WRITTEN BY NORMAN STILES
ILLUSTRATED BY JOE MATHIEU

Cloth: Random House
Published: 1984

An adaptation of the thoughtful television episode of *Sesame Street* (which aired only once) in which Big Bird, the program's emblematic four-year-old, dealt with the death of Mr. Hooper from the candy store. Today's *Sesame Street* viewers won't remember Mr. Hooper, but the story remains helpful as a book for preschool children.

I'M TERRIFIC   [392]

WRITTEN BY MARJORIE WEINMAN SHARMAT
ILLUSTRATED BY KAY CHORAO
Cloth: Holiday
Paper: Scholastic
Published: 1977

A gently comic story about Jason Bear, who tries many ways of being different until he accepts himself.

IN COAL COUNTRY   [393]

WRITTEN BY JUDITH HENDERSHOT
ILLUSTRATED BY THOMAS B. ALLEN
Cloth: Knopf
Published: 1987

An unflinching and evocative account of childhood in a coal-mining town in the 1930s, remembered with pride and affection, and illustrated in the same spirit.

IN THE NIGHT KITCHEN   [394]

WRITTEN AND ILLUSTRATED BY MAURICE SENDAK
Cloth: Harper
Paper: Harper   PRIZES: NEW YORK TIMES BEST ILLUSTRATED BOOK,
Published: 1970   CALDECOTT HONOR BOOK

Mickey's dream adventure carries him into the night kitchen, where the bakers are making cake for the morning. The brilliant illustrations are also about movies and New York City in the 1930s. Some adults have found the story, not to mention Mickey's frontal nudity, alarming, but children, especially boys, adore the book.

IRA SLEEPS OVER   [395]

WRITTEN AND ILLUSTRATED BY BERNARD WABER
Cloth: Houghton Mifflin
Paper: Houghton Mifflin
Published: 1972

A first sleepover, even if it is at the house of a friend who lives right next door, is a big event, and here it is handled tenderly, and almost entirely in pricelessly accurate-sounding dialogue. The important question is whether a boy takes his teddy bear along.

THE IRON LION [396]

WRITTEN BY PETER DICKINSON
ILLUSTRATED BY PAULINE BAYNES
Cloth: Bedrick
Published: 1984

A droll modern fairy tale about Mustapha, a charming, impoverished prince who is determined to restore the family fortunes and marry the Emperor's daughter Yasmin. He makes the Iron Lion laugh, becomes his friend, and cures his rustiness. The full-color illustrations in lavish and exotic style combining Persian miniatures and medieval illumination are both exquisite and funny.

ISLAND WINTER [397]

WRITTEN AND ILLUSTRATED BY CHARLES MARTIN
Cloth: Greenwillow
Published: 1983

A pleasant catalog of month-to-month life off-season on an island almost surely off the Northeastern coast of the United States. The illustrations detail family and community life and the happy activities of a third-grader named Heather and her seven friends. Other titles in the series include *For Rent, Island Rescue,* and *Summer Business.*

IT COULD ALWAYS BE WORSE:
A YIDDISH FOLK TALE [398]

WRITTEN AND ILLUSTRATED BY MARGOT ZEMACH
Cloth: Farrar, Straus
Paper: Scholastic
Published: 1977

PRIZES: CALDECOTT HONOR BOOK,
NEW YORK TIMES BEST ILLUSTRATED BOOK

A poor man thinks his crowded household in an Eastern European town is so intolerably crowded that he goes to the rabbi to ask for advice. Amazingly, amusingly, astonishingly, his life gets worse, and the man learns to count his blessings. A familiar folktale told and illustrated with charm.

IT HAPPENED IN PINSK   [399]

WRITTEN BY ARTHUR YORINKS
ILLUSTRATED BY RICHARD EGIELSKI
Cloth: Farrar, Straus
Paper: Farrar, Straus
Published: 1983

Irv Irving, a cranky Russian shoe salesman, literally loses his head before breakfast and runs around Pinsk looking for it. The full-color illustrations are folkloric, Slavic, and stylishly zany all at once.

JELLY BELLY   [400]

WRITTEN BY DENNIS LEE
ILLUSTRATED BY JUAN WIJNGAARD
Cloth: Bedrick
Paper: Bedrick
Published: 1985

An exuberant collection of raucous and rowdy verses illustrated with gusto.

JERUSALEM, SHINING STILL   [401]

WRITTEN BY KARLA KUSKIN
ILLUSTRATED BY DAVID FRAMPTON
Cloth: Harper
Published: 1987

The wood-block illustrations that accompany this poetic evocation of the history of Jerusalem are as golden, spare, and appealing as the text itself. Good to read aloud for families of all faiths.

JONAH AND THE GREAT FISH   [402]

WRITTEN AND ILLUSTRATED BY WARWICK HUTTON
Cloth: McElderry
Published: 1984   PRIZES: NEW YORK TIMES BEST ILLUSTRATED BOOK

A beautiful retelling of the story of Jonah by a British artist whose watercolor illustrations, unusually rich and textured, carry the narrative with greater power than the simple text taken from the King James Bible.

JOSEPH WHO LOVED THE SABBATH [403]

WRITTEN BY MARILYN HIRSH
ILLUSTRATED BY DEVIS GREBU
Cloth: Viking
Published: 1986

A very handsome retelling of this traditional Jewish story about Joseph, the devout but poor man who bought the finest things to celebrate the Sabbath and was eventually rewarded for his devotion.

JUMANJI [404]

WRITTEN AND ILLUSTRATED BY CHRIS VAN ALLSBURG
Cloth: Houghton Mifflin
Published: 1981

PRIZES: CALDECOTT MEDAL,
NEW YORK TIMES BEST ILLUSTRATED BOOK

Two bored children find a board game in the park. They take it home and somehow unleash jungle creatures in the house. Complex, haunting pencil illustrations create a real sense of threat and excitement before a safe return to reality.

KATIE MORAG AND THE TWO GRANDMOTHERS [405]

WRITTEN AND ILLUSTRATED BY MAIRI HEDDERWICK
Cloth: Little, Brown
Published: 1986

The setting is a remote Scottish island, and young Katie Morag figures out how to reconcile her island granny, bluff and hearty, and her refined mainland granny who comes to visit. Another title, about the birth of her brother, is *Katie Morag and the Tiresome Ted*.

THE KING IN THE GARDEN [406]

WRITTEN BY LEON GARFIELD
ILLUSTRATED BY MICHAEL BRAGG
Cloth: Lothrop
Published: 1985

This distinguished British children's writer has retold several Old Testament stories, this one being Nebuchadnezzer's dream. The text is excellent. The illustrations are not quite its equal. *King Nimrod's Tower* is the story of the Tower of Babel.

KING ISLAND CHRISTMAS [407]

WRITTEN BY JEAN ROGERS
ILLUSTRATED BY RIE MUNOZ
Cloth: Greenwillow
Published: 1985

The Eskimo community of King Island has to rescue their new priest and get him from his stranded ship in the Bering Sea to their village in time for Christmas. An unusual story with distinctive illustrations in the myriad blues of the North.

THE KING OF THE PIPERS [408]

WRITTEN AND ILLUSTRATED BY PETER ELWELL
Cloth: Macmillan
Published: 1984

Our young piper hero makes terrible sounds on his bagpipe. In comic opera style laced with Monty Python humor, he encounters a cowardly king, a beautiful princess, and a lucky dwarf. The pen-and-ink illustrations are ornate.

THE KNEE-HIGH MAN AND OTHER TALES [409]

WRITTEN BY JULIUS LESTER
ILLUSTRATED BY RALPH PINTO
Cloth: Dial
Paper: Dial
Published: 1972

A collection of six animal stories from the American black folklore tradition. The author has also retold some of the Uncle Remus stories.

LIBBY'S NEW GLASSES [410]

WRITTEN AND ILLUSTRATED BY TRICIA TUSA
Cloth: Holiday
Published: 1984

Embarrassed to be seen in her first pair of glasses, Libby runs away from home and meets an ostrich who has buried his head in the sand to hide his own spectacles. Together they learn to see the light clearly, through their glasses.

LIKE JAKE AND ME   [411]

WRITTEN BY MAVIS JUKES
ILLUSTRATED BY LLOYD BLOOM
Cloth: Knopf
Paper: Knopf
Published: 1984   PRIZES: NEWBERY HONOR BOOK

Alex, who is quiet and rather shy, probably like his father, is trying to cope with his stepfather—a brash cowboy. The turning point comes when Alex rescues Jake from a wolf spider. A well-written story about the formation of new families that carries special conviction.

THE LITTLE BOOKROOM   [412]

WRITTEN BY ELEANOR FARJEON
ILLUSTRATED BY EDWARD ARDIZZONE
Cloth: Godine
Paper: Godine
Published: 1984   PRIZES: HANS CHRISTIAN ANDERSEN

This collection of illustrated stories, which represents some of the best work of the renowned and beloved British author and artist, has been reissued by an American publisher.

A LITTLE BOX OF
BALLET STORIES   [413]

WRITTEN BY MARGARET GREAVES
ILLUSTRATED BY FRANCESCA CRESPI
Cloth: Dial
Published: 1986

The little box contains three brightly illustrated palm-size volumes with the stories of "Firebird" and "Petruska" by Stravinsky and "Coppelia" by Delibes. *A Little Box of Witches* and *A Little Box of Fairy Tales* are by the same author and illustrator.

THE LITTLE HOUSE [414]

WRITTEN AND ILLUSTRATED BY VIRGINIA LEE BURTON
Cloth: Houghton Mifflin
Paper: Houghton Mifflin
Published: 1942   PRIZES: CALDECOTT MEDAL

This is the now-classic story of a little house that was built upon a hill
long ago and how, as time passed, the city closed in upon it. The little
house was rescued and brought back to rural peace and calm. With its
windows, door, and stoop that together look like a smiling face, the
little house is back on its hill. Beneath the charm and sweetness there is
a profound antiurbanism to both text and illustration, which many
adults see clearly.

LITTLE RABBIT'S LOOSE TOOTH [415]

WRITTEN BY LUCY BATE
ILLUSTRATED BY DIANE de GROAT
Cloth: Crown
Paper: Crown
Published: 1975

The title tells all, but perhaps does not convey the charm of the heroine
and the dialogue as she moves through one of life's crises, inevitably
faced by six-year-olds—the first loose tooth. Little Rabbit reappears
addressing another threatening issue in *Little Rabbit's Baby Brother.*

THE LITTLE RED LIGHTHOUSE AND THE GREAT GRAY BRIDGE [416]

WRITTEN BY HILDEGARDE HOYT SWIFT
ILLUSTRATED BY LYND WARD
Cloth: Harcourt Brace
Paper: Voyager/HBJ
Published: 1942

There really is a little red lighthouse that sits in the shadow of the
George Washington Bridge, which spans the Hudson River in New
York City. A picture book favorite for generations.

LITTLE RED RIDING HOOD [417]

WRITTEN BY THE BROTHERS GRIMM
ILLUSTRATED BY TRINA SCHART HYMAN
Cloth: Holiday
Paper: Holiday House
Published: 1983   PRIZES: CALDECOTT HONOR BOOK

The illustrator of this version of the classic tale has a distinctive style—lush, romantic, and anxious at the same time—that suits the story well. There are many other editions, including cartoonish ones illustrated by Paul Galdone, James Marshall, and Harriet Pincus, and a very provocative one illustrated with photographs by Sarah Moon. Consider the age of the reader when choosing—younger children find the lighter, more cartoonish versions easier to handle.

LITTLE SISTER AND THE MONTH BROTHERS [418]

WRITTEN BY BEATRICE SCHENK de REGNIERS
ILLUSTRATED BY MARGOT TOMES
Published: 1976
Cloth: Clarion
Paper: Clarion

A bright retelling of the Russian fairy tale about how the Month Brothers help Little Sister meet the seasonally impossible demands of her greedy stepmother. The illustrations are witty and suitable.

LITTLE TIM AND THE BRAVE SEA CAPTAIN [419]

WRITTEN AND ILLUSTRATED BY EDWARD ARDIZZONE
Paper: Puffin
Published: 1936, reissued 1977

This beloved English picture book adventure, now only available in paperback, tells how young Tim stows away on a steamship and nearly goes down with the captain. The watercolor illustrations capture the changing moods of the sea beautifully. A thrilling book with a happy ending. Other Tim books include: *Tim and Ginger*, *Tim and Charlotte*, and *Tim and Towser*.

[418]

LOUHI, WITCH OF NORTH FARM [420]

WRITTEN BY TONI de GEREZ
ILLUSTRATED BY BARBARA COONEY
Cloth: Viking
Paper: Puffin
Published: 1986

This is a story from the epic Finnish cycle, the Kalevala, about naughty Louhi, the witch. In this episode she steals both the sun and moon and locks them away in Copper Mountain. But Vainamoinen the Great Knower outwits her, of course. The text and the carefully detailed illustrations, in a muted northern palate, perfectly complement each other.

LOUIS THE FISH [421]

WRITTEN BY ARTHUR YORINKS
ILLUSTRATED BY RICHARD EGIELSKI
Cloth: Farrar, Straus
Paper: Farrar, Straus
Published: 1980

Here is a perfectly executed, scaley fantasy in which Louis, a respectable, aproned butcher, turns into a large fish. A salmon, actually. And he looks really ridiculous lying in bed under the covers, wearing striped pajamas over his fins. It's the kind of zany story that often appeals to parents as much as children.

LULLABIES AND NIGHT SONGS [422]

WRITTEN BY WILLIAM ENGVICK
ILLUSTRATED BY MAURICE SENDAK
Cloth: Harper
Published: 1965

The music for these forty-eight songs, whose lyrics are taken from nursery rhymes and poems, is by Alec Wilder. The color illustrations are by another master, Maurice Sendak. If you are musical enough to pick out the graceful melodies, this is worth having at home.

THE LULLABY SONGBOOK [423]

WRITTEN BY JANE YOLEN
ILLUSTRATED BY CHARLES MIKOLAYCAK
Cloth: Harcourt Brace
Published: 1986

This is a pleasing collection of bedtime songs, old and new, from around the world, with handsome illustrations and simple piano and guitar arrangements.

LYLE, LYLE, CROCODILE [424]

WRITTEN AND ILLUSTRATED BY BERNARD WABER
Cloth: Houghton Mifflin
Paper: Houghton Mifflin
Published: 1965

The crocodile who lives in *The House on East 88th Street* wants to make friends with Loretta the cat. The Primm family copes, of course. Other titles in the much-loved series include *Lovable Lyle*, *Lyle and the Birthday Party*, and *Lyle Finds His Mother.*

MAGGIE DOESN'T WANT TO MOVE [425]

WRITTEN BY ELIZABETH LEE O'DONNELL
ILLUSTRATED BY AMY SCHWARTZ
Cloth: Four Winds
Published: 1987

This is bibliotherapy, but so laced with wit and humor, and further enhanced by winsome comic illustrations, that it is also a good story book. Simon, who is seven, insists that he doesn't really mind moving, it's Maggie, his little sister, who would miss the slide at the playground and his teacher, Mrs. Acosta, and the neighborhood. But when they go to visit the new house, new neighborhood, and new school, Simon thinks maybe Maggie might change her mind.

[421]

THE MAGIC SCHOOL BUS   [426]

WRITTEN BY JOANNA COLE
ILLUSTRATED BY BRUCE DEGAN
Cloth: Scholastic
Paper: Scholastic
Published: 1986

Ms. Frizzle may be the strangest teacher in the school, but the trip she takes her class on, going into the reservoir system and through the waterworks back to school is magic. The author delivers straight science and information in sidebar notes. The whole is a model of witty, imaginative, and accurate science writing with equally accomplished and funny illustrations. The second title in the series is *The Magic School Bus: Inside the Earth*.

THE MAN WHO COULD CALL DOWN OWLS   [427]

WRITTEN BY EVE BUNTING
ILLUSTRATED BY CHARLES MIKOLAYCAK
Cloth: Macmillan
Published: 1984

A fable about a sorcerer, deep in the woods, who calls down the owls each night. An evil stranger envies his power. The black-and-white illustrations are full of mystery and slightly scary shadows.

THE MAN WHOSE MOTHER WAS A PIRATE   [428]

WRITTEN BY MARGARET MAHY
ILLUSTRATED BY MARGARET CHAMBERLIN
Cloth: Viking
Paper: Puffin
Published: 1986

He's an office-worker wimp, his mother was a pirate, and now she wants to go home to the sea. So, with only a wheelbarrow and a kite, Sam takes her. The illustrations to this grand story are broad and funny; the text, however, is far, far better still, and includes lyric praise of the sea. While the illustrations are fun, this book is worth reading aloud again and again just for the pleasure of the language.

MANY MOONS [429]

WRITTEN BY JAMES THURBER
ILLUSTRATED BY LOUIS SLOBODKIN
Cloth: Harcourt Brace
Paper: Voyager/HBJ
Published: 1943   PRIZES: CALDECOTT MEDAL

There was once a little princess who wanted the moon. And she got it.
A classic story with pale, subtle, haunting illustrations.

MARGUERITE, GO WASH
YOUR FEET! [430]

SELECTED AND ILLUSTRATED BY WALLACE TRIPP
Cloth: Houghton Mifflin
Paper: Houghton Mifflin
Published: 1985

A collection of funny verse from Shakespeare to Spike Milligan, with
suitably sharp illustrations, many of which contain cartoonish rendi-
tions of famous people.

MAZEL AND SHLIMAZEL:
OR THE MILK OF A LIONESS [431]

WRITTEN BY ISAAC BASHEVIS SINGER
ILLUSTRATED BY MARGOT ZEMACH
Cloth: Farrar, Straus
Published: 1967

This story, told in the manner of an Eastern European folktale, is about
the contest between good and evil, who take the forms of the happy and
good Mazel and the wicked old Shlimazel. The illustrations perfectly
complement the wise tale.

[429]

141

A MEDIEVAL FEAST [432]

WRITTEN AND ILLUSTRATED BY ALIKI

Cloth: Crowell
Paper: Harper
Published: 1983

What happens when the king announces that he and his attendants plan to visit the lord of the manor? In this remarkably accomplished historical story book, the detailed illustrations, in the medieval style, show how manor life was structured and the elaborate preparations that must take place before the king arrives—how the food is prepared and served, the entertainment is organized, and so on. Joe Lasker's *Merry Ever After* and *A Tournament of Knights* are fine companion titles.

MERRY CHRISTMAS, STREGA NONA [433]

WRITTEN AND ILLUSTRATED BY TOMIE de PAOLA

Cloth: Harcourt
Published: 1986

The Calabrian witch, heroine of a whole series of books, refuses to use her magic to fix the Christmas feast. Big Anthony, her doltish assistant, triumphs. There's *Strega Nona* (published 1975; Caldecott Honor Book), *Big Anthony and the Magic Ring* (which is about spring fever), and *Strega Nona's Magic Lessons*.

[433]

MERRY EVER AFTER: THE STORY OF TWO MEDIEVAL WEDDINGS [434]

WRITTEN AND ILLUSTRATED BY JOE LASKER

Cloth: Viking
Paper: Puffin
Published: 1976   PRIZES: NEW YORK TIMES BEST ILLUSTRATED BOOK

The celebration of two weddings offers a fine explanation of class and custom in the Middle Ages. The illustrations are detailed and high-spirited. *A Tournament of Knights* by the same author is another good story book about medieval life, as is *A Medieval Feast* by Aliki.

MIKE MULLIGAN AND HIS STEAM SHOVEL [435]

WRITTEN AND ILLUSTRATED BY VIRGINIA LEE BURTON

Cloth: Houghton Mifflin
Paper: Houghton Mifflin
Published: 1939

A classic picture book with a message that has pleased generations of young readers. Mike Mulligan and his steam shovel, Mary Anne, are being declared obsolete, but, fiercely determined, they find one last one-day job in a small town. They dig their way to a new career and a happy ending.

MING LO MOVES THE MOUNTAIN [436]

WRITTEN AND ILLUSTRATED BY ARNOLD LOBEL

Cloth: Greenwillow
Paper: Scholastic
Published: 1982

Ming Lo asks the wise man's help in moving the mountain away from his house. The wise man puffs away on his water pipe and eventually comes up with the perfect solution that convinces Ming Lo and his wife that indeed the mountain has moved.

THE MIRACLE CHILD [437]

WRITTEN BY ELIZABETH LAIRD WITH
    ABBA AREGAWEI WOLDE GABRIEL
ILLUSTRATED WITH REPRODUCTIONS
Cloth: Holt
Published: 1985

The story of Ethiopian Saint Tekla Heymanot, a thirteenth-century monk, is simply told and illustrated with fine paintings from an eighteenth-century manuscript collection. All profits go to Ethiopian relief agencies.

MISS FLORA McFLIMSEY'S
EASTER BONNET [438]

WRITTEN AND ILLUSTRATED BY MARIANA
Cloth: Lothrop
Published: 1951; reissued 1987

One of a series of enchanting old-fashioned books about a pretty doll from long ago. Other titles include *Miss Flora McFlimsey's May Day* and *Miss Flora McFlimsey's Valentine*. Miss Flora's adventures require charming costume changes—the sort that please little girls who also like to play with dolls and paper dolls.

MISS NELSON IS MISSING! [439]

WRITTEN BY HARRY ALLARD
ILLUSTRATED BY JAMES MARSHALL
Cloth: Houghton Mifflin
Paper: Houghton Mifflin
Published: 1977

The first in a raucous trio of books about the students in Room 207, their dear teacher, Miss Nelson, and her mean, hideous, lunatic substitute, Miss Viola Swamp. Other titles are *Miss Nelson Has a Field Day* and *Miss Nelson Is Back*.

MISS RUMPHIUS   [440]

WRITTEN AND ILLUSTRATED BY BARBARA COONEY

Cloth: Viking
Paper: Puffin
Published: 1982

Miss Rumphius was told as a child that she must do something to make the world more beautiful. She traveled, had adventures, and found her calling as the Lupine Lady, sowing the seed of the blue and purple flowers by the seacoast where she lives. She is very old now, and quite magical. A small, jewel-like picture book that carries its moral imperative lightly.

[439]

MOLLY'S PILGRIM   [441]

WRITTEN BY BARBARA COHEN
ILLUSTRATED BY MICHAEL J. DERANEY

Cloth: Lothrop
Published: 1983

The Pilgrim doll that Molly makes for her third-grade Thanksgiving class assignment reflects her experiences as a recent immigrant and the only Jewish child in the class. An unusual and provocative book.

MOON MAN   [442]

WRITTEN AND ILLUSTRATED BY TOMI UNGERER

Cloth: Harper
Paper: Harper
Published: 1967

The Man in the Moon comes to earth for a night of fun, but getting there and getting home requires a simple lesson in periodicity, because a fat moon cannot escape an earthly prison. Fine fantasy that young children enjoy and older children also find provocative.

MOON TIGER   [443]

WRITTEN BY PHYLLIS ROOT
ILLUSTRATED BY ED YOUNG
Cloth: Holt
Paper: Holt
Published: 1985

A dream of adventure and revenge. Jessica Ellen and her little brother are sent to bed. She dreams that the moon tiger will carry her off to the Arctic and to jungles, and finally, of course, home. Intense, vibrant illustrations in startling colors make this an unusual bedtime book.

MOSS GOWN   [444]

WRITTEN BY WILLIAM H. HOOKS
ILLUSTRATED BY DONALD CARRICK
Cloth: Clarion
Published: 1987

This story, drawn from Carolina folklore and set in the antebellum South, mixes elements of *King Lear* and "Cinderella." Candace is rejected by her father for loving him "as much as meat loves salt." Magically transformed to "Moss Gown," she becomes the mistress of a great plantation and years later is reconciled with her father. The language is rich, and the illustrations are mysterious.

MOTHER GOOSE: A COLLECTION OF CLASSIC NURSERY RHYMES   [445]

SELECTED AND ILLUSTRATED BY MICHAEL HAGUE
Cloth: Holt
Published: 1984

A collection of the illustrator's favorites from the Mother Goose canon. The artist's lush style is often reminiscent of the work of artists from an earlier era.

THE MOUNTAINS OF TIBET   [446]

WRITTEN AND ILLUSTRATED BY MORDICAI GERSTEIN

Cloth: Harper

Published: 1987   PRIZES: NEW YORK TIMES BEST ILLUSTRATED BOOK

The life cycle of a child who grows up to become a woodcutter in a valley in Tibet is told in a brilliant story book adaptation of the Tibetan Book of the Dead. At his death the woodcutter has the choice of becoming part of heaven or living another life. The illustrations help carry the story from that faraway valley into the cosmos itself and back to the valley. This is an awesomely accomplished book that can be read repeatedly by both children and adults.

MRS. MOSKOWITZ AND THE SABBATH CANDLESTICKS   [447]

WRITTEN AND ILLUSTRATED BY AMY SCHWARTZ

Cloth: Jewish Publication Society

Published: 1983

Mrs. Moskowitz and her cat, Fred, have moved to a new apartment. Finding her Sabbath candlesticks in a packing box prompts the widow into unpacking and making their new quarters into a welcoming home. Droll illustrations and an unself-conscious text explain Jewish Sabbath rituals in an affecting way.

MUFARO'S BEAUTIFUL DAUGHTERS: AN AFRICAN TALE   [448]

WRITTEN AND ILLUSTRATED BY JOHN STEPTOE

Cloth: Lothrop

Paper: Mulberg

Published: 1987   AWARDS: CALDECOTT HONOR BOOK

A West African tale about Mufaro's two beautiful but totally different daughters—Manyara, who is ambitious and mean, and Nyasha, who is kind and helpful. Guess which one ends up marrying the king? The illustrations are sumptuous.

MUMMIES MADE IN EGYPT [449]

WRITTEN AND ILLUSTRATED BY ALIKI
Cloth: Crowell
Paper: Harper
Published: 1979

This is a well-organized and very well illustrated introduction to ancient Egyptian beliefs and funerary practices, especially, of course, the fascinating mummies.

MY FIRST PICTURE DICTIONARY [450]

WRITTEN BY KATHERINE HOWARD
ILLUSTRATED BY HUCK SCARRY
Paper: Random House
Published: 1978

A slim, well-organized paperback that is a useful dictionary—over two hundred words are illustrated in cheerful fashion—but also an introduction to the idea of dictionaries and reference books.

MY LITTLE ISLAND [451]

WRITTEN AND ILLUSTRATED BY FRAN'E LESSAC
Cloth: Lippincott
Paper: Harper
Published: 1985

The lucky narrator describes a visit to an island in the Caribbean, which he takes with his best friend, who was born there. Their holiday trip is captured in exuberant, brightly colored, primitive-style paintings.

THE MYSTERIES OF HARRIS BURDICK [452]

WRITTEN AND ILLUSTRATED BY CHRIS VAN ALLSBURG
Cloth: Houghton Mifflin
Published: 1984   PRIZES: NEW YORK TIMES BEST ILLUSTRATED BOOK

Strange, even weird, fragments of text, illustrated in totally unexpected ways by a master draftsman. This is one of the contemporary picture books that speaks to teenagers and adults as strongly as to older children. A book for discussion and to use in making up games and plays.

A NEW COAT FOR ANNA [453]

WRITTEN BY HARRIET ZIEFERT
ILLUSTRATED BY ANITA LOBEL
Cloth: Knopf
Paper: Knopf
Published: 1986

Someplace in Europe after World War II, Anna's mother bargains and barters with a sheep farmer, a spinner, a weaver, and a tailor so that Anna will have a new coat the following winter. Evocative illustrations. This story is of greatest interest to early-grade children, especially girls, but holds the attention of younger listeners.

THE NIGHTINGALE [454]

WRITTEN BY HANS CHRISTIAN ANDERSEN
ILLUSTRATED BY LISBETH ZWERGER
Cloth: Picture Book
Published: 1985

The Viennese illustrator's version of the familiar story of the emperor and the real and mechanical songbirds is very fragile and subtle. The emperor and his court seem, somehow, like child dolls, possibly made of porcelain. There are other handsome but very different versions illustrated by Demi (delicate), Beni Montresor (lush), and Nancy E. Burkhert (large faces).

NOAH AND THE GREAT FLOOD [455]

WRITTEN AND ILLUSTRATED BY WARWICK HUTTON
Cloth: McElderry
Published: 1977

The familiar Bible story is told here by the contemporary English artist whose watercolors capture the sea and storm with startling power.

NOAH'S ARK [456]

WRITTEN AND ILLUSTRATED BY PETER SPIER
Cloth: Doubleday
Paper: Doubleday   PRIZES: CALDECOTT MEDAL,
Published: 1977   NEW YORK TIMES BEST ILLUSTRATED BOOK

The only text in this prize-winning version of the story of Noah is a
seventeenth-century Dutch poem describing the menagerie. The rest
of this account is wordless, narrative illustration. There are double-
page spreads showing minute details of the construction of the ark and
habits of the animals, contrasted with double-page spreads of the tiny
boat on wind-tossed, rainy seas. The crowding, chaos, and tension of
the ark just before the end is palpable. This book holds the attention of
a wide age range, from toddlers through the middle grades.

NO MORE SECRETS FOR ME [457]

WRITTEN BY ORALEE WACHTER
ILLUSTRATED BY JANE AARON
Cloth: Little, Brown
Paper: Little, Brown
Published: 1983

Perhaps the best-known and most widely distributed book for children
about how to recognize and deal with sexual abuse. Four plausible stories about when "someone you know...touches you, and you don't like
it." The language used is simple enough so that lower-grade children
can read it for themselves. The subject is so potent that older children

who are concerned, for themselves or others, can and will read it without feeling it is babyish.

OH, BOY! BABIES! [458]

WRITTEN BY ALISON CRAGIN HERZIG
   AND JANE LAWRENCE MALI
ILLUSTRATED BY KATRINA THOMAS
Cloth: Little, Brown
Paper: Little, Brown
Published: 1980
This photo-documentary about a one-semester course in baby and
infant care taught in a proper, preppy boys' school contains a great deal
of practical advice and information for older siblings disguised with a
thin story line.

OLD HENRY [459]

WRITTEN BY JOAN W. BLOS
ILLUSTRATED BY STEPHEN GAMMELL
Cloth: Morrow
Published: 1987
Old Henry just doesn't keep house the way his neighbors think he
ought to, but when he up and leaves they find they miss him. A small
morality play about tolerance illustrated with great style and wit in a
style reminiscent of *The Relatives Came*.

[456]

OL' PAUL, THE MIGHTY LOGGER [460]

WRITTEN AND ILLUSTRATED BY GLEN ROUNDS

Cloth: Holiday
Paper: Holiday
Published: 1936

A dandy collection of stories about the giant logger's adventures and achievements. Rounds is the author/illustrator of an additional title, called *The Morning the Sun Refused to Rise*, that is also comic and far-fetched. There are other Paul Bunyan stories in print, including Stephen Kellogg's exuberant full-color picture book version, and a reissue of a distinguished volume illustrated by Rockwell Kent.

ONE DAY IN PARADISE [461]

WRITTEN AND ILLUSTRATED BY HELME HEINE

Cloth: McElderry
Published: 1986

Beautiful watercolor illustrations by a distinguished German artist make this charming version of the biblical story of Creation unique. It shows God as the kindliest and most dignified of elderly gardeners.

ONE SUMMER AT GRANDMOTHER'S HOUSE [462]

WRITTEN AND ILLUSTRATED BY POUPA MONTAUFIER

Cloth: Carolrhoda
Published: 1986

A memoir, illustrated with charming, primitive-style paintings, of a summer the author spent with her grandmother Oma in the Alsace region of France.

OUTSIDE OVER THERE [463]

WRITTEN AND ILLUSTRATED BY MAURICE SENDAK

Cloth: Harper
Published: 1981

AWARDS: CALDECOTT HONOR BOOK,
NEW YORK TIMES BEST ILLUSTRATED BOOK

This most visually lavish Sendak book has a spare text but addresses potent, emotional issues—siblings and abandonment. Ida is left in charge of her baby sister, who is kidnapped. Ida determines to rescue the baby and enters a baffling dream world from which they both emerge with new understanding. The painterly illustrations, full of elaborate symbolism and literary, musical, and historical references, are worth studying closely.

OVER THE MOON: A BOOK OF NURSERY RHYMES [464]

WRITTEN AND ILLUSTRATED BY CHARLOTTE VOAKE
Cloth: Crown
Published: 1985

A collection of familiar rhymes, riddles, lullabies, and songs, mostly Mother Goose, with distinctive, delicate, pen-and-ink-over-water-color-painting illustrations.

OWL MOON [465]

WRITTEN BY JANE YOLEN
ILLUSTRATED BY JOHN SCHOENHERR
Cloth: Philomel
Published: 1987   PRIZES: CALDECOTT MEDAL

This is the sort of book that makes city children achingly wish to live in the country. The very idea of going out late on a moonlight winter's night with your father and calling for owls is quite magical, as is this story, with its snowy, night-lit illustrations.

OX-CART MAN [466]

WRITTEN BY DONALD HALL
ILLUSTRATED BY BARBARA COONEY
Cloth: Viking
Paper: Puffin   PRIZES: CALDECOTT MEDAL,
Published: 1979   NEW YORK TIMES BEST ILLUSTRATED BOOK

[466]

History can be conveyed to young children, as this splendid book clearly shows. The text is by a distinguished writer and poet; the beautiful, prize-winning illustrations are in the folk tradition. Their collaborative evocation of a year of domestic life in a nineteenth-century rural New England area is rich with detail and insight.

THE OX OF THE WONDERFUL HORNS AND OTHER AFRICAN FOLKTALES [467]

WRITTEN AND ILLUSTRATED BY ASHLEY BRYAN

Cloth: Atheneum

Published: 1981

A collection of five African folktales told in the traditional style, with handsome illustrations.

PAMELA CAMEL [468]

WRITTEN AND ILLUSTRATED BY BILL PEET

Cloth: Houghton Mifflin

Paper: Houghton Mifflin

Published: 1984

Circus life makes Pamela Camel cross and irritable. She runs away, along a railroad track, and happens upon a broken tie, recognizes the danger it represents, and later is able to prevent a wreck by bravely stopping a train. A hero, she returns to the circus a star. There are several dozen books by Bill Peet in print. They are lightly told, often rhymed fables, with illustrations that suggest his background as a Walt Disney artist. They are endearing, unpretentious and satisfying. Among the best are *Kermit the Hermit*, *Buford, the Little Bighorn*, *Ella*, and *The Pinkish, Bluish Purplish Egg*.

PAPER JOHN [469]

WRITTEN AND ILLUSTRATED BY DAVID SMALL

Cloth: Farrar, Straus

Published: 1987

Paper John is a mysterious fellow who makes wonderful things, including his own house, out of folded paper. He does battle with a devil who has only one trick, but it is the potent one of controlling the winds, and threatens to destroy Paper John and the town as well. Handsomely illustrated fable.

[468]

PA'S BALLOON AND OTHER PIG TALES   [470]

WRITTEN AND ILLUSTRATED BY ARTHUR GIESERT
Cloth: Houghton Mifflin
Published: 1984

Pa takes the whole pig family flying in a hot-air balloon, and they have a series of adventures set out in hand-colored copper-plate prints. The thrill of being airborne is almost palpable.

THE PATCHWORK QUILT   [471]

WRITTEN BY VALERIE FLOURNOY
ILLUSTRATED BY JERRY PINKNEY
Cloth: Dial
Published: 1985

As she cuts and stitches pieces from old family clothes, Tanya's grandmother tells her about the quilt she is making. Grandmother becomes ill, and the family works together to complete her masterpiece. The full-color illustrations capture the richness and strength of Tanya's loving family as well as the quilt.

PATRICK'S DINOSAURS   [472]

WRITTEN BY CAROL CARRICK
ILLUSTRATED BY DONALD CARRICK
Cloth: Clarion
Paper: Clarion
Published: 1983

Patrick listens carefully to his big brother Hank's description of dinosaurs and then scares himself with some fine fantasies about what it would be like if they were around today. In the even funnier *Return of Patrick's Dinosaurs*, he claims that they are back, and the illustrations show clearly how they enrich the ordinary things in modern life.

PAUL BUNYAN   [473]

WRITTEN AND ILLUSTRATED BY STEVEN KELLOGG

Cloth: Morrow
Paper: Mulberry
Published: 1984

A rambunctious version of the legend of the mighty logger and his blue ox, Babe. The illustrations are exuberant. The author/illustrator has also retold *Pecos Bill*.

A PEACEABLE KINGDOM: THE SHAKER ABECEDARIUS   [474]

WRITTEN AND ILLUSTRATED BY ALICE AND MARTIN PROVENSEN

Cloth: Viking
Paper: Puffin
Published: 1978   PRIZES: NEW YORK TIMES BEST ILLUSTRATED BOOK

A memorable abecedarius (or alphabet book), which shows a grand procession of real and imaginary animals parading in a setting that is also a vision of Shaker society.

PERFECT THE PIG   [475]

WRITTEN AND ILLUSTRATED BY SUSAN JESCHKE

Cloth: Holt
Paper: Scholastic
Published: 1981

Sometimes getting what you wish for leads to serious complications. Perfect the Pig wishes for wings, but the results are not what he expected, although he and his friend Olive end up just where they want to be in this charming and roundabout story.

[478]

PETER AND THE WOLF   [476]

WRITTEN BY SERGEI PROKOFIEV
ILLUSTRATED BY JÖRG MÜLLER
Published: 1986
Cloth: Knopf

This version of the story with music that is so often a child's real introduction to the orchestra is persuasively placed in a lush theatrical setting—a European opera house. The relationship of the musical instruments to the characters thus becomes clear, and even the role of the conductor makes sense. There are other good editions around by such illustrators as Charles Mikolaycak and Warren Chappell. There is a pop-up version by Barbara Cooney.

PETER THE GREAT   [477]

WRITTEN AND ILLUSTRATED BY DIANE STANLEY
Cloth: Four Winds
Published: 1986
A brightly told and well-illustrated biography of one of Western history's truly larger than life figures.

THE PHILHARMONIC GETS DRESSED   [478]

WRITTEN BY KARLA KUSKIN
ILLUSTRATED BY MARC SIMONT
Cloth: Harper
Paper: Harper
Published: 1982
As a winter day ends, 105 people bathe, get dressed, and go to work. They are members of an orchestra who live in and around a big city. The text and illustrations are both witty and accomplished and offer a great deal to talk about at bedtime (or any other time, for that matter). The equally delightful companion book is *The Dallas Titans Get Ready for Bed*.

PIGS FROM A TO Z   [479]

WRITTEN AND ILLUSTRATED BY ARTHUR GEISERT
Cloth: Houghton Mifflin
Published: 1986   PRIZES: NEW YORK TIMES BEST ILLUSTRATED BOOK
A rich and imaginative alphabet book in which seven piglets build a tree house. The illustrations are, in fact, intricate etchings. This alphabet book seems especially appealing to boys.

[478]

157

THE PILGRIMS OF PLIMOTH   [480]

WRITTEN AND ILLUSTRATED BY MARCIA SEWALL

Cloth: Atheneum

Published: 1986

A narrator gives a detailed and appreciative account of daily life in the Plymouth colony, as well as a brief history of its establishment. The illustrations are unusually evocative, luminous paintings that are precise in their details.

PINKERTON, BEHAVE   [481]

WRITTEN AND ILLUSTRATED BY STEVEN KELLOGG

Cloth: Dial

Paper: Dial

Published: 1979

Even as a puppy, Pinkerton (who is really a Great Dane) is as big as a pony, as eager as a monkey, not to mention amiable, awkward, and full of mischief and goodwill. In *A Rose for Pinkerton*, the family gives him a kitten, who, it turns out, wants to be a Great Dane, too. There's also *Tallyho, Pinkerton*, and *Prehistoric Pinkerton*, all with illustrations in the author's recognizable, wild, funny style.

THE POLAR EXPRESS   [482]

WRITTEN AND ILLUSTRATED BY CHRIS VAN ALLSBURG

Cloth: Houghton Mifflin

Published: 1985   PRIZES: CALDECOTT MEDAL, NEW YORK TIMES BEST ILLUSTRATED BOOK

An unseen adult narrator remembers a mysterious Christmas Eve when he rode the special train to the North Pole and was selected by Santa Claus to receive the first Christmas gift. Haunting illustrations in rich, subtle colors make this a very special book indeed.

THE PORCELAIN CAT   [483]

WRITTEN BY MICHAEL PATRICK HEARN
ILLUSTRATED BY LEO AND DIANE DILLON
Cloth: Little, Brown
Published: 1987

There are rats in the sorcerer's library, so he wants to cast a spell to bring his porcelain cat to life. But first, Nickon, his assistant, must go out into the night to fetch a vial of basilisk blood. Nickon meets a witch, a centaur, and an undine. The structure is traditional; the illustrations are mysterious and full of surprises for searching eyes. The result is a very satisfying, read-it-again story.

A PRAIRIE BOY'S WINTER   [484]

WRITTEN AND ILLUSTRATED BY WILLIAM KURELEK
Cloth: Houghton Mifflin
Paper: Houghton Mifflin
Published: 1973   PRIZES: NEW YORK TIMES BEST ILLUSTRATED BOOK

A prairie farm in winter during the 1930s is vividly recalled in a book distinguished by the quality of both prose and full-page illustrations. The companion volume is A Prairie Boy's Summer.

THE PURPLE COAT   [485]

WRITTEN BY AMY HEST
ILLUSTRATED BY AMY SCHWARTZ
Cloth: Four Winds
Published: 1986

Every year Gabrielle's grandfather makes her a new navy blue coat in his tailor shop in the city. This year Gabrielle wants a purple coat, and her mother says no. Grandfather finds a way. The illustrations, with their quirky, cartoonish quality, are precise and full of details to explore, especially the ones of the tailor shop.

THE RANDOM HOUSE BOOK OF MOTHER GOOSE   [486]

SELECTED AND ILLUSTRATED BY ARNOLD LOBEL
Cloth: Random House
Published: 1986

This generous edition of the canon, including 306 verses, shows a fine artist at the top of his roly-poly form. An ebullient collection, with selections appropriate for all ages.

THE RANDOM HOUSE BOOK OF POETRY FOR CHILDREN   [487]

SELECTED BY JACK PRELUTSKY
ILLUSTRATED BY ARNOLD LOBEL
Cloth: Random House
Published: 1983

A rich and distinctly optimistic anthology of poetry, including many familiar gems, with zestful illustrations of distinctly Arnold Lobelish owls, cats, and frogs, among other other creatures.

THE RED BALLOON   [488]

WRITTEN AND ILLUSTRATED BY ALBERT LAMORISSE
Cloth: Doubleday
Paper: Doubleday
Published: 1957   PRIZES: NEW YORK TIMES BEST ILLUSTRATED BOOK

It's Paris just a shiver of time back in the past. The book, like the film on which it is based, captures the adventures of a little boy and his best friend, a glorious red balloon that follows him everywhere. An enduring favorite, illustrated with color photographs from the film.

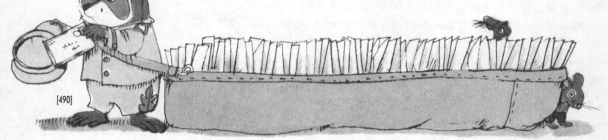

[490]

RICHARD SCARRY'S PIG WILL AND PIG WON'T   [489]

WRITTEN AND ILLUSTRATED BY RICHARD SCARRY
Cloth: Random House
Published: 1984

Siblings. Guess which one minds his manners and cooperates and gets to go interesting places? Guess which one learns some lessons in these three short stories? Good lessons, well taught.

RICHARD SCARRY'S WHAT DO PEOPLE DO ALL DAY?   [490]

WRITTEN AND ILLUSTRATED BY RICHARD SCARRY
Cloth: Random House
Published: 1968

Well, what *do* people do? Here, in typical Scarry fashion (that is, very busy pictures featuring many of his regular cast of animals), are a series of stories about building houses, baking bread, laying roads, going on a railroad, going on a boat, and more. Preschoolers can pour over the pages for hours, and many's the adult who has been intrigued by the clarity of the explanations. The present edition is abridged, alas.

THE RIDICULOUS STORY OF GAMMER GURTON'S NEEDLE   [491]

WRITTEN BY DAVID LLOYD
ILLUSTRATED BY CHARLOTTE VOAKE
Cloth: Crown
Published: 1987

The classic sixteenth-century English farce about Diccon, the trouble-maker in the village where the imposing old lady called Gammer Gurton lives, has been imaginatively retold and illustrated in a cartoonish style that is both delicate and raucous. Appealing to older children, adults, English majors, and even graduate students.

THE ROOM   [492]

WRITTEN AND ILLUSTRATED BY MORDICAI GERSTEIN
Cloth: Harper
Published: 1984

Over a period of time, perhaps half a century, a series of improbable characters—a married pair of musicians, some acrobats, a dentist, a great many animals—inhabit a rented room in a house. The bright little book is filled with vivid people and fascinating objects. The subtle theme is the passage of time.

ROSALIE   [493]

WRITTEN BY JOAN HEWETT
ILLUSTRATED BY DONALD CARRICK
Cloth: Lothrop
Published: 1987

Rosalie is an old dog. She can't run, and her hearing isn't so good, but every member of the family loves her and makes adjustments for her infirmities.

ROTTEN ISLAND   [494]

WRITTEN AND ILLUSTRATED BY WILLIAM STEIG
Cloth: Godine
Published: 1969

A revised edition of the splendid fantasy first published in the 1960s, about a horrible, ghastly, ugly, vicious island populated with hideous monsters, disgusting creatures, thorny plants, and awful things. The wondrously imaginative illustrations are printed in fluorescent color. Although one of the best books in the Steig canon, it was unavailable for many years.

RUMPELSTILTSKIN   [495]

ADAPTED AND ILLUSTRATED BY PAUL O. ZELINSKY
Cloth: Dutton
Published: 1986   PRIZES: CALDECOTT HONOR BOOK

A version of the familiar Grimm tale placed in a medieval setting—turreted castles, peasants in the fields—executed in technically accomplished oil paintings. The straw and gold truly gleam. The text is from

Grimm. Adults may be distracted by the resemblance between Rumpelstiltskin and the late comedian Marty Feldman. The illustrator has done an equally lavish setting of "Hansel and Gretel" in the style of seventeenth-century Dutch landscape painting. There are other Rumpelstiltskin's, including an almost cartoonishly high-spirited one illustrated by Paul Galdone.

SECRETS OF A SMALL BROTHER   [496]

WRITTEN BY RICHARD J. MARGOLIS
ILLUSTRATED BY DONALD CARRICK
Cloth: Macmillan
Published: 1984

A collection of poems, pointed and poignant, about what it is like being a younger brother. The pencil illustrations are a perfect complement to the verses.

THE SELFISH GIANT   [497]

WRITTEN BY OSCAR WILDE
ILLUSTRATED BY LISBETH ZWERGER
Cloth: Picture Book
Published: 1984

The Christian parable about children seeking access to a giant's garden is illustrated here by an unusually talented Viennese artist who takes an oblique view of the tale in her delicate watercolor paintings. She has also illustrated Wilde's *The Canterville Ghost*. The story reads aloud well and has an enduring appeal for adults as well as school-age children.

[495]

THE SELKIE GIRL [498]

WRITTEN BY SUSAN COOPER
ILLUSTRATED BY WARWICK HUTTON
Cloth: McElderry
Published: 1986

The haunting tale from the Irish and Scots islands of the young lad who loves and marries the maiden who is really a seal is beautifully told in this distinguished collaboration. The author and illustrator also did the Welsh tale "The Silver Cow."

SHADOW [499]

WRITTEN BY BLAISE CENDRARS
ILLUSTRATED BY MARCIA BROWN
Cloth: Scribners
Paper: Aladdin
Published: 1982   PRIZES: CALDECOTT MEDAL

The text, translated from the French, describes the mysterious eeriness of the Shadow figure in African tribal life. The illustrations are dramatic collages.

SHAKER LANE [500]

WRITTEN AND ILLUSTRATED BY ALICE AND
  MARTIN PROVENSEN
Cloth: Viking
Published: 1987

This is a cautionary tale about real estate development and environmental preservation most artfully disguised as a handsome children's book about a somewhere place called Shaker Lane. It tells about the folks who have always lived there, newcomers, and the changes that come along in very modern times. The illustrations are so simple and so sophisticated at the same time that readers of many ages can find different but equally rewarding stories and lessons in the book.

THE SIGN IN MENDEL'S WINDOW [501]

WRITTEN BY MILDRED PHILLIPS
ILLUSTRATED BY MARGOT ZEMACH
Cloth: Macmillan
Published: 1985

A retelling of an old Jewish story about Mendel, who rents half his butcher shop to Tinker the thinker, who tries to swindle everyone. Folk wisdom, wryly told, with illustrations that capture Mendel's bemusement.

SIR CEDRIC [502]

WRITTEN AND ILLUSTRATED BY ROY GERRARD
Cloth: Farrar, Straus
Paper: Sunburst/Farrar, Straus
Published: 1984   PRIZES: NEW YORK TIMES BEST ILLUSTRATED BOOK

A gallant tale of knights of old—in this case, the very round Sir Cedric the Good, who travels with his horse, Walter, and cucumber sandwiches. He wins the hand of the fair Fat Matilda. Very droll, with lavish detailed illustrations. Sir Cedric Rides Again continues the story and introduces their daughter, Edwina the Pest.

THE SLEEPING BEAUTY [503]

WRITTEN AND ILLUSTRATED BY TRINA SCHART HYMAN
Cloth: Little, Brown
Paper: Little, Brown
Published: 1977

This adaptation of the Grimm Brothers' tale is distinguished by the artist's characteristically intense and dramatic illustrations. Other fine versions have been illustrated by Arthur Rackham, Warwick Hutton, Warren Chappell, and Mercer Mayer.

Story Books

A SNAKE IS TOTALLY TAIL   [504]

WRITTEN BY JUDI BARRETT
ILLUSTRATED BY LONNI SUE JOHNSON
Cloth: Atheneum
Paper: Aladdin
Published: 1983

Epigrams that encapsulate twenty-eight animals, suitably illustrated.
Bees, of course, buzz.

SOME SWELL PUP OR ARE YOU SURE YOU WANT A DOG?   [505]

WRITTEN BY MAURICE SENDAK AND MATTHEW MARGOLIS
ILLUSTRATED BY MAURICE SENDAK
Cloth: Farrar, Straus
Paper: Michael di Capua/Sunburst/Farrar, Straus
Published: 1976

Before you consider bringing a puppy into your home, you should con-
sult this guidebook for young owners. The information, presented in
comic strip form, comes from a dog trainer and stresses the need for
patience and kindness in training a dog. The illustrations are vintage
Sendak and show clearly that he is a dog lover.

SOMETHING ON MY MIND   [506]

WRITTEN BY NIKKI GRIMES
ILLUSTRATED BY TOM FEELINGS
Cloth: Dial
Paper: Dial
Published: 1978

Poems about thoughts, hopes, and fears of black children, with sensi-
tive illustrations.

[494]

THE SOMETHING   [507]

WRITTEN AND ILLUSTRATED BY NATALIE BABBITT

Cloth: Farrar, Straus
Paper: Michael di Capua/Sunburst/Farrar, Straus
Published: 1970

A soothing book about a common fear. Mylo, a hairy sort of cave mon-
sterish little fellow, worries about Something coming through his window at night. His mother gives him some clay, and he eventually
manages to make a statue of it. Later, he is not afraid when he meets
the Something in a dream. The black-and-white line drawings are
simultaneously amusing and comforting.

SPACE CASE   [508]

WRITTEN BY EDWARD MARSHALL
ILLUSTRATED BY JAMES MARSHALL

Cloth: Dial
Paper: Dial
Published: 1980

A creature from outer space named Space Case comes to visit Buddy
and his family one Halloween. The sequel is *Merry Christmas, Space Case*.
These silly adventures, like those of the Stupids, appeal strongly to children, especially boys, in the early grades.

SPIRIT CHILD: A STORY
OF THE NATIVITY   [509]

WRITTEN BY JOHN BIERHORST
ILLUSTRATED BY BARBARA COONEY

Cloth: Morrow
Published: 1984

An Aztec version of the Nativity, translated into modern English. The
exciting text is matched by the fine, evocative illustrations.

STEVIE [510]

WRITTEN AND ILLUSTRATED BY JOHN STEPTOE

Cloth: Harper
Paper: Harper
Published: 1969

The frustrations of family life: a black boy tells about the problems a younger foster brother caused in the house, and then acknowledges gruffly that he misses him very much. This was a stunning and innovative book when first published and remains poignant and appealing to new generations of young readers.

SAINT GEORGE AND THE DRAGON [511]

WRITTEN BY MARGARET HODGES
ILLUSTRATED BY TRINA SCHART HYMAN

Cloth: Little, Brown
Published: 1984

PRIZES: CALDECOTT MEDAL,
NEW YORK TIMES BEST ILLUSTRATED BOOK

Based on Spenser's *Faerie Queen*, this is a retelling of Saint George's three-day battle with the dragon. The prize-winning illustrations are in the style of illuminated manuscripts; the text has been simplified but remains courtly.

[512]

THE STORY ABOUT PING [512]

WRITTEN BY MARJORIE FLACK
ILLUSTRATED BY KURT WIESE

Cloth: Viking
Paper: Puffin
Published: 1933

Ping lives with his large extended family on a boat on the great Yangtze River. One day, to avoid getting a spanking for being last back on board at the end of the day, Ping ventures off. Miraculously, he finds his way home. After more than half a century this remains a compelling, even thrilling story of nearly universal appeal to children just discovering the wide world beyond their own daily routines.

THE STORY OF BABAR   [513]

WRITTEN AND ILLUSTRATED BY JEAN de BRUNHOFF

Cloth: Random House

Published: 1933

This is the classic French tale of a baby elephant, cruelly orphaned, who reaches the city, is civilized (even acquiring a handsome green suit), and eventually returns home to be king. The cast of characters includes his wife, Queen Celeste, their children, relatives, and the splendid Old Lady. Some readers have seen the politics of colonialism in the stories, but that has not deterred children in many countries from adoring them. The series includes *The Travels of Babar*, *Babar and His Children*, and *Babar the King*. The originals are handsome large-format books with script rather than type, reproduced in *Babar's Anniversary Album*, a large-format title that includes six of the stories. There are some other less satisfying Babar stories and a variety of paperback adaptations that are diluted but popular nonetheless.

THE STORY OF MRS. LOVEWRIGHT AND PURRLESS HER CAT   [514]

WRITTEN BY LORE SEGAL

ILLUSTRATED BY PAUL O. ZELINSKY

Cloth: Knopf

Published: 1985   PRIZES: NEW YORK TIMES BEST ILLUSTRATED BOOK

Mrs. Lovewright, who lives alone, inherits a kitten and plans on being cozy with it. But Purrless, who grows to giant size, has a different, sometimes bruising definition of cozy. Adults may detect a wry parable on marriage here, but children take the story more literally. The illustrations are stylized and raucous.

THE STORY OF THE DANCING FROG   [515]

WRITTEN AND ILLUSTRATED BY QUENTIN BLAKE

Cloth: Knopf

Published: 1985

A young widow befriends a frog who can dance. She puts him on the stage, and he becomes world famous before retiring to domestic life, or so the mother who tells the story claims. The loose, cartoonish illustrations add to the silly fun.

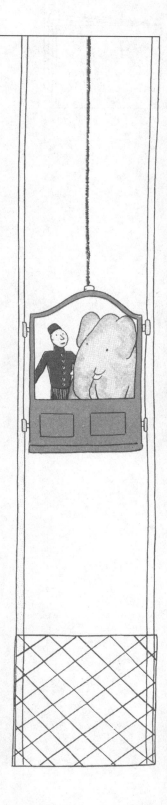

[513]

169

THE STORY OF THE NUTCRACKER BALLET [516]

WRITTEN BY DEBORAH HAUTZIG
ILLUSTRATED BY DIANE GOODE
Paper: Random House
Published: 1986
Based on the version George Balanchine created for the New York City Ballet that is now standard holiday fare around the country, this behind-the-scenes look is perfect for before and after that annual outing.

STREGA NONA [517]

WRITTEN AND ILLUSTRATED BY TOMIE de PAOLA
Cloth: Prentice-Hall
Paper: Treehouse, Prentice-Hall
Published: 1975   PRIZES: CALDECOTT HONOR BOOK
The first of the inspired story books about the magic witch of Calabria, in which we meet Strega Nona and her doltish helper, Big Anthony, and are introduced to Strega Nona's powers. Delightful to read aloud.

THE STUPIDS HAVE A BALL [518]

WRITTEN BY HARRY ALLARD
ILLUSTRATED BY JAMES MARSHALL
Cloth: Houghton Mifflin
Paper: Houghton Mifflin
Published: 1978
The Stupid family manages to justify their name in this series of silly, dumb, funny books by the Allard/Marshall team that also produced the manic Miss Nelson. In this installment, the Stupids celebrate the fact that Buster and Petunia have failed every school subject—including recess. Don't miss *The Stupids Step Out* and *The Stupids Die*. Children in the middle grades grow weak with laughter.

SULEIMAN THE ELEPHANT [519]

WRITTEN AND ILLUSTRATED BY MARGRET RETTICH
Cloth: Lothrop
Published: 1986

Based on the fact that Prince Max (later Emperor Maximilian II) and
Princess Maria were given an elephant when they married in Spain in
1551 and had to transport themselves and the creature to their home in
Vienna, this is a fine piece of illustrated history for young readers.

SUSAN AND GORDON
ADOPT A BABY [520]

WRITTEN BY JUDY FREUDBERG AND TONY GEISS
ILLUSTRATED BY JOE MATHIEU
Cloth: Random House
Published: 1986

This book is based on the *Sesame Street* episodes when Susan and Gordon
adopted baby Miles. Its reassuring story addresses not only adoption
but sibling rivalry. There is a note to parents with some suggestions
about discussions.

SUSANNA OF THE ALAMO:
A TRUE STORY [521]

WRITTEN BY JOHN JAKES
ILLUSTRATED BY PAUL BACON
Cloth: Gulliver/HBJ
Published: 1986

Susanna Dickinson played a crucial role in the early history of Texas.
She and her baby survived the siege of the Alamo in 1836, and she
brought General Santa Anna's warning and challenge to Sam Houston. Her story was lost or overlooked for a long time, and this book
helps straighten out the record.

TALES OF A GAMBLING GRANDMA   [522]

WRITTEN AND ILLUSTRATED BY DAYAL KAUR KHALSA

Cloth: Potter

Published: 1986

A little girl considers her gambling grandmother, who came from Russia, married Louis the plumber, and played poker. Grandmother taught many lessons, including card games. The primitive-style illustrations are whimsical. The story has a refreshing bittersweet tone.

TALES OF PAN   [523]

ILLUSTRATED BY MORDICAI GERSTEIN

Cloth: Harper

Published: 1986

A giddy, boisterous, infectious, and therefore utterly suitable collection of stories about the Greek god Pan and his mischievous ways. The colorful line drawing illustrations are as light as confetti.

TELEPHONE TIME: A FIRST BOOK OF TELEPHONE DO'S AND DON'T'S   [524]

WRITTEN BY ELLEN WEISS

ILLUSTRATED BY HILARY KNIGHT

Paper: Random House

Published: 1986

Ringalina the Telephone Fairy has some "sound" advice for the whole family about using the telephone—taking messages, what to do in emergencies, safety, and even some social monsters such as the Tie-Uppasaurus. The illustrations are perky and bright.

TELL ME A MITZI   [525]

WRITTEN BY LORE SEGAL

ILLUSTRATED BY HARRIET PINCUS

Cloth: Farrar, Straus

Paper: Scholastic

Published: 1970

Three memorable stories about Mitzi and her little brother Jacob: their secret attempt to visit Grandma, the whole family's cold, and an encounter with a presidential procession. The funny, awkward illustrations combine fantasy and vivid detail in a way that complements the text perfectly. There is a related title, *Tell Me a Trudy*.

THE TENTH GOOD THING ABOUT BARNEY [526]

WRITTEN BY JUDITH VIORST
ILLUSTRATED BY ERIC BLEGVAD
Cloth: Atheneum
Paper: Aladdin
Published: 1971

When Barney the cat dies, his young owner struggles to think of good things about his pet and understand both the finality of death and the unity of life. This is a splendid book, a deserved classic, suitable for readers of all ages. In its simplicity and the genuine comfort it offers, it is one of the best books for children about death.

THAT NEW PET! [527]

WRITTEN BY ALANE FERGUSON
ILLUSTRATED BY CATHERINE STOCK
Cloth: Lothrop
Published: 1986

The arrival of a new baby as seen by the household pets—Siam the cat, Bones the dog, and Crackers the parrot—who are all deeply affronted by the intruder, but eventually accept and even adore the baby. The full-color illustrations are very winning.

THE THREE BEARS & FIFTEEN OTHER STORIES [528]

WRITTEN AND ILLUSTRATED BY ANNE ROCKWELL
Cloth: Crowell
Paper: Harper
Published: 1975

A collection of classic stories from La Fontaine, Aesop, Grimm, and others, economically told with bright, witty illustrations. Good for beginning readers as well as reading aloud.

[528]

Story Books

THREE DAYS ON A RIVER IN A RED CANOE [529]

WRITTEN AND ILLUSTRATED BY VERA B. WILLIAMS

Cloth: Greenwillow
Paper: Mulberry
Published: 1981

Just what the title promises—an account of the trip a little girl, her cousin, and their mothers took, complete with instructions on how to set up a tent, make a fire, and cook. A charming travelogue.

THROUGH GRANDPA'S EYES [530]

WRITTEN BY PATRICIA MACLACHLAN
ILLUSTRATED BY DEBORAH RAY

Cloth: Harper
Paper: Harper
Published: 1980

On his visits to his grandparents, John has learned to appreciate that although Grandpa is blind, he sees and moves through a rich and detailed world.

TODAY WAS A TERRIBLE DAY [531]

WRITTEN BY PATRICIA REILLY GIFF
ILLUSTRATED BY SUSANNA NATTI

Cloth: Viking
Paper: Puffin
Published: 1984

Ronald Morgan is a hapless hero and suffers from acute bumbling and the problems of the second grade. His struggles continue in *Watch Out,*

Ronald Morgan! which is almost as funny as *The Almost Awful Play*, in which Ronald is the star, sort of, of the class play. He is Winky the Cat.

TOMIE de PAOLA'S FAVORITE NURSERY TALES [532]

SELECTED AND ILLUSTRATED BY TOMIE de PAOLA
Cloth: Putnam
Published: 1986

A bright companion volume to de Paola's *Mother Goose* that includes more than twenty-five well-loved stories such as "Rumpelstiltskin," "The Frog Prince," and "The Emperor's New Clothes."

THE TOMTEN AND THE FOX [533]

WRITTEN BY ASTRID LINDGREN
ILLUSTRATED BY HARALD WILERG
Cloth: Coward
Paper: Coward
Published: 1965

The Tomten is a Swedish troll who guards farms. In this version of a traditional tale, the author of *Pippi Longstocking* tells about the wise and canny Tomten who wards off the fox who slinks silently around in the moonlight. The midwinter illustrations are snowy and fine. Other Tomten stories include *The Tomten* and *The Christmas Tomten*.

TOUGH EDDIE [534]

WRITTEN BY ELIZABETH WINTHROP
ILLUSTRATED BY LILLIAN HOBAN
Cloth: Dutton
Published: 1985

Everyone thinks Eddie is a tough little boy until his sister mentions his dollhouse. He sorts out his pals and deals with the problems of sexual stereotyping in a believable way. The illustrations are engaging.

THE TOWN MOUSE AND THE COUNTRY MOUSE   [535]

WRITTEN AND ILLUSTRATED BY LORINDA BRYAN CAULEY

Cloth: Putnam
Paper: Putnam
Published: 1984

This charming retelling of the familiar fable from Aesop is set lovingly in the nineteenth century, with fine domestic and culinary detail. The illustrator has also done a jolly version of *The Owl and the Pussycat.*

TURKEYS, PILGRIMS AND INDIAN CORN: THE STORY OF THE THANKSGIVING SYMBOLS   [536]

WRITTEN AND ILLUSTRATED BY EDNA BARTH

Cloth: Clarion
Paper: Clarion
Published: 1975

A simple introduction to the symbols and ideas of Thanksgiving. One of a series of books about holidays that includes *Witches, Pumpkins and Grinning Ghosts*, *Lilies, Rabbits, and Painted Eggs*, and *Shamrocks, Harps and Shillelaghs.*

THE TWELVE DANCING PRINCESSES: RETOLD FROM A STORY BY THE BROTHERS GRIMM   [537]

ILLUSTRATED BY ERROL LE CAIN

Paper: Puffin
Published: 1981

A very pretty, ornamented version of the story of the princesses who danced the nights away and fooled all their prospective suitors until a poor soldier manages to follow them to their subterranean pleasure grounds.

THE TWENTY-ONE BALLOONS   [538]

WRITTEN AND ILLUSTRATED BY WILLIAM PÈNE DU BOIS

Cloth: Viking
Paper: Puffin
Published: 1947   PRIZES: NEWBERY MEDAL

A wonderfully illustrated account of what happens when Professor William Waterman Sherman is found in the middle of the ocean with what is left of twenty-one balloons. A delightful fantasy that continues to appeal.

THE TWO OF THEM   [539]

WRITTEN AND ILLUSTRATED BY ALIKI

Cloth: Greenwillow
Paper: Mulberry
Published: 1979

This is a quiet story about a grandfather who loved his granddaughter from the time she was born, and how, when he died, she was able to remember things he had made for her and time they had spent together and absorb their special relationship.

TY'S ONE-MAN BAND   [540]

WRITTEN BY MILDRED PITTS WALTER
ILLUSTRATED BY MARGOT TOMES

Cloth: Four Winds
Paper: Scholastic
Published: 1979, reprinted 1987

A little boy named Andro tells about the hot summer day a peg-legged man came into town. He was a one-man band, and he brought music and dancing into the night and then slipped away. This is a magical story, and the subtle full-color illustrations capture the heat and shadows of summer days and nights.

THE UGLY DUCKLING   [541]

WRITTEN BY HANS CHRISTIAN ANDERSEN
ILLUSTRATED BY ROBERT VAN NUTT
Cloth: Knopf
Published: 1986   PRIZES: NEW YORK TIMES BEST ILLUSTRATED BOOK

A muted edition of the story of the duckling who turns into a swan, with handsome illustrations that focus close up on the cygnet and the other creatures. This edition can be purchased with an audio tape or as a book alone. There are other interesting editions illustrated by Thomas Locker, whose style is very painterly; Monica Laimbgruber, who does richly colored, fine pen-and-ink drawings; and Lorinda Bryan Cauley, whose work typically has a sweet and old-fashioned air.

UP NORTH IN WINTER   [542]

WRITTEN BY DEBORAH HARTLEY
ILLUSTRATED BY LYDIA DABCOVICH
Cloth: Dutton
Published: 1986

Grandpa Ole misses the last train home one bitter cold night a long time ago. He has to walk, and encounters what he thinks is a frozen fox, which he picks up and uses as a scarf as he trudges home. The surprise ending is startling and funny.

THE VELVETEEN RABBIT   [543]

WRITTEN BY MARGERY WILLIAMS
ILLUSTRATED BY WILLIAM NICHOLSON
Cloth: Doubleday
Paper: Avon
Published: 1922

The slightly syrupy tale of the toy that so loved its boy that it did, ultimately, become real, was a modest standard title until a surge of popularity with college students and younger adults gave it visibility in the late 1970s and early 1980s. Through carelessness, the copyright was allowed to expire, and presto, a half-dozen other editions appeared, including those illustrated by Michael Hague, David Jorgensen, and Tien Ho. This is the original and most affecting edition, and comes plain or in a fancy slipcase.

VERY LAST FIRST TIME [544]

WRITTEN BY JAN ANDREWS
ILLUSTRATED BY IAN WALLACE
Cloth: McElderry
Published: 1986

A fine and unusual picture book about Eva, an Inuit girl, and her first trip under the sea ice to gather mussels for her family to eat for a winter meal. Eerie and exciting.

THE VILLAGE OF ROUND AND SQUARE HOUSES [545]

WRITTEN AND ILLUSTRATED BY ANN GRIFALCONI
Cloth: Little, Brown
Published: 1986   PRIZES: CALDECOTT HONOR BOOK

There is a reason that in one small East African village the men live in square houses and the women live in round ones. A fascinating story with mysterious full-color illustrations.

A VISIT TO THE SESAME STREET HOSPITAL [546]

WRITTEN BY DEBORAH HAUTZIG
ILLUSTRATED BY JOE MATHIEU
Paper: Random House
Published: 1985

One of the best of the *Sesame Street* guidebooks. Grover, Ernie, Bert, and Grover's mother go to visit the hospital in preparation for Grover's tonsilectomy. Full of detail and reassurance for preschoolers and older children as well. The full-color illustrations are interesting without being obtrusive.

A VISIT TO THE SESAME STREET LIBRARY [547]

WRITTEN BY DEBORAH HAUTZIG
ILLUSTRATED BY JOE MATHIEU
Paper: Random House
Published: 1986

Big Bird visits the public library and discovers some of the things there are to do there. This inexpensive paperback could lead a child to corners he or she might miss on an early library visit.

A VISIT TO WILLIAM BLAKE'S INN: POEMS FOR INNOCENT AND EXPERIENCED TRAVELERS [548]

WRITTEN BY NANCY WILLARD
ILLUSTRATED BY ALICE AND MARTIN PROVENSEN
Cloth: Harcourt Brace
Paper: Voyager/HBJ   PRIZES: NEWBERY HONOR BOOK,
Published: 1981   CALDECOTT HONOR BOOK

A collection of intriguing poems inspired by William Blake's "Songs of Innocence" and "Songs of Experience," with stylized, witty illustrations capturing a sense of London and a sense of mystery. While this is a book meant for older children and adults, younger children who are used to listening to poetry may be interested.

[548]

WALK TOGETHER CHILDREN: BLACK AMERICAN SPIRITUALS [549]

WRITTEN AND ILLUSTRATED BY ASHLEY BRYAN
Cloth: Atheneum
Paper: Aladdin
Published: 1974

A rich, handsomely illustrated collection of spirituals, including songs that are generally familiar and some that are less so. There is a companion volume, *I'm Going to Sing*. Wonderful for bedtime singing.

THE WAY TO START A DAY [550]

WRITTEN BY BYRD BAYLOR
ILLUSTRATED BY PETER PARNALL
Cloth: Scribner
Paper: Aladdin
Published: 1978   PRIZES: CALDECOTT HONOR BOOK

A lyric evocation of the simple fact that all over the world, in many
different cultures and throughout history, people have welcomed
the sun.

A WEEKEND IN THE COUNTRY [551]

WRITTEN AND ILLUSTRATED BY LEE LORENZ
Cloth: Prentice-Hall
Paper: Simon and Schuster Books for Young Readers
Published: 1985

Two dear friends are cordially—oh, so cordially—invited to come
spend a summer weekend in the country, but it turns out there is no
way to get there. An old joke told in high-style cartoon fashion.

WHATEVER HAPPENED TO THE DINOSAURS? [552]

WRITTEN AND ILLUSTRATED BY BERNARD MOST
Cloth: Harcourt Brace
Paper: Voyager/HBJ
Published: 1984

Some possible and some impossible answers to a very commonly asked
question. The illustrations—putting the great lizards in improbable
settings such as pirate ships and large cities—are bright and amusing.
The companion title is *If the Dinosaurs Came Back*.

[548]

WHEN THE DARK COMES DANCING: A BEDTIME POETRY BOOK   [553]

WRITTEN BY NANCY LARRICK
ILLUSTRATED BY JOHN WALLNER
Cloth: Philomel
Published: 1983

This collection of lullabies and poems particularly suitable for reading aloud was chosen by a distinguished anthologist and is charmingly illustrated.

WHEN WE WERE VERY YOUNG   [554]

WRITTEN BY A. A. MILNE
ILLUSTRATED BY ERNEST H. SHEPARD
Cloth: Dutton
Paper: Dell
Published: 1924

A collection of verse for young children that has been considered classic for generations—full of fantasy and vignettes to remember for a lifetime. Household pets, kings and queens, games, illness, pirates and prayers, and lilting, sometimes silly rhymes. The line drawings are models of illustration, balancing the sometimes fey poems. *Now We Are Six* is the companion volume.

[555]

WHERE THE BUFFALOES BEGIN   [555]

WRITTEN BY OLAF BAKER
ILLUSTRATED BY STEPHEN GAMMELL
Cloth: Warne
Paper: Puffin
Published: 1981

PRIZES: NEW YORK TIMES BEST ILLUSTRATED BOOK,
CALDECOTT HONOR BOOK

This is a handsomely illustrated retelling of the American Indian legend of Little Wolf, the boy who led the stampeding buffaloes away from his people.

WHITE DYNAMITE AND CURLY KIDD [556]

WRITTEN BY BILL MARTIN, JR., AND JOHN ARCHAMBAULT

ILLUSTRATED BY TED RAND

Cloth: Holt

Published: 1986

A grand account of White Dynamite, a mean old bull, and Curly Kidd, the toughest rodeo rider around. Designed for reading aloud.

WHY MOSQUITOES BUZZ IN PEOPLE'S EARS: A WEST AFRICAN TALE [557]

WRITTEN BY VERNA AARDEMA

ILLUSTRATED BY LEO AND DIANE DILLON

Cloth: Dial

Paper: Dial

Published: 1975   PRIZES: CALDECOTT MEDAL

This is an eccentric and quite wonderful story based on an odd chain of events. Mosquito tells a lie that results ultimately in the sun not rising. When the animals, led by Lion, figure out just what happened, Mosquito is punished. A fine read-aloud text is supported by stunning illustrations.

THE WILD SWANS [558]

WRITTEN BY HANS CHRISTIAN ANDERSEN

ILLUSTRATED BY SUSAN JEFFERS

Cloth: Dial

Paper: Dial

Published: 1981

The contemporary illustrator with a distinctive style featuring large, luminous faces has done a series of Andersen tales. In addition to this version of the familiar and haunting tale of the flock of swans, she has done *Thumbelina* and *The Snow Queen*. The text adaptations are by Amy Ehrlich. Another handsome edition of *The Wild Swans* is illustrated by Angela Barrett.

WILL I HAVE A FRIEND? [559]

WRITTEN BY MIRIAM COHEN
ILLUSTRATED BY LILLIAN HOBAN
Cloth: Macmillan
Paper: Aladdin
Published: 1967

The first of three books dealing with some of the perfectly reasonable fears and anxieties about kindergarten. The answer to the question, happily, is yes. Paul makes friends with Jim on the very first day. In *The New Teacher* they cope with a mid-year replacement, and in *Best Friends* they cope with an emergency.

THE WINTER WREN [560]

WRITTEN AND ILLUSTRATED BY BROCK COLE
Cloth: Farrar, Straus
Cloth: Sunburst/Farrar, Straus
Published: 1984

Simon, a simple boy, and his little sister Meg hear that Spring is asleep at Winter's farm. When they get there and Meg disappears, a winter wren intercedes. The story has the tone and richness of a fable, and the watercolor illustrations are perfectly evocative.

[560]

THE WITCH WHO LIVES DOWN THE HALL [561]

WRITTEN BY DONNA GUTHRIE
ILLUSTRATED BY AMY SCHWARTZ
Cloth: Harcourt Brace
Published: 1985

An urban Halloween story about a little boy who is quite sure his neighbor is a witch and explains why with unerring, but incorrect, logic. Funny illustrations.

WORSE THAN WILLY! [562]

WRITTEN AND ILLUSTRATED BY JAMES STEVENSON
Cloth: Greenwillow
Published: 1984

One of the raucous, improbable, impossible, and soothing stories Grandpa tells Louie and Mary Ann about the childhood he shared with Uncle Wainwright. The form is half storybook, half cartoon. This one, about sibling rivalry, has Grandpa captured by pirates and an octopus and rescued by Wainey. Other titles in the series include: *Could Be Worse*, *That Dreadful Day*, and *What's Under My Bed?* They are quite wonderful.

YERTLE THE TURTLE AND OTHER STORIES [563]

WRITTEN AND ILLUSTRATED BY DR. SEUSS
Cloth: Random House
Published: 1958

Dr. Seuss from his classic period. Three modern fables with improbable characters, illustrations, and story lines all in verse—but with very real morals.

YOU READ TO ME, I'LL READ TO YOU   [564]

WRITTEN BY JOHN CIARDI
ILLUSTRATED BY EDWARD GOREY
Cloth: Lippincott
Paper: Harper
Published: 1962, reprinted 1981

A collection of thirty-five poems, mostly amusing, organized for a child
and an adult to read out loud alternately and together. The illustrations
are appropriately amusing, too.

[373]

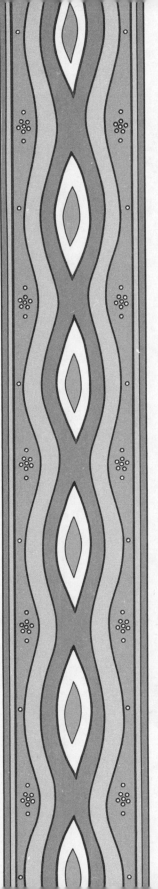

Early
Reading
Books

These well-illustrated books are designed for children who are learning to read and making the transition into "chapter books." Some of them are a particular pleasure to read aloud to younger children.

AMANDA PIG AND HER BIG BROTHER OLIVER [565]

WRITTEN BY JEAN VAN LEEUWEN
ILLUSTRATED BY ANN SCHWENINGER
Cloth: Dial (Easy to Read)
Paper: Dial
Published: 1982

One of the finest early-reader series is also particularly acute on sibling rivalry and sibling strength and affection. It features a family of plausible pigs and their endearing children in a range of domestic adventures that will resonate in the lives of most young readers. These books are a pleasure to read to children until they can read them to each other. Titles include *Tales of Oliver Pig*, *More Tales of Oliver Pig*, and *More Tales of Amanda Pig*.

AMELIA BEDELIA [566]

WRITTEN BY PEGGY PARISH
ILLUSTRATED BY FRITZ SEIBEL
Cloth: Harper
Paper: Harper
Published: 1963

The eleven Amelia Bedelia books have been published in two series by Harper & Row and Greenwillow with no diminution in their wacky charm and appeal. The literal-minded housekeeper was first hired by Mr. and Mrs. Rogers more than a quarter of a century ago, when class was less of an issue, and she remains beloved by beginning readers. She goes on "dressing" chickens, "separating" the eggs, and earnestly misunderstanding. However, she always puts "a little of this" and "a little of that" together and bakes her way into job security. Other titles: *Come Back, Amelia Bedelia*, *Good Work, Amelia Bedelia*, *Amelia Bedelia and the Baby*, *Amelia Bedelia Goes Camping*, and *Merry Christmas, Amelia Bedelia*.

A, MY NAME IS ALICE [567]

WRITTEN BY JANE E. BAYER
ILLUSTRATED BY STEVEN KELLOGG
Cloth: Dial
Paper: Dial
Published: 1984

An assortment of animals jump rope and bounce balls to those familiar rhymes that pass from generation to generation with only minor and gradual changes.

AND THEN WHAT HAPPENED, PAUL REVERE? [568]

WRITTEN BY JEAN FRITZ
ILLUSTRATED BY MARGOT TOMES
Cloth: Coward
Paper: Coward
Published: 1973

A biography of Paul Revere for young readers that is good-natured and accessible as well as accurate and good history. The prize-winning author has written a veritable history course of lighthearted but provocative biographies for children. Other fine titles include *Can't You Make Them Behave, King George?*, *Why Don't You Get a Horse, Sam Adams?* and *What's the Big Idea, Ben Franklin?* There is a boxed set of six biographies of figures from the American Revolution available in both hardcover and paperback.

[585]

ARE YOU MY MOTHER? [569]

WRITTEN AND ILLUSTRATED BY P. D. EASTMAN
Cloth: Random House
Published: 1960

A classic beginning reader—a baby bird falls from the nest and tries to find his mother. The simple text is augmented by bright pictures.

ARTHUR'S HONEY BEAR [570]

WRITTEN AND ILLUSTRATED BY LILLIAN HOBAN
Cloth: Harper (I Can Read)
Paper: Harper
Published: 1974

Arthur the chimpanzee and his little sister Violet are two favorite siblings in the world of early-reader books. Their relationship and adventures are plausible and entertaining. Here Arthur decides he can sell his old Honey Bear. The other titles include *Arthur's Prize Reader*, *Arthur's Pen Pal* (which has a good antisexist surprise in the plot), *Arthur's Christmas Cookies*, and *Arthur's Funny Money*.

A BEAR CALLED PADDINGTON [571]

WRITTEN BY MICHAEL BOND
ILLUSTRATED BY PEGGY FORTNUM
Cloth: Houghton Mifflin
Paper: Dell
Published: 1960

The first book about the lovable bear from darkest Peru found by Mr. and Mrs. Brown in London's Paddington Station. There are ten books in the original series and nearly half a dozen others, plus all sorts of franchise paraphernalia and merchandise to be found everywhere. The original stories are still delightfully funny. The same author created Olga De Polga, a very imaginative guinea pig. She appears in three books.

[571]

BETSY-TACY   [572]

WRITTEN BY MAUD HART LOVELACE
ILLUSTRATED BY LOIS LENSKI
Cloth: Harper
Paper: Harper
Published: 1940

The Betsy-Tacy series, set in Deep Valley, Minnesota, around the turn of the century, follows three girls—Betsy (Wasp), Tacy (Irish), and Tib (German)—from the time they are five on through high school, college, and marriage. It is a model of an enduring and appealing kind of series fiction in which the text increases in complexity with each book and the characters are fully developed. The girls' concerns and adventures are more than plausible, they ring true even now. The first six titles are the childhood sequence and are available in a boxed paperback edition. They include *Betsy, Tacy and Tib*, *Betsy and Tacy Go over the Big Hill*, *Betsy and Tacy Go Downtown*, *Heavens to Betsy*, and *Betsy in Spite of Herself*. The illustrations in the first books are by Lois Lenski, in the later books they are by Vera Neville; both are fine.

B IS FOR BETSY   [573]

WRITTEN AND ILLUSTRATED BY CAROLYN HAYWOOD
Cloth: Harcourt Brace
Paper: Voyager/HBJ
Published: 1939

The first of four easy-to-read and perennially popular chapter books that follow Betsy from first to fourth grade. Other titles include *Back to School with Betsy*, *Betsy and the Boys*, and *Betsy and Billy*.

THE CAT IN THE HAT   [574]

WRITTEN AND ILLUSTRATED BY DR. SEUSS
Cloth: Beginner Books
Published: 1957

The one, not the only, but certainly the original, contemporary beginning reader. (It makes no difference that it is over thirty years old.) One rainy afternoon when Mother is out and there is nothing to do, that Cat in the Hat comes to visit, and mayhem ensues.

CAT'S CRADLE, OWL'S EYES: A BOOK OF STRING GAMES [575]

WRITTEN BY CAMILLA GRYSKI
ILLUSTRATED BY TOM SANKEY
Cloth: Morrow
Paper: Morrow Jr.
Published: 1984

A collection of forty string games, with clear instructions and fine photographs, beginning, of course, with "Cat's Cradle." If you think about it, string games are more than fun, they are an introduction to math as well. If you get hooked on string, there is a sequel, *Many Stars, and More String Games*.

THE CHALK BOX KID [576]

WRITTEN BY CLYDE ROBERT BULLA
ILLUSTRATED BY THOMAS B. ALLEN
Paper: Random House
Published: 1987

Gregory's family's fortunes are on the decline; they have moved into a new house, and the lonely boy searches for a place to play. He makes a secret garden in a surprising way. This story is one title in the Stepping Stone Series of paperback originals for readers who are between early reading books and real chapter books. Other titles include *Next Spring an Oriole*, *Lily and the Runaway Baby*, and *Julian's Glorious Summer*.

[772]

COMMANDER TOAD IN SPACE [577]

WRITTEN BY JANE YOLEN
ILLUSTRATED BY BRUCE DEGEN
Cloth: Coward
Paper: Coward
Published: 1980

This is the first in a series of ridiculously funny early-reader texts that spin wildly off *Star Wars*, a movie the current generation of beginning readers may know only from videos. Which goes to prove that you didn't have to be there to enjoy this set of jokes. Other titles include *Commander Toad and the Planet of the Grapes*, *Commander Toad and the Intergalactic Spy*, *Commander Toad and the Dis-Asteroid*, and *Commander Toad and the Space Pirates*.

DANNY AND THE DINOSAUR [578]

WRITTEN AND ILLUSTRATED BY SYD HOFF
Cloth: Harper (I Can Read)
Paper: Harper
Published: 1958

A museum dinosaur spends a perfectly wonderful day wandering around the city with Danny. There is a Spanish language edition of this perennial favorite in print as well. The author also created *Sammy the Seal* and *Chester the Horse* in the early-reader series.

DID YOU CARRY THE FLAG TODAY, CHARLEY? [579]

WRITTEN BY REBECCA CAUDILL
ILLUSTRATED BY NANCY GROSSMAN
Cloth: Holt
Paper: Holt
Published: 1966

At Charley's school in Appalachia, you don't get to carry the flag unless you learn to behave. Mischievous Charley wins the honor in the end.

[574]

DIGGING UP DINOSAURS [580]

WRITTEN AND ILLUSTRATED BY ALIKI

Cloth: Crowell
Paper: Crowell
Published: 1981

All right, dinosaur fans, just how did those bones get from the ground into the museums? This book provides serious answers in a light-hearted and informative way sure to please young scientists.

DINNIEABBIESISTER-R-R [581]

WRITTEN BY RIKI LEVINSON
ILLUSTRATED BY HELEN COGANCHERRY

Cloth: Bradbury
Published: 1987

This gentle story of family life in a Jewish family in Brooklyn in the 1930s is slightly longer than an early reader, but is set out in fourteen short chapters that are indeed easy to read.

DINOSAURS ARE DIFFERENT [582]

WRITTEN AND ILLUSTRATED BY ALIKI

Cloth: Crowell
Paper: Crowell
Published: 1985

This dinosaur book explains in simple text and clear illustrations the differences among the giant creatures—for example, how to tell the meat eaters from the vegetarians. Essential for the fanatics, interesting to the merely curious.

[574]

FISH FACE [583]

WRITTEN BY PATRICIA REILLY GIFF
ILLUSTRATED BY BLANCHE SIMS

Cloth: Delacorte
Paper: Dell
Published: 1984

One of the twelve titles in the Kids of the Polk Street School Series that follows the adventures of the children in Ms. Rooney's room,

especially Emily Arrow and Richard "Beast" Best, throughout the year. Here, Emily Arrow discovers that the girl who sits next to her, Dawn Tiffanie Bosco, is a thief. The illustrations are cheerful. The series is very popular with beginning readers. Some of the other titles are *The Beast in Ms. Rooney's Room*, *The Valentine Star*, *Snaggle Doodles*, and *Say "Cheese."*

FOX AND HIS FRIENDS   [584]

WRITTEN BY EDWARD MARSHALL
ILLUSTRATED BY JAMES MARSHALL
Cloth: Dial
Paper: Dial
Published: 1982

The first of a series of funny early readers about Fox, an eager fellow, and his assorted friends. The titles include *Fox at School*, *Fox in Love*, *Fox on Wheels*, and *Fox All Week*.

FROG AND TOAD TOGETHER   [585]

WRITTEN AND ILLUSTRATED BY ARNOLD LOBEL
Cloth: Harper (I Can Read)
Paper: Harper
Published: 1972

There are four books about those amiable friends, Frog and Toad, and their modest but utterly engrossing adventures and activities—everything from planting a garden or dreaming of grandeur to getting the house clean or flying a kite. The language is pleasing, the illustrations

[585]

amusing. *Days with Frog and Toad, Frog and Toad Are Friends*, and *Frog and Toad All Year* are the other titles. Younger children love hearing them, beginning readers pore over them, and adults remember them with abiding affection.

GIVE US A GREAT BIG SMILE, ROSY COLE   [586]

WRITTEN AND ILLUSTRATED BY SHEILA GREENWALD

Cloth: Atlantic-Little, Brown

Paper: Dell

Published: 1981

The first of a series of amiable, easy-to-read chapter books about Rosy Cole, who is growing up middle-class in New York City with ordinary problems and quandaries. *Rosy Cole's Great American Guilt Club* takes a sharp look at fad fashions, family budgets, and the consequences of lying.

GREEN EGGS AND HAM   [587]

WRITTEN AND ILLUSTRATED BY DR. SEUSS

Cloth: Beginner Books

Published: 1960

One of the fine Seuss early readers with a limited vocabulary, this book has a narrator who keeps insisting, "I do not like them, Sam I am," until he tastes those eggs.

GROVER LEARNS TO READ   [588]

WRITTEN BY DAN ELLIOTT

ILLUSTRATED BY NORMAND CHARTIER

Cloth: Random House

Published: 1985

Grover is worried that if he learns to read, his mother won't read to him anymore, so he decides not to learn how. Of course he does, but the story has a nice twist.

HUGH PINE   [589]

WRITTEN BY JANWILLEM VAN DE WETERING
ILLUSTRATED BY LYNN MUNSINGER
Cloth: Houghton Mifflin
Paper: Bantam
Published: 1980

The first of a delightful pair of easy-to-read books about a very wise porcupine in the Maine woods who learns to dress in boots, coat, and hat and dispenses advice. In *Hugh Pine and the Good Place* he just has to get away from all his responsibilities. Good for reading aloud to younger children.

I AM NOT GOING TO GET UP TODAY!   [590]

WRITTEN BY DR. SEUSS
ILLUSTRATED BY JAMES STEVENSON
Cloth: Beginner Books
Published: 1987

The narrator of this funny Seussian verse is a lad who firmly insists that he is not getting up today no matter what happens—send neighbors, bands, even the United States Marines. The illustrations are suitably frenzied.

IN A DARK, DARK ROOM   [591]

WRITTEN BY ALVIN SCHWARTZ
ILLUSTRATED BY DIRK ZIMMER
Cloth: Harper (I Can Read)
Paper: Harper
Published: 1984

A nicely nasty collection of mysterious stories based on traditional folktales, but written for the beginning reader.

IT'S ME, HIPPO! [592]

WRITTEN BY MIKE THALER
ILLUSTRATED BY MAXIE CHAMBLISS
Cloth: Harper (I Can Read)
Published: 1983

A lighthearted early reader about Hippo and his jungle friends, who disagree about most things—like what constitutes a home, art, and games. But they all love Hippo. A sequel is *Hippo Lemonade*. Preschoolers like to listen to these stories, too.

JANE MARTIN, DOG DETECTIVE [593]

WRITTEN BY EVE BUNTING
ILLUSTRATED BY AMY SCHWARTZ
Cloth: Harcourt Brace
Published: 1984

For a fee of just twenty-five cents a day Jane Martin finds missing dogs. Three short, easy-to-read detective stories with whimsical illustrations.

KEEP THE LIGHTS BURNING, ABBIE [594]

WRITTEN BY PETER AND CONNIE ROOP
ILLUSTRATED BY PETER E. HANSON
Cloth: Carolrhoda
Paper: Carolrhoda
Published: 1985

An easy-to-read and well-illustrated version of the true story of Abbie Burgess, a little girl who kept the lighthouse lamps burning when a storm hit the coast of Maine in 1856 and her father, the lighthouse keeper, was ashore. There is a story book version of the same incident in *The Lighthouse Keeper's Daughter*.

Early
Reading
Books

THE KID NEXT DOOR
AND OTHER HEADACHES:
STORIES ABOUT ADAM JOSHUA [595]

WRITTEN BY JANICE LEE SMITH
ILLUSTRATED BY DICK GACKENBACH
Cloth: Harper
Paper: Harper
Published: 1984

Adam Joshua and Nelson are best friends and next-door neighbors, and they play and battle as best friends do. Their finest hour is coping with a visit from Nelson's truly horrid cousin Cynthia. Funny, realistic stories. There is a second volume—*The Kid Next Door & Other Headaches: More Stories About Adam Joshua.*

LITTLE BEAR [596]

WRITTEN BY ELSE HOLMELUND MINARIK
ILLUSTRATED BY MAURICE SENDAK
Cloth: Harper (I Can Read)
Paper: Harper
Published: 1957

One of the first and very finest series of early-reader books features Little Bear and his considerate friends, including Hen, Duck, Cat, his doting parents in their Victorian dress, and eventually his friend Emily and her doll Lucy. The use of a controlled vocabulary does not inhibit the stories, which appeal to toddlers and preschoolers almost as much as they appeal to beginning readers. The other titles are *Little Bear's*

[596]

200

Friend, *Father Bear Comes Home*, *Little Bear's Visit*, and *A Kiss for Little Bear*, in which the various animals deliver the kiss Grandma sends Little Bear in return for a picture.

LITTLE HOUSE IN THE BIG WOODS [597]

WRITTEN BY LAURA INGALLS WILDER
ILLUSTRATED BY GARTH WILLIAMS
Cloth: Harper
Paper: Harper
Published: 1932

The Little House books are perhaps the classic American childhood series. They follow the Ingalls family as they moved from Wisconsin west into Indian lands and finally settled in the Dakota territory. The stories begin in the 1870s, when Laura, the central character, is not quite five, and continue through her girlhood and adolescence to her marriage to Almanzo Wilder, a young settler. His boyhood in New York State is described in *Farmer Boy*. The prose becomes more sophisticated as Laura grows up. The details of pioneer life are vivid and exact, and the books are thrilling in their artless didacticism and their portrayal of close and rewarding family life. There is an endlessly replaying television series very loosely based on the books, but with none of their charm. The other titles include *Little House on the Prairie*, *On the Banks of Plum Creek*, *By the Shores of Silver Lake*, *The Long Winter*, *Little Town on the Prairie*, and *These Happy Golden Years*. There is a boxed paperback edition of nine titles. *The Little House Cookbook: Frontier Foods from Laura Ingalls Wilder's Classic Stories*, is a good cookbook for children, drawing on the recipes that occur so naturally in the stories.

LITTLE WITCH'S BIG NIGHT [598]

WRITTEN BY DEBORAH HAUTZIG
ILLUSTRATED BY MARC BROWN
Paper: Random House (Step into Reading)
Published: 1984

Little Witch has been so good that she is punished and has to stay at home on Halloween. She takes three friends—a pirate, an astronaut, and a devil—riding on her broomstick. In *Little Witch's Birthday*, her friends manage to come to her birthday party.

[596]

201

LOTTA ON TROUBLEMAKER STREET [599]

WRITTEN BY ASTRID LINDGREN
ILLUSTRATED BY JULIE BRINKLOE
Cloth: Macmillan
Published: 1984

Lotta, who is five, wakes up cranky, and things get worse from there. By the author of *Pippi Longstocking*, and in the same rebellious spirit.

MORRIS AND BORIS: THREE STORIES [600]

WRITTEN AND ILLUSTRATED BY BERNARD WISEMAN
Cloth: Dodd
Paper: Scholastic
Published: 1974

Morris the Moose and Boris the Bear are friends, and their early-reader adventures are consistently funny. The other titles in the series include *Halloween with Morris and Boris, Morris Has a Cold,* and *Morris Tells Boris Mother Moose Stories and Rhymes.*

we have

MOUSE TALES [601]

WRITTEN AND ILLUSTRATED BY ARNOLD LOBEL
Cloth: Harper (I Can Read)
Paper: Harper
Published: 1972

Papa Mouse promises his boys one story each before bedtime. There are seven, all short, some funny, some wise, all quite wonderful. There's a talking wishing well, a tall and a short mouse, a flood, and more. Engrossing for a beginning reader. *Mouse Soup* is a sequel of sorts.

[606]

we have

MR. POPPER'S PENGUINS [602]

WRITTEN BY RICHARD AND FLORENCE ATWATER
ILLUSTRATED BY ROBERT LAWSON
Cloth: Little, Brown
Paper: Dell
Published: 1938   PRIZES: NEWBERY HONOR BOOK

The truly, after half a century, classic tale of Mr. Popper, a kindly housepainter in a town called Stillwater, who loved penguins, and how his family coped with the gift of one, Captain Cook, who was joined by another, Greta, and begat a small flock of penguins. The illustrations capture the humor of both penguins and the story. The essential curiosity of the penguins and Mr. Popper's goodwill are something readers remember all their lives.

MY FATHER'S DRAGON *we have* [603]

WRITTEN BY RUTH STILES GANNETT
ILLUSTRATED BY RUTH CHRISMAN GANNETT
Cloth: Random House
Paper: Knopf
Published: 1948   PRIZES: NEWBERY HONOR BOOK

The narrator's father, Elmer Elevator, sets out to rescue a baby dragon from the Wild Island. He uses his wits and imagination and only a few props. The illustrations, and especially the endpapers, are enchanting. Good early chapter book for reading aloud or reading alone. There is a boxed paperback set that includes two other dragon titles, *Elmer and the Dragon* and *The Dragons of Blueland*.

NO MORE MONSTERS FOR ME [604]

WRITTEN BY PEGGY PARRISH
we have
ILLUSTRATED BY MARC SIMONT
Cloth: Harper (I Can Read)
Paper: Harper
Published: 1981

Minneapolis Simpkin is quite desperate to have a pet, and her mother didn't say she couldn't have a monster. So she brings home a weird baby monster and then tries to keep it fed and hidden. A fine, farcically funny early reader. The single child/single parent household is a given.

NO ONE IS GOING TO NASHVILLE [605]

WRITTEN BY MAVIS JUKES
ILLUSTRATED BY LLOYD BLOOM
Cloth: Knopf
Paper: Knopf
Published: 1983

An unusually well written but easy-to-read book about how new families evolve, in this case a *weekend family*—stepmother, father, and child— and a stray dog.

[603]

we have ## OLD MOTHER WEST WIND [606]

WRITTEN BY THORNTON W. BURGESS
ILLUSTRATED BY HARRISON CADY
Cloth: Little, Brown
Paper: Little, Brown
Published: 1910

This delightful collection of short, easy-to-read stories about Reddy Fox, Peter Rabbit, Danny Meadow Mouse, and the other creatures of the meadow and woods has been a favorite for generations, and with good reason. In addition to the charm of the stories, the type is large and clear, the illustrations old-fashioned and simple. Good for reading aloud to younger children, too.

OWL AT HOME [607]

we have

WRITTEN AND ILLUSTRATED BY ARNOLD LOBEL
Cloth: Harper
Paper: Harper
Published: 1975

A fine set of stories about Owl, a rather-stay-at-home fellow, who lets winter come in to visit with chilling results, makes tear-water tea, and finds a friend in the moon. A splendid early reader, good for reading aloud to lap listeners.

PIPPI LONGSTOCKING [608]

WRITTEN BY ASTRID LINDGREN
ILLUSTRATED BY LOUIS S. GLANZMAN
Cloth: Viking
Paper: Puffin
Published: 1950

Pippi is a scamp, a mischief maker, and a very nice little girl all in one. She lives all alone in a little house at the edge of the village. Her manners, housekeeping methods, and everything else about her are unconventional. The translations from the Swedish are slightly awkward and clumsy to read aloud, but listeners invariably want another chapter, please, and then reread the books for themselves. Other Pippi books include *Pippi Goes on Board, Pippi on the Run*, and *Pippi in the South Seas*.

RAMONA [609]

WRITTEN BY BEVERLY CLEARY
Cloth: Morrow
Paper: Dell
Published: 1952–1984

Ramona is a national treasure and an institution. This series of novels about the Quimby family and their neighbors, written over a thirty-year period but bringing Ramona only to the third grade, is a mine of information about loving, ordinary, day-to-day modern family life, told with increasing skill and laced with irresistible humor. Read one, read 'em all, learn to love Ramona, Beezus, and the rest. Enjoy kindergarten and the early grades again. It's not all sunshine, but it all rings true. The illustrations by Louis Darling in the early books and Allen Tiegreen in the later ones are a perfect fit. Some of the best titles are *Henry and Beezus*, *Beezus and Ramona*, *Ramona the Pest*, *Ramona the Brave*, and *Ramona Quimby, Age 8*.

RICHARD KENNEDY: COLLECTED STORIES [610]

WRITTEN BY RICHARD KENNEDY
ILLUSTRATED BY MARCIA SEWALL
Cloth: Harper
Published: 1987

These sixteen tales were originally published separately as picture and story books. They work very well as a large volume of relatively easy reading chapters and are accompanied by fourteen new illustrations. The stories are mostly a little bit fantastic, like the one about a porcelain man glued together from a broken vase.

SAM THE MINUTEMAN [611] *we have*

WRITTEN BY NATHANIEL BENCHLEY
ILLUSTRATED BY ARNOLD LOBEL
Cloth: Harper (I Can Read)
Paper: Harper
Published: 1969

This remarkably well written story gives one little boy's version of the beginnings of the American Revolution. The story is both accurate

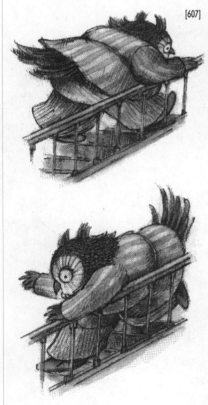

[607]

and clear, and makes a number of sophisticated points about the causes of the Revolution in ways young children can absorb. The companion volume is *George the Drummer Boy,* about a British drummer boy.

THE SHRINKING OF TREEHORN   [612]

WRITTEN BY FLORENCE PARRY HEIDE
ILLUSTRATED BY EDWARD GOREY
Cloth: Holiday
Paper: Dell
Published: 1971   PRIZES: NEW YORK TIMES BEST ILLUSTRATED BOOK

The first of three wistfully comic tales about Treehorn, the sort of boy who is ignored by others, even his parents and teachers. He is actually fading away and they don't notice. The morbid and hilarious illustrations are by a master. The other two titles are *Treehorn's Treasure* and *Treehorn's Wish.*

SOMETHING SLEEPING
IN THE HALL   [613]

WRITTEN AND ILLUSTRATED BY KARLA KUSKIN
Cloth: Harper (I Can Read)
Published: 1985

A collection of twenty-eight short, mostly funny poems about pets that a beginning reader can enjoy independently. The line drawing illustrations are droll.

THE STORIES JULIAN TELLS   [614]

WRITTEN BY ANN CAMERON
ILLUSTRATED BY ANN STRUGNELL
Cloth: Pantheon
Paper: Knopf
Published: 1981

A chapter book for beginning readers—six stories about Julian and his modest, cheerful, middle-class black family, including his engaging little brother, Huey. There is an appealing everydayness—losing a tooth, ordering a cat from a catalog. The sequel is *More Stories Julian Tells.*

SUGARING TIME [615]

WRITTEN BY KATHRYN LASKY
ILLUSTRATED BY CHRISTOPHER G. KNIGHT
Cloth: Macmillan
Paper: Aladdin
Published: 1983

PRIZES: NEWBERY HONOR BOOK

A fine collaborative effort in photojournalism that tells about the Lacey family in Vermont and how they make maple syrup.

SURPRISES [616]

WRITTEN BY LEE BENNETT HOPKINS
ILLUSTRATED BY MEGAN LLOYD
Cloth: Harper
Paper: Harper
Published: 1984

An anthology of thirty-eight easy-to-read and surprising poems, with inviting illustrations.

TIKTA'LIKTAK: AN ESKIMO LEGEND [617]

WRITTEN AND ILLUSTRATED BY JAMES HOUSTON
Cloth: Harcourt Brace
Published: 1965

A fine account of a young hunter's adventures, which include surviving terrible weather, encountering a polar bear, and struggling to get home.

THE TOUGH PRINCESS [618]

WRITTEN BY MARTIN WADDELL
ILLUSTRATED BY PATRICK BENSON
Cloth: Philomel
Published: 1987

Princess Rosamund, a very independent snippet of royalty born late in life to a doting king and queen, sets off to find her own prince and has some dandy adventures. The cartoonish illustrations are funny.

[613]

Early Reading Books

UNCLE ELEPHANT [619]

WRITTEN AND ILLUSTRATED BY ARNOLD LOBEL

Cloth: Harper (I Can Read)
Paper: Harper
Published: 1981

A little elephant who thinks his parents have been lost at sea is rescued by an elderly uncle. The book addresses separation anxieties carefully; even so, adults may find themselves teary.

A VERY YOUNG DANCER [620]

WRITTEN AND ILLUSTRATED BY JILL KREMENTZ

Cloth: Knopf
Paper: Dell
Published: 1976

A lavishly illustrated photo essay about a ten-year-old girl's experience playing Marie under the direction of George Balanchine in his New York City Ballet production of *The Nutcracker*. The photographs of Mr. Balanchine have certain historic value, and this book in particular is much loved by aspiring young ballerinas. The production, of course, continues. Other titles in the "Very Young" Series are about gymnasts, circus riders, skaters, and horseback riders.

WAKE UP, SUN [621]

WRITTEN BY DAVID L. HARRISON
ILLUSTRATED BY HANS WILHELM

Paper: Random House
Published: 1986

An entertaining early reader about a silly dog who wakes up in the middle of the night, can't find the sun, and then wakes up his friends to help him find it.

THE WEAVER'S GIFT [622]

WRITTEN BY KATHRYN LASKY
ILLUSTRATED BY CHRISTOPHER G. KNIGHT
Cloth: Warne
Paper: Warne
Published: 1981

A fine work of photojournalism that follows wool from the sheep's back
to its final incarnation as a child's blanket.

THE WHITE STALLION [623]

WRITTEN BY ELIZABETH SHUB
ILLUSTRATED BY RACHEL ISADORA
Cloth: Greenwillow
Published: 1982

As her family heads across Texas in a Conestoga wagon, Gretchen falls
asleep tied on the back of an old mare. She awakes in the midst of a
band of wild horses. It's a thrilling story, handsomely illustrated.

[613]

209

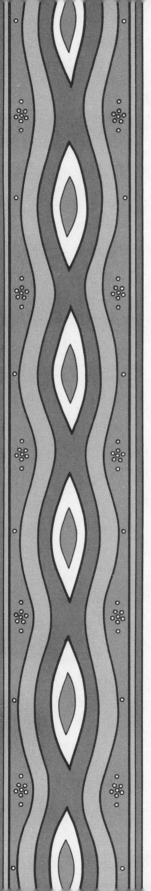

MIDDLE READING BOOKS

The books in this section are part of the rich treasure chest of childhood—adventures, fairy stories, folktales, chapter books, series—books to listen to, read, reread and then reread again for the pleasure of knowing what is going to happen next. The appropriate age range for listening to these stories in very wide. Preschoolers can follow some of them; many teen-agers comfortably read others. A number of the titles were once considered appropriate for adolescent readers only. For good or ill, our children grow up too soon these days, and in a world made small by television and the electronic media, a parent should use judgment about what individual children know and understand. The annotations make such distinctions clear.

ABEL'S ISLAND   [624]

WRITTEN AND ILLUSTRATED BY WILLIAM STEIG

Cloth: Farrar, Straus
Paper: Sunburst/Farrar, Straus
Published: 1976   PRIZES: NEWBERY HONOR BOOK

Abelard Hassam di Chirico Flint, an artist and a mouse, is swept away
in a rainstorm and is stranded for a year on an island in the middle of a
river. Splendid Steig for independent readers or reading aloud.

ABOUT WISE MEN AND SIMPLETONS: TWELVE TALES FROM GRIMM   [625]

WRITTEN BY ELIZABETH SHUB
ILLUSTRATED BY NONNY HOGROGIAN

Cloth: Macmillan
Published: 1971

A fine collection of some of the best-known Grimm tales, told gently
and directly, illustrated with haunting line drawings.

AN ACTOR'S LIFE FOR ME   [626]

WRITTEN BY LILLIAN GISH AS TOLD TO SELMA LANES
ILLUSTRATED BY PATRICIA HENDERSON LINCOLN

Cloth: Viking
Published: 1987

Here's an engaging memoir of life in the American theater at the turn
of the century, before there were movies, let alone television or VCRs,
as told by an actress whose later work may be familiar to some readers.
Fascinating story, well told, with particularly insightful and handsome
illustrations.

THE ADVENTURES OF PINOCCHIO   [627]

WRITTEN BY CARLO COLLODI
ILLUSTRATED BY GERALD MCDERMOTT

Cloth: Four Winds
Published: 1981

The adventures of the little wooden puppet who wants to become a real
boy have enchanted generations and been subject to many adaptations

and versions. This translation and adaptation by Marianna Mayer is a good one, although the illustrations are slightly awkward. There are, however, a number of other editions available, although none is unusually distinguished. Children weaned on the Disney version, which is quite wonderful in its own right (some, including Maurice Sendak, claim that it is better), should be warned that the book is quite different.

ALAN AND NAOMI [628]

WRITTEN BY MYRON LEVOY
Cloth: Harper
Paper: Harper
Published: 1977

Naomi is a refugee child from Paris who moves into Alan Silverman's New York City apartment building during World War II. She seems very peculiar, and he avoids her at first, but a genuine friendship ensues in the honestly told story.

ALL-OF-A-KIND FAMILY [629]

WRITTEN BY SYDNEY TAYLOR
ILLUSTRATED BY HELEN JOHN
Paper: Yearling
Published: 1951, reissued 1966

The first of a series of books about a loving, close-knit Jewish family living on New York City's Lower East Side in the early part of this century. The five daughters are high-spirited and make their own good times. The sequel is *All-of-a-Kind Family Downtown*. This is a favorite with younger readers, and a good read-aloud selection particularly for Jewish families. The other titles are out of print.

[631]

AMY'S EYES [630]

WRITTEN BY RICHARD KENNEDY
ILLUSTRATED BY RICHARD EGIELSKI
Cloth: Harper
Paper: Harper
Published: 1985

A big, rollicking fantasy adventure that begins in an orphanage. Amy pines away for her sailor doll who turns into a real captain, then she herself turns into a doll, and off they go with a crew of animals, seeking more than gold.

ANASTASIA KRUPNIK [631]

WRITTEN BY LOIS LOWRY
ILLUSTRATED BY DIANE DE GROAT
Cloth: Houghton Mifflin
Paper: Bantam, Dell
Published: 1979

The beginning of an affectionate, comic series about the Krupnik family and Anastasia in particular, growing up bright and articulate in a Boston suburb. The other members of the family, especially her little brother, Sam, are vivid. The series begins in the fourth grade, and by the fifth book Anastasia is in junior high school. Other titles include *Anastasia at Your Service, Anastasia, Ask Your Analyst, Anastasia On Her Own,* and *Anastasia and Her Chosen Career.*

...AND NOW MIGUEL [632]

WRITTEN BY JOSEPH KRUMGOLD
ILLUSTRATED BY JEAN CHARLOT
Cloth: Harper
Paper: Harper
Published: 1953   PRIZES: NEWBERY MEDAL

Miguel Chaven, a twelve-year-old boy, lives with his family of sheepherders in the Sangre de Christo Mountains in New Mexico. He tells how he wishes to accompany the men and the sheep to their summer pasture, a journey that is both a rite of passage and a symbol of belonging to the community. This book has passed the test of time and remains engrossing.

ANGRY WATERS [633]

WRITTEN BY WALT MOREY
ILLUSTRATED BY RICHARD CUFFARI
Cloth: Dutton
Published: 1969

An adventure story about a troubled fifteen-year-old boy who is placed on a dairy farm in Oregon for parole. It has had lasting appeal for boys.

THE ANIMAL FAMILY [634]

WRITTEN BY RANDALL JARRELL
ILLUSTRATED BY MAURICE SENDAK
Cloth: Pantheon
Paper: Knopf   PRIZES: NEW YORK TIMES BEST ILLUSTRATED BOOK,
Published: 1965   NEWBERY HONOR BOOK

This is a facsimile of the handsome original edition of the distinguished American poet's memorable fantasy about a solitary hunter who miraculously acquires a family, including a mermaid, a bear, a lynx, and finally a boy. Extraordinary writing and fine, restrained decorations. Splendid for reading aloud again and again.

ANNE FRANK: THE DIARY OF A YOUNG GIRL HIDING FROM THE NAZIS [635]

WRITTEN BY ANNE FRANK
Cloth: Doubleday
Paper: Pocket Books
Published: 1967

The diary of the thirteen-year-old Jewish girl, hidden in an attic during the Nazi occupation of Holland, remains a powerful and poignant book. The universally appealing aspects—the simple problems of adolescence and Anne's family relationships as well as her optimism—are in shocking contrast to the terror of her situation. And, of course, there was no happy ending. Children often read it to themselves, so it needs to be discussed, often at length and sometimes in the middle of the night. The introduction to the hardcover edition is by Eleanor Roosevelt, who may herself require some introduction for contemporary readers.

ANNE OF GREEN GABLES [636]

WRITTEN BY L. M. MONTGOMERY
ILLUSTRATED BY JODY LEE
Cloth: Grosset & Dunlap
Paper: Bantam
Published: 1908; reissued 1983

Anne Shirley, the heroine of the perennially popular series, lives on Canada's Prince Edward Island at the turn of the century. As the series begins she is eleven and full of troubles till she sorts out her relationship to her foster mother. In later installments she goes to college, returns to the island to teach, and eventually marries. The other titles include *Anne of Avonlea*, *Anne of the Island*, *Anne of Windy Poplars*, *Anne's House of Dreams*, and *Anne of Ingleside*.

ANNO'S COUNTING HOUSE [637]

WRITTEN AND ILLUSTRATED BY MITSUMASA ANNO
Cloth: Philomel
Published: 1982

In the generosity of his genius, this world-renowned Japanese artist has embarked on a dazzling set of illustrated picture books that teach mathematical theory and logic. This one deals with numbers, addition, subtraction, number sets, and game theory. *Anno's Hat Tricks* is about binary logic, *Anno's Mysterious Multiplying Jar* is about factorials, *Socrates and the Three Little Pigs* is about combinatorial analysis, and *Anno's Math Games* is an introduction to mathematics. These remarkable books are not to be handed out lightly. They are rich, delicious, and difficult. However beautiful to look at, they can be daunting to those with math aversion (adults as well as children). Equally, if you enjoy working with children, they are a wonderful way to do mathematics at home for the pure fun of it.

ARE YOU THERE, GOD? IT'S ME, MARGARET [638]

WRITTEN BY JUDY BLUME
Cloth: Bradbury
Paper: Dell
Published: 1970

Almost twelve, both longing for and fearing adolescence, Margaret, who chats with God on a regular basis about her worries, is a heroine most children identify with, at least for a minute, as they move along the path toward growing up. Controversial when they were first published, the Blume books are part of the rites of passage for many, if not most, American children. Some of the other most popular titles are: *Then Again, Maybe I Won't, Otherwise Known as Sheila the Great*, and *Tiger Eyes. Are You There God?* is also available in Spanish.

ARTHUR, FOR THE VERY FIRST TIME [639]

WRITTEN BY PATRICIA MACLACHLAN
ILLUSTRATED BY LLOYD BLOOM
Cloth: Harper
Paper: Scholastic
Published: 1980

It is a transitional summer for Arthur, a fussy ten-year-old boy who is spending time at his eccentric aunt and uncle's farm while his mother awaits a new baby at home. A charmingly illustrated and well-written story of self-discovery and assertion.

ASK ANOTHER QUESTION: THE STORY AND MEANING OF PASSOVER [640]

WRITTEN BY MIRIAM CHAIKIN
ILLUSTRATED BY MARVIN FRIEDMAN
Cloth: Clarion
Paper: Clarion
Published: 1985

A welcoming explanation of the story, symbols, and rituals of Passover, full of nuggets of information and points for conversation. One of a series of books on the Jewish holidays, including *Light Another Candle*, for

Hanukkah, *Make Noise, Make Merry* for Purim, and *Shake a Palm Branch* for Sukkot. These books are useful for family reference, and can be read aloud or excerpted for younger children.

ASK ME NO QUESTIONS   [641]

WRITTEN BY ANN SCHLEE
Cloth: Holt
Published: 1982

A compelling historical novel about what happens when an epidemic of cholera sweeps through a boarding school in the nineteenth century.

BADGER ON THE BARGE AND OTHER STORIES   [642]

WRITTEN BY JANNI HOWKER
Cloth: Greenwillow
Paper: Penguin
Published: 1985

A deeply affecting collection of five fine short stories, all set in England, all involving lonely young people who come into contact with elderly strangers. Beautifully written.

THE BAGTHORPE SAGA   [643]

WRITTEN BY HELEN CRESSWELL
Cloth: Macmillan
Paper: Puffin
Published: 1977

A series of madcap novels about an eccentric British family. The Bagthorpes are fiercely competitive, terribly clever, and slightly nutty. The saga is in six parts: *Ordinary Jack, , Absolute Zero, Bagthorpes Unlimited, Bagthorpes v. the World, Bagthorpes Abroad*, and *Bagthorpes Haunted*.

BALLET SHOES [644]

WRITTEN BY NOEL STREATFEILD
Paper: Yearling
Published: 1937, reissused 1979

The first in an internationally popular series of books for girls. This one tells the story of the three Fossil girls, adopted by the ever-traveling professor, who has sent them to be raised in London and trained for the stage. They are plucky and determined and beguilingly British. Similarly appealing, other families and their adventures are told in *Movie Shoes*, *Dancing Shoes*, *Skating Shoes*, *Theatre Shoes*, and other titles.

THE BAT-POET [645]

WRITTEN BY RANDALL JARRELL
ILLUSTRATED BY MAURICE SENDAK
Cloth: Macmillan
Paper: Aladdin
Published: 1964   PRIZES: NEW YORK TIMES BEST ILLUSTRATED BOOK

A little brown bat cannot sleep during the day—he keeps waking up and looking at the world. This collaboration between a fine poet and a fine artist is also properly considered a classic.

THE BEAR'S HOUSE [646]

WRITTEN BY MARILYN SACHS
Cloth: Dutton
Paper: Avon
Published: 1971

Fran Ellen is a nine-year-old with a great many real problems with her family and in school. Her greatest pleasure is in visiting the classroom dollhouse, the Bear's House, which she loves. This is a beautifully written short novel about struggle and maturation, and a steady favorite among middle-grade readers. The sequel is *Fran Ellen's House*.

BEAUTY: A RETELLING OF THE STORY OF BEAUTY AND THE BEAST [647]

WRITTEN BY ROBIN MCKINLEY

Cloth: Harper
Paper: NAL
Published: 1978

A first-person fantasy novel that retells the fairy tale with great style, particularly appealing to older grade readers.

BEN AND ME [648]

WRITTEN AND ILLUSTRATED BY ROBERT LAWSON

Cloth: Little, Brown
Paper: Little, Brown
Published: 1939

Here is one of a series of confidential biographies of historical figures as narrated by a pet or animal with inside information and a lighthearted view of history—in this case, Benjamin Franklin as seen by a mouse. Other titles include *Mr. Revere and I* and *Captain Kidd's Cat.* Middle-grade schoolchildren for generations have adored these books.

BERRIES GOODMAN [649]

WRITTEN BY EMILY CHENEY NEVILLE

Cloth: Harper
Paper: Harper
Published: 1964

A modern novel about the kinds of problems and prejudices a big city boy encounters on moving to the suburbs. Times change, but the core problems remain.

THE BEST CHRISTMAS PAGEANT EVER [650]

we have

WRITTEN BY BARBARA ROBINSON
ILLUSTRATED BY JUDITH GWYN BROWN
Cloth: Harper
Paper: Harper
Published: 1972

What is the true meaning of Christmas? When the ramshackle, cha-otic, impossible Herdman children are cast in the annual Christmas pageant, some important lessons are learned all around the community. This could have been treacle, but it's told so deftly it has become a classic. Good to read aloud.

THE BEST KEPT SECRET OF THE WAR [651]

WRITTEN BY LEONARD TODD
Cloth: Knopf
Published: 1984

A complex adventure novel set in the Blue Ridge Mountains at the end of World War II. Because his father is off fighting, and his mother is distracted, ten-year-old Cam Reed makes friends with a mountain man, Jeddah Whitmire, who is in hiding.

BIG RED [652]

WRITTEN BY JIM KJELGAARD
ILLUSTRATED BY BOB KUHN
Cloth: Holiday
Paper: Bantam
Published: 1945

An enduring and appealing dog-and-boy story, in this case a champion Irish setter and a trapper's son. The sequels are *Irish Red* and *Outlaw Red*.

BLACK BEAUTY [653]

WRITTEN BY ANNA SEWELL
ILLUSTRATED BY SUSAN JEFFERS
Cloth: Random House
Published: 1986

An award-winning contemporary novelist, Robin McKinley, tells the ultimate horse story in somewhat simplified language. The lush illustrations fairly gallop across the page. This abridgment works well for younger readers.

BLACK BEAUTY [654]

WRITTEN BY ANNA SEWELL
ILLUSTRATED BY FRITZ EICHENBERG
Cloth: Grosset & Dunlap
Paper: Grosset & Dunlap
Published: 1877; reissued 1945

There are many abridged editions of the best-known horse story of all. This is the full text of the story of the beautiful black horse who is traded into many adventures and ultimately rescued.

THE BLACK CAULDRON [655]

WRITTEN BY LLOYD ALEXANDER
Cloth: Holt
Paper: Dell
Published: 1965   PRIZES: NEWBERY HONOR BOOK

The first of a favorite fantasy quintet about the imaginary land of Prydain, which has some basis in Welsh legend and traditional mythology. In this volume, a council of warriors faces villainy. The other titles are *The Book of Three*, *The Castle of Llyr*, *Taran Wanderer*, and *The High King*. The last title won the Newbery Medal in 1968.

THE BLACK PEARL [656]

WRITTEN BY SCOTT O'DELL
Cloth: Houghton Mifflin
Paper: Dell
Published: 1967   PRIZES: NEWBERY HONOR BOOK

This is a thrilling adventure story set off the Baja California coast, about a village of pearl divers, rivalry, and a giant manta guarding a huge black pearl.

THE BLACK STALLION [657]

WRITTEN BY WALTER FARLEY
Cloth: Random House
Paper: Random House
Published: 1941

One of the all-time-favorite animal series—there are nineteen tales about that mighty champion, the black stallion, and his various relations. Titles include *The Black Stallion and Flame*, *The Black Stallion Challenged!*, and *The Black Stallion's Sulky Colt*.

BLOWFISH LIVE IN THE SEA [658]

WRITTEN BY PAULA FOX
Cloth: Bradbury
Paper: Aladdin
Published: 1970

His stepsister is the narrator of this novel about eighteen-year-old Ben Felix, an unhappy, erratic boy trying to come to terms with himself and his real father.

BLUE WILLOW [659]

WRITTEN BY DORIS GATES
ILLUSTRATED BY PAUL LANTZ
Cloth: Viking
Paper: Puffin
Published: 1940   PRIZES: NEWBERY HONOR BOOK

This story of migrant workers in California is nearly a half century old but remains fresh and affecting. Janey, who is an only child, longs to live in a house and have an orderly life. The only possession she and her parents have of value or beauty is a blue willow plate.

A BOOK OF AMERICANS [660]

WRITTEN BY ROSEMARY AND STEPHEN VINCENT BENET
ILLUSTRATED BY CHARLES CHILD
Cloth: Holt
Paper: Holt
Published: 1933; reissued 1986

A collection of fifty-six poems about historic Americans, lesser and well known, written with style and wit more than half a century ago and reissued in 1987 for new generations to enjoy. Perfect for reading aloud. The woodcut illustrations are dramatic.

THE BORROWERS [661]

WRITTEN BY MARY NORTON
ILLUSTRATED BY BETH AND JOE KRUSH
Cloth: Harcourt Brace
Paper: Voyager/HBJ
Published: 1953

The first volume of a grand series of novels about Pod, Homily, and Arrietty, a family of little people who live under the kitchen floor in a quiet house some time not so very long ago. The idea of these little people often appeals to children who otherwise have no taste for whimsy. The fine line illustrations certainly add to their charm. Other titles include *The Borrowers Afield*, *The Borrowers Afloat*, *The Borrowers Aloft*, and *The Borrowers Avenged*. A boxed paperback edition is available.

[661]

BOY: TALES OF CHILDHOOD [662]

WRITTEN BY ROALD DAHL
Cloth: Farrar, Straus
Paper: Puffin
Published: 1984

The story of the author's childhood in Norway and (mostly) in England is filled with incidents as peculiar, sharp, funny, and sometimes awful as those in his stories. The memoir is illustrated with excerpts from schoolboy letters and photographs. The second volume, *Going Solo*, is for older readers, and describes Dahl's experiences in Africa and as a pilot during World War II.

THE BRAVE LITTLE TOASTER [663]

WRITTEN BY THOMAS M. DISCH
ILLUSTRATED BY KAREN SCHMIDT
Cloth: Doubleday
Published: 1986

Five domestic appliances—a vacuum cleaner, a tensor lamp, an electric blanket, a clock radio, and a toaster—have been left at a cabin in the woods. Thinking they have been abandoned, they set off to find their master. The toaster is the leader. This is the kind of fantasy that requires a sure hand. The author, who writes science fiction for adults, has one. Well done.

BRIDGE TO TERABITHIA [664]

WRITTEN BY KATHERINE PATERSON
ILLUSTRATED BY DONNA DIAMOND
Cloth: Crowell
Paper: Harper
Published: 1977   PRIZES: NEWBERY MEDAL

This is an astonishingly powerful novel about an improbable friendship between Jess, a poor local boy, and Leslie, a willful, brilliantly imaginative girl who moves into a house nearby. They have a secret hiding place they call Terabithia and a rich friendship that is severed when Leslie is accidentally killed. There are only a few novels for children about death; this one succeeds brilliantly. But because the writing is so fine and persuasive, the impact on readers of all ages is deep. This is a six-Kleenex and late-night-talk-time story, and worth the effort for parents as well as children.

THE BRONZE BOW   [665]

WRITTEN BY ELIZABETH GEORGE SPEARE
Cloth: Houghton Mifflin
Paper: Houghton Mifflin
Published: 1961   PRIZES: NEWBERY MEDAL

A novel about a young Jewish fugitive who is brought to hear the teacher Jesus and must choose his own path. The subject is gripping.

BROTHERS OF THE HEART   [666]

WRITTEN BY JOAN BLOS
Cloth: Scribner
Paper: Aladdin
Published: 1985

A historical novel set in the far north in the mid-nineteenth century during a bitterly cold winter. Shem, a boy from an Ohio family moved to Michigan, and later hired as clerk to a fur-trading expedition, is found in an isolated cabin by an elderly Ottowan Indian woman. Their relationship becomes the core of the story.

BUNNICULA: A RABBIT TALE OF MYSTERY   [667]

WRITTEN BY DEBORAH AND JAMES HOWE
ILLUSTRATED BY ALAN DANIEL
Published: 1979
Cloth: Atheneum
Paper: Avon

Is Bunnicula really a vegetarian vampire bunny? The Monroe's family cat thinks so. This is the first of a comic trio of novels starring Nighty the cat. Middle-grade readers find them very entertaining. *The Celery Stalks at Midnight* is followed by *Nighty Nightmare*.

CADDIE WOODLAWN [668]

WRITTEN BY CAROL RYRIE BRINK
ILLUSTRATED BY TRINA SCHART HYMAN
Cloth: Macmillan
Paper: Aladdin
Published: 1935   PRIZES: NEWBERY MEDAL

A popular novel about pioneer life in Wisconsin in the 1860s, reillustrated in 1973. It is still convincing and compelling reading.

CALL IT COURAGE [669]

WRITTEN AND ILLUSTRATED BY ARMSTRONG SPERRY
Cloth: Macmillan
Paper: Collier
Published: 1939   PRIZES: NEWBERY MEDAL

Set in the South Pacific, this is a timelessly interesting adventure story about Mafatu, the son of the Great Chief of Hikueru, who conquers his fear of the sea.

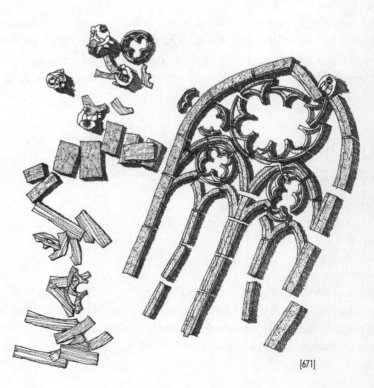

[671]

CANYON WINTER [670]

WRITTEN BY WALT MOREY
Cloth: Dutton
Published: 1972

Pete, a fifteen-year-old boy, is stranded in a canyon after a plane crash; he finds his way to the cabin of Omar, a solitary old man, and spends the whole winter with him. There is an underlying theme of conservation and concern for ecology and nature. Among Morey's other popular boys-and-nature books are *The Lemon Meringue Dog*, *Sandy and the Rock Star*, and *The Year of the Black Pony*.

CATHEDRAL: THE STORY OF ITS CONSTRUCTION [671]

WRITTEN AND ILLUSTRATED BY DAVID MACAULAY
Cloth: Houghton Mifflin
Paper: Houghton Mifflin
Published: 1973   PRIZES: NEW YORK TIMES BEST ILLUSTRATED BOOK

A remarkable re-creation of the building of a French Gothic cathedral. The illustrations are pen and ink, the text is utterly clear. If you are mesmerized by this explanation, then look for *Castle* and *Pyramid* or the brilliant fantasy *Unbuilding*.

THE CAT WHO WENT TO HEAVEN [672]

WRITTEN BY ELIZABETH COATSWORTH
Cloth: Macmillan
Paper: Aladdin
Published: 1930   PRIZES: NEWBERY MEDAL

A prize-winning and timeless novel about a Japanese artist, a little cat, and a miracle.

THE CHANGES [673]

WRITTEN BY PETER DICKINSON
Cloth: Delacorte
Paper: Dell
Published: 1970

A splendid trilogy of early novels by a distinguished British author who writes for both adults and younger readers has been collectively reissued as *The Changes*. It includes *The Devil's Children*, *Heartsease*, and *The Weathermonger*. As the series begins, there has been a revolt in Britain; twelve-year-old Nicola Gore is alone in London, which is now a deserted city. The society advances into a kind of superstitious medievalism. Readers who ordinarily don't like fantasy or science fiction get caught up in these books.

CHARLIE AND THE CHOCOLATE FACTORY [674]

WRITTEN BY ROALD DAHL
ILLUSTRATED BY JOSEPH SCHINDELMAN
Cloth: Knopf
Paper: Bantam, Viking Penguin
Published: 1964

The story of how poor but honest Charlie Bucket came to visit Willie Wonka's fantastic and marvelous Chocolate Factory in the company of a memorable band of truly obnoxious children (all of whom get their just desserts) is one of the deserved, and certainly the most delicious, modern classics. There is an adaptation in play form available in paperback from Penguin, and a sequel, *Charlie and the Great Glass Elevator*.

[675]

CHARLOTTE'S WEB [675]

WRITTEN BY E. B. WHITE
ILLUSTRATED BY GARTH WILLIAMS
Cloth: Harper
Paper: Harper
Published: 1952

Wilbur, an innocent and amiable pig, is saved from slaughter by a true friend and a fine writer, Charlotte, the gray spider in the barnyard door. The language, the subplots, the details (especially the science and nature observations), and the moral seem more insightful and rewarding with each reading. The feature-length cartoon is not a travesty and does not usually dissuade children from actually listening to, or reading, the book. As Charlotte herself wrote, "Terrific."

CHEAPER BY THE DOZEN [676]

WRITTEN BY ERNESTINE CAREY AND FRANK B. GILBRETH
Cloth: Crowell
Paper: Bantam
Published: 1948

This memoir of growing up in the Gilbreth family with twelve children
and dozens of ideas and adventures is lighthearted and entertaining, as
is the sequel, *Belles on Their Toes*.

THE CHILDREN'S HOMER: THE ADVENTURES OF ODYSSEUS AND THE TALE OF TROY [677]

WRITTEN BY PADRAIC COLUM
ILLUSTRATED BY WILLY POGANY
Paper: Macmillan
Published: 1918

This is a splendid use of paperback publishing—making the beautifully illustrated 1918 edition of Homer as told by the distinguished
Irish poet available to new readers. The prose is brilliant, the fine line
drawings are fairly breathtaking. The companion volume, *The Golden
Fleece: And the Heroes Who Lived Before Achilles*, which tells many Greek
myths within the framework of the story of Jason and the Argonauts,
is also available.

[678]

A CHILD'S CHRISTMAS IN WALES [678]

WRITTEN BY DYLAN THOMAS
ILLUSTRATED BY TRINA SCHART HYMAN
Cloth: Holiday
Published: 1985

The Welsh poet's short evocative memoir of Christmas early in this
century is full of snow, cats, aunties, and boyish adventure. This is a
handsome edition with affectionate watercolor illustrations (the cats in
the snow are specially fine), nicely sized to hold in small hands. There
is another beautifully drawn edition illustrated by the British artist
Edward Ardizzone.

CHIMNEY SWEEPS: YESTERDAY AND TODAY [679]

WRITTEN BY JAMES CROSS GIBLIN
ILLUSTRATED BY MARGOT TOMES
Cloth: Crowell
Paper: Harper
Published: 1982

An entertaining and well-illustrated history of an old and colorful profession, full of folklore and stories going back to the fifteenth century.

CHOCOLATE FEVER [680]

WRITTEN BY ROBERT KIMMEL SMITH
ILLUSTRATED BY GIOIA FIAMMENGHI
Paper: Yearling
Published: 1978

Chocoholics, beware! Henry Green ate so much of the stuff he caught chocolate fever. How was he cured? Read and find out. Funny enough to read aloud to middle-grade listeners.

THE CHOCOLATE TOUCH [681]

WRITTEN BY PATRICK SKENE CATLING
ILLUSTRATED BY MARGOT APPLE
Cloth: Morrow
Paper: Bantam
Published: 1979

Imagine the Midas story turned from gold to rich, dark, chocolatey brown. Here it is, and imagine what happens to John when everything he touches turns to...chocolate. Delicious fantasy.

[679]

A CHRISTMAS CAROL [682]

WRITTEN BY CHARLES DICKENS
ILLUSTRATED BY TRINA SCHART HYMAN
Cloth: Holiday
Published: 1983

Bless us one and all. Here's a setting of the familiar text handsomely set off with decorated initials and six color plates by a well-known contemporary artist. There is another good edition illustrated by Michael Foreman.

[678]

THE CHRONICLES OF NARNIA [683]

WRITTEN BY C. S. LEWIS
ILLUSTRATED BY PAULINE BAYNES
Cloth: Macmillan
Paper: Collier
Published: 1950

This seven-volume allegorical Christian fantasy has steadily gained worldwide popularity since it was first published in the 1950s. In the beginning, Alsan, the white lion, freed Narnia from the spell of the White Witch, but that was just the beginning. These tales are very good for reading aloud. The titles are *The Lion, the Witch and the Wardrobe*, *Prince Caspian*, *The Voyage of the 'Dawn Treader'*, *The Silver Chair*, *The Horse and His Boy*, *The Magician's Nephew*, and *The Last Battle*.

CITY: A STORY OF ROMAN PLANNING AND CONSTRUCTION [684]

WRITTEN AND ILLUSTRATED BY DAVID MACAULAY
Cloth: Houghton Mifflin
Paper: Houghton Mifflin
Published: 1974

The planning and construction of an imaginary Roman city is set forth in clear pen-and-ink illustrations and lucid text. The idea of rational city planning is explicit.

CLEVER GRETCHEN AND OTHER FORGOTTEN FOLK TALES [685]

WRITTEN BY ALISON LURIE
ILLUSTRATED BY MARGOT TOMES
Cloth: Crowell
Published: 1980

A good selection of fourteen stories with active heroines—young women who are doers and clever thinkers whether they are princesses or commoners. There is a refreshing tartness to both the text and the illustrations.

COLOUR FAIRY BOOKS [686]

WRITTEN BY ANDREW LANG
ILLUSTRATED BY VARIOUS ARTISTS
Cloth: Viking
Paper: Dover
Published: 1978

The famed colour fairy books—Blue, Green, Pink, Red, and Yellow—have been slightly revised from their original 1889/1890/1892 editions in the hardback series and illustrated by John Lawrence, Antony Maitland, Colin McNaughton, Faith Jacques, and Eric Blegvad. Facsimilies of the original editions are available in paperback from Dover. Either way, they are a trove of lore and provide nearly endless hours of delight for readers who like fairy tales.

COME SING, JIMMY JO [687]

WRITTEN BY KATHERINE PATERSON
Cloth: Lodestar
Paper: Avon
Published: 1985

A fine novel about an eleven-year-old boy who has been content to live in the mountains with his grandmother. When he joins the family bluegrass troupe, he confronts not only family problems but also the realities of fame. This is an interesting inside look at the peculiar invasive dynamic of modern celebrity that children can begin to understand.

COMMODORE PERRY IN THE LAND OF THE SHOGUN [688]

WRITTEN BY RHODA BLUMBERG

Cloth: Lothrop
Published: 1985   PRIZES: NEWBERY HONOR BOOK

The story of the American expedition to Japan led by Commodore Matthew Perry in 1853. Not only is the text well written, but the large-format book is unusually well designed and is illustrated with reproductions of Japanese art of the period.

COWBOYS OF THE WILD WEST [689]

WRITTEN BY RUSSELL FREEDMAN

Cloth: Clarion
Published: 1985

Terrific period photographs enliven this introduction to the trail drivers of the later nineteenth century, the most romantic of American heros.

CRACKER JACKSON [690]

WRITTEN BY BETSY BYARS

Cloth: Viking
Paper: Puffin
Published: 1985

In this compellingly plausible novel, twelve-year-old Cracker realizes that Alma, his former baby-sitter, is being beaten by her husband. It isn't his problem, but it is.

THE CRICKET IN TIMES SQUARE [691]

WRITTEN BY GEORGE SELDEN
ILLUSTRATED BY GARTH WILLIAMS

Cloth: Farrar, Straus
Paper: Dell
Published: 1960   PRIZES: NEWBERY HONOR BOOK

The first of a fine series of heartwarming adventures involving Harry the cat, Tucker the mouse, Chester the musical cricket, and their friends in the Times Square newsstand. Other titles include *Tucker's Countryside*, *Chester Cricket's New Home*, *Harry Cat's Pet Puppy*, and the prequel *Harry Kitten and Tucker Mouse*.

THE CUNNING LITTLE VIXEN   [692]

WRITTEN BY RUDOLF TESNOHLIDEK
ILLUSTRATED BY MAURICE SENDAK
Cloth: Farrar, Straus
Published: 1985

This rich and engrossing Czech novel, on which the opera of the same name is based, tells the story of Bartos, the forester, and Vixen Sharp-Ears, the clever innocent. The illustrations are closely related to Maurice Sendak's inventive staging of the opera. The translation by Tatiana Firkusny, Maritza Morgan, and Robert T. Jones is exemplary. This is for reading aloud and for older, sophisticated children and their parents.

CUSTARD AND COMPANY   [693]

WRITTEN BY OGDEN NASH
ILLUSTRATED BY QUENTIN BLAKE
Cloth: Little, Brown
Paper: Little, Brown
Published: 1980

A hilarious collection of eighty poems—including, of course, "Custard the Dragon," that "realio, trulio cowardly dragon"—written by the popular American poet, illustrated by a distinguished British artist.

DADDY LONG-LEGS   [694]

WRITTEN BY JEAN WEBSTER
Paper: Bantam
Published: 1912

Today's young readers may be infinitely more sophisticated, but this remains a timeless, romantic favorite. Miraculously, a mysterious benefactor sends seventeen-year-old Jerusha, an orphan, to college. Her only obligation is to write him progress reports.

DADDY'S GIRL   [695]

WRITTEN BY J. D. LANDIS
Cloth: Morrow
Paper: Bantam
Published: 1984

Jennie, thirteen, beloved only offspring of a "perfect marriage," sees her father passionately kissing a strange woman on a street corner. This novel develops the dramatic contemporary situation with sensitivity and also great wit. A hilarious subplot involves Ms. Richter's Feminist Day School.

DAN ALONE   [696]

WRITTEN BY JOHN ROWE TOWNSEND
Cloth: Lippincott
Published: 1983

In this novel by a popular English writer, a boy's adventure of self-discovery is set in a provincial British city in 1922, as eleven-year-old Dan Lunn tries to straighten out a complex set of family relationships.

THE DARK IS RISING   [697]

WRITTEN BY SUSAN COOPER
ILLUSTRATED BY ALAN COBER
Cloth: McElderry
Paper: Aladdin
Published: 1973

The first in a thrilling quartet of fantasy novels—including *Greenwitch*, *The Grey King*, and *Silver on the Tree*—that deal with Will Stanton, his siblings, the ancient sleepers, a crystal sword, as well as good and, of course, evil. *The Grey King* won both the Newbery and the Carnegie medals.

[832]

237

DARWIN AND THE
VOYAGE OF THE *BEAGLE*   [698]

WRITTEN BY FELICIA LAW
ILLUSTRATED BY JUDY BROOK
Cloth: Deutsch
Published: 1985

A fictionalized account of the voyage to the Galapagos based on the
diaries of Charles Darwin and Robert Fitzroy, the captain of the *Beagle*.
Lucid explanation of how Darwin reached his conclusions.

DEAR MR. HENSHAW   [699]

WRITTEN BY BEVERLY CLEARY
ILLUSTRATED BY PAUL O. ZELINSKY
Cloth: Morrow
Paper: Dell
Published: 1983   PRIZES: NEWBERY MEDAL

A fine novel about that painful issue—divorce. Leigh Botts, who is not
only the new kid in school, but also is adjusting to his parents' divorce,
follows a class assignment and writes to his favorite author.

THE DEVIL IN VIENNA   [700]

WRITTEN BY DORIS ORGEL
Cloth: Dial
Paper: Viking Penguin
Published: 1978

An affecting autobiographical novel, told in diary form, of a Jewish
girl in Vienna and her friend, the daughter of a Nazi, during the
Anschluss.

THE DEVIL'S STORYBOOK   [701]

WRITTEN AND ILLUSTRATED BY NATALIE BABBITT
Cloth: Farrar, Straus
Paper: Sunburst/Farrar, Straus
Published: 1974

The Devil seen in these ten stories is a clever joker who, when restless,
comes to earth and plays dirty tricks on unsuspecting types. The Devil

returns in *The Devil's Other Storybook*. There is interesting moral fiction hidden in the supple prose.

DINOSAURS WALKED HERE AND OTHER STORIES FOSSILS TELL [702]

WRITTEN BY PATRICA LAUBER
Cloth: Bradbury
Published: 1987

If you are past entry-level, cute-and-funny books about dinosaurs, this well-written photo essay is a particularly good discussion of fossil formation and the fossil record.

DIRT BIKE RACER [703]

WRITTEN BY MATT CHRISTOPHER
ILLUSTRATED BY BARRY BOMZER
Cloth: Little, Brown
Paper: Little, Brown
Published: 1979

An action-filled boy's book by a popular writer whose other fiction mostly deals with team sports. Typically, a strong character with an obsession works his way through a problem...just watch his dust.

A DOG ON BARKHAM STREET [704]

WRITTEN BY MARY STOLZ
ILLUSTRATED BY LEONARD SHORTALL
Cloth: Harper
Paper: Harper
Published: 1960

Edward wants a dog, and he wants to be free of Martin Hastings, the bully who lives next door. *The Bully of Barkham Street* reveals Martin's problems clearly. There is also *The Explorer of Barkham Street*. Good books about preadolescent boys, and favorite first books for independent reading.

THE DOG WHO WOULDN'T BE   [705]

WRITTEN BY FARLEY MOWAT
ILLUSTRATED BY PAUL GALDONE
Cloth: Atlantic-Little, Brown
Published: 1957
Adventure fiction by a distinguished Canadian writer.

THE DOLL'S HOUSE   [706]

WRITTEN BY RUMER GODDEN
Paper: Puffin
Published: 1948
The story of Charlotte and Emily's great-grandmother's dollhouse, restored after World War II for the dolls who think of themselves as the Plantagenet family. The heroine is Tottie, the brave farthing doll; the villain is Marchpane, too beautiful to be played with, only admired. A grand girl's book.

DOMINIC   [707]

WRITTEN AND ILLUSTRATED BY WILLIAM STEIG
Cloth: Farrar, Straus
Paper: Sunburst/Farrar, Straus
Published: 1972
Dominic is a hero and a multitalented gent, as well as being a dog. He sets out to see the world, and tests his many talents to wide acclaim.

DRAGONWINGS   [708]

WRITTEN BY LAURENCE YEP
Cloth: Harper
Paper: Harper
Published: 1975   PRIZES: NEWBERY HONOR BOOK
The setting is San Francisco in the first years of the century. A Chinese immigrant father and son build a flying machine shortly after the Wright brothers build theirs. The immigrant perspective on the turbulent period and place is particularly interesting.

THE EGYPT GAME [709]

WRITTEN BY ZILPHA KEATELY SNYDER
ILLUSTRATED BY ALTON RAIBLE

Cloth: Atheneum
Paper: Dell
Published: 1967   PRIZES: NEWBERY HONOR BOOK

April and Melanie are eleven years old and best friends in a small town
in California. They are deeply interested in ancient Egypt, and the
game they invent leads them into real-life criminal investigation.
Inventive plotting and great fun for middle-grade readers.

EINSTEIN ANDERSON, SCIENCE SLEUTH [710]

WRITTEN BY SEYMOUR SIMON
ILLUSTRATED BY FRED WINKOWSKI

Cloth: Viking
Paper: Puffin
Published: 1980

The first in a series of short, lighthearted "mystery" adventures by a
fine science writer for children. Adam "Einstein" Anderson, boy
detective, applies scientific principles to everyday problems. Other
titles include *Einstein Anderson Shocks His Friends*, *Einstein Anderson Makes
Up for Lost Time*, *Einstein Anderson Tells a Comet's Tale*, *Einstein Anderson Goes
to Bat*, *Einstein Anderson Lights Up the Sky*, and *Einstein Anderson Sees Through
the Invisible Man*.

ENCYCLOPEDIA BROWN, BOY DETECTIVE [711]

WRITTEN BY DONALD J. SOBOL
ILLUSTRATED BY LEONARD SHORTALL

Cloth: Lodestar/Morrow
Paper: Bantam
Published: 1963

Idaville's Chief of Police Brown nicknamed his son Leroy "Encyclopedia" because of all the facts he knows and his methodical way of observ-
ing and using his mind. Thus a hero is born. There are several dozen

books available from several publishers in both hardbound and soft-cover. Most of the books consist of ten cases the boy detective solves. Some of the titles are *Encyclopedia Brown and the Case of the Midnight Visitor*, and *Encyclopedia Brown Finds the Clues*. In addition to the series, there is the Encyclopedia Brown Wacky-but-True Series about animals, crimes, spies, sports, and weird and wonderful facts.

EVERY LIVING THING   [712]

WRITTEN BY CYNTHIA RYLANT
ILLUSTRATED BY S. D. SCHINDLER
Cloth: Bradbury
Paper: Aladdin
Published: 1985

A collection of well-written short stories about people whose lives are affected by animals ranging from a stray puppy and other household pets to nesting robins.

THE EYES OF THE AMARYLLIS   [713]

WRITTEN BY NATALIE BABBITT
Cloth: Farrar, Straus
Paper: Sunburst/Farrar, Straus
Published: 1977

A fine novel about Geneva Reade's grandmother, who lives in a cabin by the sea and has been struggling for over thirty years to get a message from the depths.

THE FINDING   [714]

WRITTEN BY NINA BAWDEN
Cloth: Lothrop
Paper: Dell
Published: 1985

Alex is eleven and adopted and unexpectedly has an inheritance that prompts him to run away from home. A short, effective novel from a British writer.

FIVE FALL INTO ADVENTURE [715]

WRITTEN BY ENID BLYTON

Cloth: Atheneum

Published: 1972

This series of British children's books has been popular for several generations. Once you acquire the taste for them they are exciting reading. There are nine other titles available in this country (many more available abroad), including *Five Caught in a Treacherous Plot*, *Five on a Treasure Island*, and *Five Run Away to Danger*.

THE FLEDGLING [716]

WRITTEN BY JANE LANGTON

Cloth: Harper

Paper: Harper

Published: 1980   PRIZES: NEWBERY HONOR BOOK

A fine fantasy, set at Walden Pond, about a girl named Georgie who longs to fly. She meets a mysterious Canada goose, and her dream comes true. Her cousins, Eleanor and Eddie, are prominent in the fantasies *The Astonishing Stereoscope* and *The Diamond in the Window*.

THE FLUNKING OF JOSHUA T. BATES [717]

WRITTEN BY SUSAN SHREVE

ILLUSTRATED BY DIANE de GROAT

Cloth: Knopf

Paper: Scholastic

Published: 1984

Sometimes children, especially boys, are held back in school even if they are smart. To his dismay, Joshua T. Bates was supposed to repeat the whole third grade, but he was lucky enough to have a very sympathetic teacher. Although a touch bibliotherapeutic, this may be helpful to read with some children who are having school troubles.

FOUR DOLLS: IMPUNITY JANE, THE FAIRY DOLL, HOLLY, CANDY FLOSS [718]

WRITTEN BY RUMER GODDEN
ILLUSTRATED BY PAULINE BAYNES
Cloth: Greenwillow
Paper: Dell
Published: 1984

A quartet of well-known and well-loved doll stories in one volume. Each story involves faith, longing, goodwill, and a good heart. "The Story of Holly and Ivy" (available separately in a paperback with illustrations by Barbara Cooney) is also one of the all-time teary Christmas confections.

THE FOX STEALS HOME [719]

WRITTEN BY MATT CHRISTOPHER
ILLUSTRATED BY LARRY JOHNSON
Cloth: Little, Brown
Paper: Little, Brown
Published: 1978

This book happens to be about baseball, and also about coping with divorce, but the author specializes in persuasive stories about boys, sports, and personal challenge. Other titles signal the sports: *Jackrabbit Goalie*, *Johnny No Hit*, *The Kid Who Only Hit Homers*, and *The Dog That Called the Signals*. Four autumn sports titles are in paperback: *Tough to Tackle*, *Ice Magic*, *Touchdown for Tommy*, and *Soccer Halfback*.

FREAKY FRIDAY [720]

WRITTEN BY MARY ROGERS
Cloth: Harper
Paper: Harper
Published: 1972

Imagine that you are Annabel Andrews, a thirteen-year-old girl, and you wake up one Friday—in your mother's body. It's a funny premise, told with great style and conviction. In *A Billion for Boris* the upstairs neighbor has a get-rich-quick scheme for exploiting his television set that shows everything one day in advance. In *Summer Switch* Annabel's twelve-year-old brother, Ben, trades bodies with his father. These books remain fresh, appealing, and popular.

FREDDY AND THE PERILOUS ADVENTURE [721]

WRITTEN BY WALTER R. BROOKS
ILLUSTRATED BY KURT WIESE
Paper: Knopf
Published: 1942

The delightful porcine detective Freddy, who first charmed readers half a century ago, is back in a paperback reissue of eight titles, including *Freddy Goes Camping, Freddy & the Perilous Adventure*, and *Freddy the Politician*. The political maxims are cooperate and organize, and some adults remember with joy the interpretation of R.S.V.P.—Refreshments Served Very Promptly. Although long chapter books, they are popular with younger independent readers.

FROM THE MIXED-UP FILES OF MRS. BASIL E. FRANKWEILER [722]

WRITTEN AND ILLUSTRATED BY E. L. KONIGSBURG
Cloth: Atheneum
Paper: Aladdin, Dell
Published: 1967   PRIZES: NEWBERY MEDAL

Living inside the Metropolitan Museum of Art in New York City turns out to have some unexpected problems for Claudia and Jamie, who try it. A prized comic novel.

GAFFER SAMSON'S LUCK [723]

WRITTEN BY JILL PATON WALSH
ILLUSTRATED BY BROCK COLE
Cloth: Farrar, Straus
Published: 1984

James Lang's family has moved to the Fens, the flatland portion of England, where he is befriended by, and in turn befriends, an elderly eccentric, Gaffer Samson. The fine nature writing, about the Fens themselves and the flooding of the marshes, becomes an integral part of the exciting plot as James searches for the "luck" Gaffer buried some seventy years earlier.

A GATHERING OF DAYS: A NEW ENGLAND GIRL'S JOURNAL, 1830-32 [724]

WRITTEN BY JOAN BLOS

Cloth: Scribners
Paper: Aladdin
Published: 1979   PRIZES: NEWBERY MEDAL

A haunting work of historical fiction, this novel takes the form of a New Hampshire farm girl's diary written in the 1830s, full of the stuff of everyday life. It is both evocative and poignant.

THE GATHERING ROOM [725]

WRITTEN BY COLBY RODOWSKY

Cloth: Farrar, Straus
Paper: Sunburst/Farrar, Straus
Published: 1981

This remarkable novel is set in a graveyard. Mudge's parents cannot cope with the world and become caretakers there, and Mudge has grown up happily in this unusual environment. An aunt wants to bring the family back into the more conventional world.

THE GENIE OF SUTTON PLACE [726]

WRITTEN BY GEORGE SELDEN

Cloth: Farrar, Straus
Paper: Sunburst/Farrar, Straus
Published: 1973

In his father's archaeological notebooks, Tim finds an ancient spell for calling up a genie he thinks he needs because his aunt is insisting that he give up his dog, Sam. The genie turns out to be trapped in a museum nearby. Delightful fantasy for those who would like a little more magic in life.

GENTLE BEN [727]

WRITTEN BY WALT MOREY
ILLUSTRATED BY JOHN SCHOENHERR
Cloth: Dutton
Paper: Avon
Published: 1965

A boy and a bear in Alaska before statehood—friendship and adventure popular for decades, especially with middle-grade boy readers.

GETTING SOMETHING ON MAGGIE MARMELSTEIN [728]

WRITTEN BY MARJORIE WEINMAN SHARMAT
ILLUSTRATED BY BEN SHECTER
Cloth: Harper
Paper: Harper
Published: 1971

The first of a series of books for middle-grade readers about Maggie Marmelstein and her friend Thad Smith. In this one, he is determined to keep her from learning his secret. There are also *Maggie Marmelstein for President*, *Sincerely Yours, Maggie Marmelstein*, and *Mysteriously Yours, Maggie Marmelstein*.

A GIRL CALLED AL [729]

WRITTEN BY CONSTANCE C. GREENE
ILLUSTRATED BY BYRON BARTON
Cloth: Viking
Paper: Dell
Published: 1969

The first of a series of books about Al (Alexandra), bright, fat, nonconformist and vulnerable. The other titles include *I Know You, Al, Your Old Pal, Al, Al(exandra) the Great*, and *Just Plain Al*. Good fiction about real-life growing up.

THE GIRL WHO CRIED FLOWERS AND OTHER TALES [730]

WRITTEN BY JANE YOLEN
ILLUSTRATED BY DAVID PALLADINI
Cloth: Crowell
Paper: Schocken
Published: 1974   PRIZES: NEW YORK TIMES BEST ILLUSTRATED BOOK

A handsomely illustrated collection of five original stories in the folk-loric manner. Themes of love and melancholy, eternally appealing to young romantics, especially girls, run through them.

THE GOLD CADILLAC [731]

WRITTEN BY MILDRED TAYLOR
ILLUSTRATED BY MICHAEL HAYS
Cloth: Dial
Published: 1987

A short, easy-to-read, but very powerful story about a black family living in Ohio in 1950. 'lois's daddy buys a gold Cadillac and tries to take the family home to Mississippi. The proud, loving family and the shock of their harsh encounter with institutionalized racism are skillfully described in a book that stands as fiction and history and is suitable for early-grade children.

THE GOLDEN KEY [732]

WRITTEN BY GEORGE MACDONALD
ILLUSTRATED BY MAURICE SENDAK
Cloth: Farrar, Straus
Paper: Sunburst/Farrar, Straus
Published: 1967; revised edition 1976

This is a handsome edition of one of the classic Victorian fairy tales. Sendak also illustrated MacDonald's *The Light Princess*.

THE GREAT BRAIN   [733]

WRITTEN BY JOHN FITZGERALD
ILLUSTRATED BY MERCER MAYER
Cloth: Dial
Paper: Dell
Published: 1967

The first of a good-natured series of books based on the author's memories of growing up in Utah at the beginning of this century—in awe of his older brother, who was called "The Great Brain." Other titles include *The Great Brain at the Academy*, *The Great Brain Does It Again*, *The Great Brain Reforms*, and *The Return of the Great Brain*. They are especially appealing to boys.

THE GREAT GILLY HOPKINS   [734]

WRITTEN BY KATHERINE PATERSON
Cloth: Crowell
Paper: Harper   PRIZES: NEWBERY HONOR BOOK,
Published: 1978   NATIONAL BOOK AWARD

Gilly Hopkins is a tough, angry girl who has been shunted from foster home to foster home and is determined not to fit in at this new house of misfits and eccentrics. But she does. A fine novel that deals sensitively with issues of racism and class as well as the more obvious problems the plot presents. It is most likely to hold young readers because of the story and Gilly's strong, absolutely believable voice.

HALF MAGIC   [735]

WRITTEN BY EDWARD EAGER
ILLUSTRATED BY N. M. BODECKER
Cloth: Harcourt Brace
Paper: Voyager/HBJ
Published: 1954

Four children double wish on an ancient coin and presto, their dull summer turns into a series of splendid, exciting adventures. Other titles in the series include *Magic or Not?* and *Magic by the Lake*. Good for reading aloud, too.

HANDLES [736]

WRITTEN BY JAN MARK
Cloth: Atheneum
Paper: Puffin
Published: 1985   PRIZES: CARNEGIE PRIZE

A fine British novel (complete with glossary) about Erica Timperley, a girl whose real passion in life is motorcycles. She's sent to a country village on holiday and stumbles into a motorcycle repair shop and a glorious summer of adventure and self-discovery.

HARRIET THE SPY [737]

WRITTEN AND ILLUSTRATED BY LOUISE FITZHUGH
Cloth: Harper
Paper: Dell
Published: 1964

A justly acclaimed modern classic about Harriet, a clever little girl who wants to be a writer, so she watches and takes notes about everything that she sees and hears. Which is fine until her notebooks fall into the wrong hands.

HAZEL RYE [738]

WRITTEN BY VERA AND BILL CLEAVER
Cloth: Lippincott
Paper: Harper
Published: 1983

Hazel is a memorable character, an eleven-year-old determined to make money, who lets a poor family live and work on restoring an orange grove on some property she owns. Hazel's own character undergoes a metamorphosis.

THE HEADLESS CUPID [739]

WRITTEN BY ZILPHA KEATLEY SNYDER
ILLUSTRATED BY ALTON RAIBLE

Cloth: Atheneum
Paper: Dell
Published: 1971   PRIZES: NEWBERY HONOR BOOK

There are several comic novels about the Stanley family. In this one, the children's new stepsister believes in the occult. In *Blair's Nightmare*, they are joined by a very large dog, two escaped convicts, and a school bully. In *The Famous Stanley Kidnapping Case*, they go to Italy. Entertaining reading.

HEAR THE WIND BLOW: AMERICAN FOLK SONGS RETOLD [740]

WRITTEN BY SCOTT R. SANDERS
ILLUSTRATED BY PONDER GOEMBEL

Cloth: Bradbury
Published: 1985

The author proposes stories that explain, with imagination and wit, the origins of twenty well-known American folk songs such as "Yankee Doodle."

THE HERO AND THE CROWN [741]

WRITTEN BY ROBIN MCKINLEY

Cloth: Greenwillow
Paper: Berkeley
Published: 1984   PRIZES: NEWBERY MEDAL

The prize-winning sequel to *The Blue Sword*, a high fantasy involving the adventures of the Damarian king's daughter, Aerin. A favorite with fantasy fans.

HITTY: HER FIRST HUNDRED YEARS [742]

WRITTEN BY RACHEL FIELD
ILLUSTRATED BY DOROTHY P. LATHROP
Cloth: Macmillan
Published: 1929   PRIZES: NEWBERY MEDAL

This is the story of Hitty, a doll who was carved out of a piece of white
ash wood one winter in Maine nearly two hundred years ago. She
belonged to Phoebe Prible, who took her everywhere. It's an old-fashioned historical novel with charm.

THE HOBBIT [743]

WRITTEN BY J. R. R. TOLKIEN
ILLUSTRATED BY MICHAEL HAGUE
Cloth: Houghton Mifflin
Published: 1937

The background volume to the Lord of the Rings Trilogy tells the story
of Bilbo Baggins and the Hobbits. It can be read to or by younger children who may not be ready to absorb the other books.

HOLIDAY TALES OF SHOLOM ALEICHEM [744]

WRITTEN BY SHOLOM ALEICHEM
ILLUSTRATED BY THOMAS diGRAZIA
Cloth: Scribners
Paper: Aladdin
Published: 1979

From the pen of the best-known Yiddish story-teller, here is a collection
of seven stories about Passover, Hanukkah, and other religious holidays as celebrated by the Jews in the shtetl town called Kasrilevka.

HOMESICK: MY OWN STORY   [745]

WRITTEN BY JEAN FRITZ

ILLUSTRATED BY MARGOT TOMES

Cloth: Putnam

Paper: Dell

Published: 1982   PRIZES: NEWBERY HONOR BOOK

A historian who writes for children, Jean Fritz was born and raised in
China. Here she remembers that world and what it was like in the mid-
1920s to be "homesick" for the United States, giving a vivid picture of
life where she actually was. Her return to China after the book was
published in 1982 is described in *China Homecoming*.

THE HOSPITAL BOOK   [746]

WRITTEN BY JAMES HOWE

ILLUSTRATED BY MAL WARSHAW

Cloth: Crown

Paper: Crown

Published: 1981

Here is a detailed introduction to both routine and unusual hospital
procedures for older children. It is illustrated with black-and-white
photographs showing everything from the insertion of intravenous
tubes to special oxygen tanks. The text is straightforward and very
informative.

THE HOUSE OF DIES DREAR   [747]

WRITTEN BY VIRGINIA HAMILTON

Cloth: Macmillan

Paper: Collier

Published: 1968

A lushly written story about a contemporary black family that buys the
house in Ohio in which, a century earlier, Dies Drear and two slaves he
had been hiding were murdered. (The house was a stop on the Under-
ground Railroad.) At its simplest level this is complex but entertaining
mystery, yet it can be read as a parable. In the sequel, *The Mystery of
Drear House,* the Small family deals with hidden treasure.

THE HOUSE WITH A CLOCK IN ITS WALLS   [748]

WRITTEN BY JOHN BELLAIRS
ILLUSTRATED BY EDWARD GOREY
Cloth: Dial
Paper: Dell
Published: 1973

The first of a mystery trilogy about a boy and his uncle, who is a wizard, illustrated by an artist whose style is, in itself, mysterious. One of the most popular mystery series for children. The other titles are *The Figure in the Shadows* and *The Letter, the Witch, and the Ring.*

HOW IT FEELS TO BE ADOPTED   [749]

WRITTEN AND ILLUSTRATED BY JILL KREMENTZ
Cloth: Knopf
Paper: Knopf
Published: 1982

The universal curiosity of adopted children and many of their special feelings and interests are reflected in first-person accounts from a group of nineteen youngsters from eight to sixteen whose pictures are shown with their stories. This reassuringly low-key book is of special interest to children, family, and friends of adoptive families.

HOW IT FEELS WHEN A PARENT DIES   [750]

WRITTEN AND ILLUSTRATED BY JILL KREMENTZ
Cloth: Knopf
Paper: Knopf
Published: 1981

Some eighteen children of different ages and backgrounds talk about the death of a parent—how it felt, how it feels. Their health and well-being in the photographs is subtle reinforcement to the implicit message that life goes on.

HOW IT FEELS WHEN PARENTS DIVORCE [751]

WRITTEN AND ILLUSTRATED BY JILL KREMENTZ
Cloth: Knopf
Paper: Knopf
Published: 1984

A group of nineteen boys and girls from eight to sixteen years old talk about their widely varying experiences of divorce in their own families.

HOW TO EAT FRIED WORMS [752]

WRITTEN BY THOMAS ROCKWELL
ILLUSTRATED BY EMILY McCULLY
Cloth: Watts
Paper: Dell
Published: 1973

Billy accepted the bet and now he has to eat fifteen worms in fifteen days. The story moves along pell-mell, in short, boisterous chapters, as Billy comes up with some pretty inventive ways to get the wigglers down. Will he succeed? This is a book that holds the attention of even the most restless listeners and readers.

HOW WAS I BORN? A PHOTOGRAPHIC STORY OF REPRODUCTION AND BIRTH FOR CHILDREN [753]

WRITTEN BY LENNART NILSSON
Cloth: Delacorte
Published: 1975

Some of the famous photographs of fetal development by the photographer of the adult book *A Child Is Born* are used in this explanation of conception and birth for children.

255

HOW YOSSI BEAT THE EVIL URGE   [754]

WRITTEN BY MIRIAM CHAIKIN
ILLUSTRATED BY PETRA MATHERS
Cloth: Harper
Published: 1983

The first of a series of books about Yossi, a yeshiva boy in Brooklyn with ordinary problems, that are funny in a believable way and are solved with piety and charm. Other titles include *Yossi Asks the Angels for Help* and *Yossi Tries to Help God.*

THE HUNDRED DRESSES   [755]

WRITTEN BY ELEANOR ESTES
ILLUSTRATED BY LOUIS SLOBODKIN
Cloth: Harcourt Brace
Paper: Voyager/HBJ
Published: 1944   PRIZES: NEWBERY HONOR BOOK

The story of Wanda Petronski, the little Polish girl whose classmates did not believe she had a hundred dresses, has been a classic for several generations, teaching quiet, painful lessons of tolerance and dignity. The pale, delicate illustrations are memorable, too. The writing is simple enough for younger readers to manage independently and so powerful that they may never forget it.

I, JUAN DE PAREJA   [756]

WRITTEN BY ELIZABETH BORTON DE TREVINO
Cloth: Farrar, Straus
Paper: Sunburst/Farrar, Straus
Published: 1965   PRIZES: NEWBERY MEDAL

This powerful historical novel takes the form of the autobiography of Juan de Pareja, the son of a black African woman and a white Spaniard who was willed to the Spanish artist Velazquez. Their lifelong relationship evolved toward equality and friendship. Challenging but worth it.

INCOGNITO MOSQUITO, PRIVATE INSECTIVE [757]

WRITTEN BY E. A. HASS
ILLUSTRATED BY DON MADDEN
Paper: Random House
Published: 1985

The world's greatest "insective" stars in a series of short, pun-infested books in which the crimes he sleuths are less serious than those he launches against the language. Hilarious. The companion titles include *Incognito Mosquito Flies Again!* Readers have to be old enough to pun.

[754]

THE INCREDIBLE JOURNEY [758]

WRITTEN BY SHEILA BURNFORD
ILLUSTRATED BY CARL BURGER
Cloth: Atlantic-Little, Brown
Paper: Bantam
Published: 1961

This immensely popular story tells about three loyal house pets, two dogs and a Siamese cat, who follow "their" family through many an adventure to their new home.

INDIAN CHIEFS [759]

WRITTEN BY RUSSELL FREEDMAN
Cloth: Holiday
Published: 1987

A good introduction to six of the great American Indian chiefs who led their people against the encroaching pioneers—Red Cloud, Santana, Quanah Parker, Washakie, Joseph, and Sitting Bull—illustrated with memorable historic photographs.

257

THE INDIAN IN THE CUPBOARD   [760]

WRITTEN BY LYNN REID BANKS
ILLUSTRATED BY BROCK COLE
Cloth: Doubleday
Paper: Avon
Published: 1981

Omri, a lonely little English boy, is given an old cupboard. The key his mother digs up to unlock it has magic powers, so that when Omri puts a miniature plastic Indian in the cupboard and locks the door, the Indian is magically brought to life. His adventures, complete with his bow and arrow, teach Omri a great deal about values. A thrilling book in its scope and style. The sequel, *The Return of the Indian*, in which Omri's friends are caught up in war, is equally rewarding.

IN THE YEAR OF THE BOAR AND JACKIE ROBINSON   [761]

WRITTEN BY BETTE BAO LORD
ILLUSTRATED BY MARC SIMONT
Cloth: Harper
Paper: Harper
Published: 1984

Shirley Temple Wong arrives in Brooklyn able to speak only two words of English. She works her way into the American dream via the classic route—baseball—turning into a fan and a player the same season Jackie Robinson joined the Dodgers. It is an old-fashioned middle-grade story, told humorously and well. The illustrations are stylish and witty.

I SHOULD WORRY, I SHOULD CARE   [762]

WRITTEN BY MIRIAM CHAIKIN
ILLUSTRATED BY RICHARD EGIELSKI
Cloth: Harper
Published: 1979

A trilogy of appealing novels about Molly, a Jewish-American girl growing up in the Depression as Hitler is rising to power in Germany. The other titles are *Finders Weepers* and *Getting Even*. The illustrations are particularly evocative.

ISLAND OF THE BLUE DOLPHINS [763]

WRITTEN BY SCOTT O'DELL

Cloth: Houghton Mifflin
Paper: Dell
Published: 1960   PRIZES: NEWBERY MEDAL

A memorable adventure and coming-of-age novel about an Indian girl who spends eighteen years alone on a rocky island off the coast of California in the early nineteenth century. *Zia* is the sequel. A popular title with older grade-school children of both sexes.

IT'S LIKE THIS, CAT [764]

WRITTEN BY EMILY CHENEY NEVILLE

Cloth: Harper
Paper: Harper
Published: 1963   PRIZES: NEWBERY MEDAL

A dandy coming-of-age novel about Dave, who is fourteen and lives near Gramercy Park in New York City. He has family troubles, acquires a cat, and is launched into adventures in the neighborhood. The absence of drugs as a fact of life gives the story an old-fashioned quality, but Dave's relationship with his parents rings true.

JACOB TWO-TWO AND THE DINOSAUR [765]

WRITTEN BY MORDECAI RICHLER
ILLUSTRATED BY NORMAN EYOLFSON

Cloth: Knopf
Published: 1987

Jacob Two-Two (who always says things twice) is brought a tiny green lizard for a pet. Dippy turns into a dinosaur who eventually has the whole Canadian government on his tail, as it were. Hilarious farce, with political commentary. *Jacob Two-Two and the Hooded Fang*, an independent and fine earlier story about Jacob, is in paperback.

[761]

259

JAMES AND THE GIANT PEACH   [766]

WRITTEN BY ROALD DAHL
ILLUSTRATED BY NANCY EKHOLM BURKERT
Cloth: Knopf
Published: 1961

A fantasy about how James escapes from dreary daily life with his two aunts by developing a giant peach. This is one of those scary, wonderful books, best read aloud the first time, that lasts a lifetime and ranks among the better novels of the century.

A JAR OF DREAMS   [767]

WRITTEN BY YOSHIKO UCHIDA
Cloth: McElderry
Paper: Aladdin
Published: 1981

The first of three novels about Rinko, a Japanese-American girl growing up in Berkeley, California, in the 1930s. The extended family, the conflicting cultural influences, and the warmth of the characters are appealing. The other titles are *The Best Bad Things* and *The Happiest Ending*.

JELLY BELLY   [768]

WRITTEN BY ROBERT KIMMEL SMITH
ILLUSTRATED BY BOB JONES
Cloth: Delacorte
Paper: Dell
Published: 1981

The kids tease Ned because he's so fat and call him Jelly Belly, so his family sends him off to diet camp. His bunkmate turns out to be a cheater, but Ned learns a lot over that summer about life as well as diet. This is good fiction for upper-grade readers, not just bibliotherapy.

JOHNNY TREMAIN   [769]

WRITTEN BY ESTHER FORBES
Cloth: Houghton Mifflin
Paper: Dell
Published: 1943   PRIZES: NEWBERY MEDAL

It's 1775 in Boston, and after a tragic accident in the silversmith's shop, the young apprentice becomes involved in political activity leading to the American Revolution. A popular favorite for generations in book and film form.

JOURNEY TO AMERICA   [770]

WRITTEN BY SONIA LEVITIN
ILLUSTRATED BY CHARLES ROBINSON
Cloth: Atheneum
Paper: Aladdin
Published: 1970

The compelling fictionalized story of how one Jewish family fled from Hitler's Germany and managed to get to Switzerland and eventually to the United States.

JULIA AND THE HAND OF GOD   [771]

WRITTEN BY ELEANOR CAMERON
ILLUSTRATED BY GAIL OWENS
Cloth: Dutton
Published: 1977

The first of three old-fashioned girl's novels about Julia, growing up in Berkeley, California, during World War I, in the custody of her aunt and grandmother. The two other titles are *That Julia Redfern* and *Julia's Magic*. For middle-grade readers who liked *Betsy, Tacy*.

JULIE OF THE WOLVES [772]

WRITTEN BY JEAN CRAIGHEAD GEORGE
ILLUSTRATED BY JOHN SCHOENHERR
Cloth: Harper
Paper: Harper
Published: 1972   PRIZES: NEWBERY MEDAL

The memorable and very exciting story of Julie, a thirteen-year-old
Eskimo girl, lost on the tundra, who is protected by a wolf pack.
Another book by the same author, *Water Sky,* also deals with the
Eskimos.

JUMP! THE ADVENTURES OF BRER RABBIT [773]

WRITTEN BY VAN DYKE PARKS AND MALCOLM JONES
ILLUSTRATED BY M. BARRY MOSER
Cloth: Harcourt Brace
Published: 1986

[773]

A cheerful retelling of the Uncle Remus stories by a Southern com-
poser and writer, with truly memorable watercolor illustrations by a
distinguished artist best known for his lavish woodcut illustrations. The
just-as-good sequel is *Jump Again!*

THE JUNGLE BOOK [774]

WRITTEN BY RUDYARD KIPLING
ILLUSTRATED BY MICHAEL FOREMAN
Cloth: Viking
Published: 1896

Here are the thrilling stories of Mowgli, the man cub, raised in the
jungle, and of other creatures including Rikki-Tikki-Tavi, the mon-
goose. As with the *Just So Stories,* these perfect-for-bedtime tales deserve
to be read aloud the first time if only for the pleasure of watching children hear the language. There are dozens of editions of individual
stories with lavish illustrations, and there are paperback editions of
the second volume as well.

THE JUNIPER TREE [775]

WRITTEN BY JACOB AND WHILHELM GRIMM
ILLUSTRATED BY MAURICE SENDAK
Cloth: Farrar, Straus
Paper: Sunburst/Farrar, Straus
Published: 1973   PRIZES: NEW YORK TIMES BEST ILLUSTRATED BOOK

This two-volume set of twenty-seven stories by the Brothers Grimm was translated with scrupulous care and tact by Lore Segal and Randall Jarrell and illustrated with equal grace by Maurice Sendak. It's a labor of love that shows no age. The stories are by turn heartbreaking and terrifying, gentle and sharp, poignant and funny. If you want one edition of Grimm, to read or to read aloud, this is the most satisfying one available.

JUST SO STORIES [776]

WRITTEN BY RUDYARD KIPLING
ILLUSTRATED BY MICHAEL FOREMAN
Cloth: Viking
Published: 1902

Listen, O Best Beloved, to the wondrous tales of animals—the little elephant child, the whale, the leopard, the cat, and others. Listen carefully, for these stories should be heard first and read independently later. They are among the greatest short fictions for children in the language and fairly roll off the reader's tongue. There are many picture book editions of individual stories; some recent ones are packaged with audio- or videotapes as well. This 1987 edition, illustrated by a distinguished British artist, is appealing and inclusive.

KATIE JOHN [777]

WRITTEN BY MARY CALHOUN
ILLUSTRATED BY PAUL FRAME
Cloth: Harper
Paper: Harper
Published: 1960

A series of novels, mostly for middle-grade girl readers, about Katie John that follow the heroine from the age of ten, when the lonely child moves into a big old house, on into junior high school, when she discovers that romance isn't like the novels she reads. The other titles are *Depend on Katie John*, *Honestly, Katie John*, and *Katie John and Heathcliff*.

THE KID FROM TOMKINSVILLE   [778]

WRITTEN BY JOHN R. TUNIS
Cloth: Harcourt Brace
Paper: Voyager/HBJ
Published: 1940

Under the general title "Baseball Diamonds," a series of splendid sports novels are being reissued. They include *World Series*, *Keystone Kids*, and *Rookie of the Year*. The writing is always deft, the baseball is sensational even to nonfans.

KIDNAPPED: BEING THE MEMOIRS OF THE ADVENTURES OF DAVID BALFOUR IN THE YEAR 1751   [779]

WRITTEN BY ROBERT LOUIS STEVENSON
ILLUSTRATED BY N. C. WYETH
Cloth: Scribners
Published: 1913

One of the classic stories of adventure and self-realization about a sixteen-year-old orphan boy who becomes involved with the Scottish Highlanders fighting British rule. This reissue of the handsome old edition is a favorite, but there are others available in both hard and soft cover.

KING MATT THE FIRST   [780]

WRITTEN BY JANUSZ KORCZAK
Cloth: Farrar, Straus
Paper: Michael di Capua/Farrar, Straus
Published: 1985

This fable, first published in 1923 in Poland, is widely known in Europe but is only recently published in the United States. It tells the utopian tale of young Matt, who becomes king on his father's death and undertakes the dramatic reform of sending adults to school and allowing children to run the country. Exciting fiction. This is a book American children are just finding.

THE KING'S FIFTH [781]
WRITTEN BY SCOTT O'DELL
ILLUSTRATED BY SAMUEL BRYANT
Cloth: Houghton Mifflin
Published: 1966

A brisk historical novel about Esteban, a seventeen-year-old mapmaker in the Spanish colonies in the seventeenth century. He is charged with murder and withholding the king's gold.

KITTY IN THE MIDDLE [782]
WRITTEN BY JUDY DELTON
Cloth: Houghton Mifflin
Paper: Dell
Published: 1979

The first in a series of books about a girl growing up in the 1940s in a Roman Catholic family in the Midwest. Other titles, which carry her into high school, include *Kitty in the Summer* and *Kitty in the High School*.

KNEEKNOCK RISE [783]
WRITTEN AND ILLUSTRATED BY NATALIE BABBITT
Cloth: Farrar, Straus
Paper: Sunburst/Farrar, Straus
Published: 1970   PRIZES: NEWBURY HONOR BOOK

The villagers of Instep think that Kneeknock Rise (which is really little more than a hill) has mysterious properties. They think a fearsome creature they call a Megrimum lives at the top of the Rise and is the source of strange sounds on stormy nights. Fine and persuasive, a little bit funny, and a great deal wise.

THE LAND I LOST: ADVENTURES OF A BOY IN VIETNAM [784]

WRITTEN BY QUANG NHUONG NHUONG
ILLUSTRATED BY VO-DINH MAI

Cloth: Harper
Paper: Harper
Published: 1982

This is the true story of the author's childhood in a Vietnamese hamlet, told with affectionate details of social customs and nature. It is one of the few easily obtainable books for children about Vietnam or Vietnamese culture.

THE LANDMARK HISTORY OF THE AMERICAN PEOPLE [785]

WRITTEN BY DANIEL J. BOORSTIN

Cloth: Random House
Paper: Random House
Published: Vol. 1, Vol. 2, 1970; revised 1987

This two-volume boxed reissue of an accessible celebratory history text for young readers is a good, serious birthday or occasion present for a middle- to upper-grade child who is already interested in history and has mastered the Jean Fritz biographies or other more narrowly focused titles. Other Landmark titles on specific aspects of American history are also available in paperback.

LASSIE, COME HOME [786]

WRITTEN BY ERIC KNIGHT

Paper: Yearling, Laurel Leaf
Published: 1940

One of the most enduring dog stories, set in the wilds of Yorkshire, it features the best collie ever.

THE LAST OF THE MOHICANS   [787]

WRITTEN BY JAMES FENIMORE COOPER
ILLUSTRATED BY N. C. WYETH
Cloth: Scribners
Published: 1826

Let us not discuss the prose or politics of Cooper (both of which have been judged often and found wanting), but suspend judgment and dive back into the second of the Leatherstocking Tales about that quintessential man of the frontier, Natty Bumppo. It's 1757, in the middle of the French and Indian War. The N. C. Wyeth edition is available in hardcover; other volumes of the tales, including *The Deerslayer*, are available in various paperback editions.

LEARNING TO SAY GOOD-BYE: WHEN A PARENT DIES   [788]

WRITTEN BY EDA LeSHAN
ILLUSTRATED BY PAUL GIAVANOPOULOS
Cloth: Macmillan
Paper: Avon
Published: 1976

This book is written like a conversation with children about some of the feelings they might encounter if they had to deal with the death of a parent. The author has a compassionate but frank tone. Among her other thoughtful books about problems are *What Makes Me Feel This Way: Growing Up with Human Emotions* and *What's Going to Happen to Me: When Parents Separate or Divorce*.

THE LEMMING CONDITION   [789]

WRITTEN BY ALAN ARKIN
ILLUSTRATED BY JOAN SANDIN
Cloth: Harper
Published: 1976

An allegory about Bubber, an unlemminglike lemming who persists in asking questions and considering the consequences. A good choice for philosophical young readers.

THE LIGHT IN THE ATTIC [790]

WRITTEN AND ILLUSTRATED BY SHEL SILVERSTEIN
Cloth: Harper
Published: 1981

This immensely popular collection of poetry, verse, and illustration is by turns happy, sad, funny, and affecting. It is idiosyncratic, but maintains a firm moral stance and appeals to all ages.

A LITTLE DESTINY [791]

WRITTEN BY VERA AND BILL CLEAVER
Cloth: Lothrop
Paper: Bantam
Published: 1979

A powerful novel set in Georgia in the early part of this century in which a fourteen-year-old girl turns grief over her father's death into desire for revenge.

THE LITTLE PRINCE [792]

WRITTEN AND ILLUSTRATED BY ANTOINE de SAINT EXUPERY
Cloth: Harcourt Brace
Paper: Voyager/HBJ
Published: 1943

This mystical fairy tale story book about a little prince who comes from another planet has been an adult cult title almost since publication and is most often read in French classes.

A LITTLE PRINCESS [793]

WRITTEN BY FRANCES HODGSON BURNETT
ILLUSTRATED BY TASHA TUDOR
Cloth: Lippincott
Paper: Harper
Published: 1905

Sara Crewe falls onto hard times and adventures after being ill treated in her own boarding school. She is, of course, rescued and brought to high estate by a rich Indian gentleman. For many years this was the only edition available in the United States. But, as with all the other Burnett novels, the copyright has expired and numerous editions in hard and soft cover have appeared. Avoid clumsy and unnecessary abridgments.

LITTLE WOMEN [794]

WRITTEN BY LOUISA MAY ALCOTT
ILLUSTRATED BY JESSIE WILCOX SMITH
Cloth: Little, Brown
Paper: Penguin/Bantam/Signet
Published: 1868

The Marsh girls—Meg, Jo, Beth, and Amy—and how they grew in Massachussetts during the Civil War. More than a century later, this is still one of the most affecting and powerful novels written for girls, although contemporary parents may wish to give some running commentary about the narrow definition of proper female roles. The sequels include *Jo's Boys and How They Turned Out* and, of course, *Little Men* and *Rose in Bloom*. Because the titles are in the public domain there are many editions: watch for clumsy abridgments. Several of the paperback editions have interesting introductions by contemporary writers.

LOOK TO THE NIGHT SKY: AN INTRODUCTION TO STAR WATCHING [795]

WRITTEN BY SEYMOUR SIMON
ILLUSTRATED BY JAN BRETT
Cloth: Viking
Paper: Puffin
Published: 1977

A good introduction to star watching, which can turn into a lifetime's avocation.

THE MAID OF THE NORTH: FEMINIST FOLK TALES FROM AROUND THE WORLD [796]

WRITTEN BY ETHEL JOHNSTON PHELPS
ILLUSTRATED BY LLOYD BLOOM

Cloth: Holt
Paper: Holt
Published: 1981

A good collection of stories from different cultures and historical periods that emphasize interesting and clever heroines. Good to read aloud or browse in.

MAN O' WAR [797]

WRITTEN BY WALTER FARLEY

Cloth: Random House
Paper: Random House
Published: 1962

A novel based on the life of the great racehorse, full of information about the racing world and the excitement of thoroughbreds.

MARY POPPINS [798]

WRITTEN BY P. L. TRAVERS
ILLUSTRATED BY MARY SHEPARD

Cloth: Harcourt Brace
Paper: Voyager/HBJ
Published: 1934; first revised edition, 1964

The first in the perennially popular series of books about the British nanny with magical abilities who arrives at the Banks family home on Cherry Tree Lane with the east wind. Other titles in the series include *Mary Poppins Comes Back*, *Mary Poppins in the Park*, and *Mary Poppins Opens the Door.* The revised edition deletes the unfortunate explicit racism of the original. The movie version is not true to the stories, which have elements of mysticism and make subtle references to classic texts.

THE MASTER PUPPETEER [799]

WRITTEN BY KATHERINE PATERSON
ILLUSTRATED BY HARU WELLS
Cloth: Crowell
Paper: Harper
Published: 1976   PRIZES: NATIONAL BOOK AWARD

[798]

This is an historical novel set mostly inside the Hanaza puppet theater in eighteenth-century Osaka, Japan, during a period of famine. Jiro, the son of a starving puppetmaker, runs away from home and apprentices himself in the theater. It is extraordinarily well written and compelling, filled with detail. The author has written two other novels set in Japanese historical periods—*Of Nightingales That Weep* and *The Sign of the Chrysanthemum*—as well many other fine books set in the United States.

M. C. HIGGINS, THE GREAT [800]

WRITTEN BY VIRGINIA HAMILTON
Cloth: Macmillan
Paper: Collier
Published: 1974   PRIZES: NEWBERY MEDAL

A remarkable novel about thirteen-year-old M. C. Higgins. The black boy helps care for the younger children and dreams of escape for himself and his family from poverty and the slow-moving slag heap left from the strip mine. He fantasizes unrealistic possibilities and then seizes some real opportunities. The author's language is rich and subtle, demanding and worthwhile.

MEMO: TO MYSELF WHEN I HAVE
A TEEN-AGE KID [801]

WRITTEN BY CAROL SNYDER
Cloth: Coward
Paper: Pacer/Putnam
Published: 1983

Karen Berman, a suburban thirteen-year-old with cute younger siblings and a father who is the class mother, can't imagine that anyone has ever felt the way she does now (rotten) until her mother shows Karen the diary she had kept at the same age. For preadolescent angst.

THE MILL GIRLS: LUCY LARCOM, HARRIET HANSON ROBINSON, SARAH G. BAGLEY [802]

WRITTEN BY BERNICE SELDEN

Cloth: Atheneum

Published: 1983

Stories of three women who, for part of their youth in the mid-nineteenth century, worked in the textile mills of Lowell, Massachusetts. Larcom went west and became a writer, Hanson became an abolitionist and later a suffragette, and Bagley was the first woman telegraph operator in the United States. Fascinating social history.

MINN OF THE MISSISSIPPI [803]

WRITTEN AND ILLUSTRATED BY HOLLING C. HOLLING

Cloth: Houghton Mifflin

Paper: Houghton Mifflin

Published: 1951

This amazing book that follows a turtle down the great river is a deserved classic of nature writing and illustration. The detailed drawings and engaging text remain fresh and absorbing.

MISHMASH [804]

WRITTEN BY MOLLY CONE

ILLUSTRATED BY LEONARD SHORTALL

Cloth: Houghton Mifflin

Paper: Archway

Published: 1962

The first of a series of books about a boy named Pete and his dog, Mishmash, growing up in a small town. In the first book, Pete finds a home for his dog and gives his teacher a super present. Other titles include *Mishmash and the Big Fat Problem* and *Mishmash and the Robot*.

MITZI'S HONEYMOON
WITH NANA POTTS   [805]

WRITTEN BY BARBARA WILLIAMS

ILLUSTRATED BY EMILY ARNOLD McCULLY

Cloth: Dutton

Paper: Dell

Published: 1983

Mitzi McAllister is stuck at home with her new stepfamily, including a
startling new grandmother, Nana Potts. One of a good-humored series
about a new or blended family. Other titles include *Mitzi and Frederick the
Great*, *Mitzi and the Terrible Tyrannosaurus Rex*, and *Tell the Truth, Marly Dee*.

THE MOFFATS   [806]

WRITTEN BY ELEANOR ESTES

ILLUSTRATED BY LOIS SLOBODKIN

Cloth: Harcourt Brace

Paper: Voyager/HBJ

Published: 1941

A classic family growing-up series. Other titles include *The Middle
Moffat*, *Rufus M.*, and *The Moffat Museum*.

MOM, THE WOLF MAN AND ME   [807]

WRITTEN BY NORMA KLEIN

Cloth: Pantheon

Paper: Avon

Published: 1972

Brett's mother never has been married, and sometimes her boyfriends
stay over. All and all it's an unusual family, but one that likes it that way.
A novel that was controversial when it first appeared and remains a
popular favorite with older children.

THE MOUSE AND THE MOTORCYCLE   [808]

WRITTEN BY BEVERLY CLEARY
ILLUSTRATED BY LOUIS DARLING
Cloth: Morrow
Paper: Dell
Published: 1965

The first of three engaging books about Ralph, a mouse who is given a toy motorcycle and finds it is the vehicle of his dreams. In *Runaway Ralph*, the generation gap intrudes, and in *Ralph S. Mouse* (illustrated by Paul O. Zelinsky), the hero goes to school.

MRS. ABERCORN AND THE BUNCE BOYS   [809]

WRITTEN BY LISA FOSBURGH
ILLUSTRATED BY JULIE DOWNING
Cloth: Four Winds
Paper: Dell
Published: 1986

Crotchety, patrician, fascinating Mrs. Abercorn gets mixed up with Otis and Will Bunce, who are fatherless and adrift in their new home while their mother is at work. An appealing novel about adjustments and friendships across generations.

MRS. FRISBY AND THE RATS OF NIMH   [810]

WRITTEN BY ROBERT C. O'BRIEN
ILLUSTRATED BY ZENA BERNSTEIN
Cloth: Atheneum
Paper: Aladdin
Published: 1971   PRIZES: NEWBERY MEDAL

A prize-winning novel about Mrs. Frisby, a widow mouse, and the rats of NIMH (National Institute of Mental Health), a well-educated group who are about to set up their own culture. The sequel is *Rasco and the Rats of NIMH*, completed by the author's daughter, Jane Conly.

MY BROTHER SAM IS DEAD [811]

WRITTEN BY JAMES LINCOLN COLLIER
AND CHRISTOPHER COLLIER
Cloth: Four Winds
Paper: Scholastic
Published: 1974   PRIZES: NEWBERY HONOR BOOK

The Revolutionary War has come to the Tory town of Redding, Connecticut, and this remarkably rich novel details how it affects the Meekers, a nonpartisan family. One of the most sophisticated and powerful historical novels written for young readers.

MY FRIEND THE VAMPIRE [812]

WRITTEN BY ANGELA SOMMER-BODENBURG
ILLUSTRATED BY AMELIE GLIENKE
Cloth: Dial
Paper: Minstrel
Published: 1984

Rudolph the vampire lands on the windowsill of Tony's bedroom in the apartment house where he lives and makes friends with the normally terrified nine-year-old boy. Their comic adventures continue in *The Vampire Moves In* and *The Vampire Takes a Trip*.

MY SIDE OF THE MOUNTAIN [813]

WRITTEN AND ILLUSTRATED BY JEAN ASIGHEAD GEORGE
Cloth: Dutton
Paper: Dutton
Published: 1959   PRIZES: NEWBERY HONOR BOOK

The author, a distinguished nature writer, skillfully blends themes of nature, courage, curiosity, and independence in this story of a boy who builds himself a tree house.

"NATIONAL VELVET" [814]

WRITTEN BY ENID BAGNOLD
ILLUSTRATED BY TED LEWIN
Cloth: Morrow
Paper: Archway
Published: 1935, reissued 1985

The Golden Anniversary edition of the story of Velvet Brown, her pie-bald horse, and their championship race has black-and-white as well as color illustrations. Children today may not know why their parents and grandparents think this book is about a grown-up actress named Elizabeth Taylor, but it's a terrific story nevertheless.

THE NIGHT JOURNEY [815]

WRITTEN BY KATHRYN LASKY
ILLUSTRATED BY TRINA SCHART HYMAN
Cloth: Viking
Paper: Puffin
Published: 1981

Nana Sashie enjoys her afternoon visits with thirteen-year-old Rachel, and eventually confides in her the story of her Jewish family's escape from Czarist Russia. Moving and well written. Good to read aloud, too.

NOBODY'S BABY NOW [816]

WRITTEN BY CAROL LEA BENJAMIN
Cloth: Macmillan
Paper: Berkley
Published: 1984

Olivia is a pudgy teenager in Manhattan who is just beginning to deal with her own life when her grandmother, who has had a stroke, moves in. In assuming some responsibilities for her grandmother's care Olivia also has a chance to get to know her.

NOBODY'S FAMILY IS GOING TO CHANGE [817]

WRITTEN AND ILLUSTRATED BY LOUISE FITZHUGH

Cloth: Farrar, Straus
Paper: Sunburst/Farrar, Straus
Published: 1974

This is a compelling story about expectations, stereotypes, and family pressures. Emma wants to be a lawyer, but it is her brother, Willie, who feels the career pressure. Moreover, Willie wants to dance on the stage like Uncle Dipsey. The Sheridan family is black, but the problems are universal. The novel was the basis of the play *The Tap Dance Kid*.

THE NOONDAY FRIENDS [818]

WRITTEN BY MARY STOLZ
ILLUSTRATED BY LOUIS S. GLANZMAN

Cloth: Harper
Paper: Harper
Published: 1965   PRIZES: NEWBERY HONOR BOOK

A novel about school and family life in Greenwich Village as experienced by two eleven-year-old girls. Life was somewhat simpler in the olden days, but preadolescence remains the same.

NOTHING'S FAIR IN FIFTH GRADE [819]

WRITTEN BY BARTHE DeCLEMENTS

Cloth: Viking
Paper: Scholastic
Published: 1981

Early adolescence is funny, sad, awkward, and consistently interesting, no less so if you are like Elsie, the "fat girl" in her class. The follow-up story, about "Bad Helen," is *Sixth Grade Can Really Kill You.* Very popular series.

THE NOT-JUST-ANYBODY FAMILY   [820]

WRITTEN BY BETSY BYARS

Cloth: Delacorte
Paper: Dell
Published: 1986

The first of a trio of books about the Blossom family, beset by goodwill and bizarre mishaps. Mother is away on the rodeo circut and Pap managed to get arrested for dumping 2,147 soda cans; Junior tried to fly and broke two legs. Adventures continue in *The Blossoms Meet the Vulture Lady* and *The Blossoms and the Green Phantom*.

THE NUTCRACKER   [821]

WRITTEN BY E. T. A. HOFFMANN
ILLUSTRATED BY MAURICE SENDAK

Cloth: Crown
Published: 1984   PRIZES: NEW YORK TIMES BEST ILLUSTRATED BOOK

Here is the ultimate *Nutcracker*. This text is the original story translated carefully by Ralph Manheim—far more complex than the familiar ballet versions such as the one George Balanchine choreographed for the New York City Ballet. The lavish illustrations derive from the Seattle Ballet's *Nutcracker*, which was designed by Maurice Sendak. A stunning and exciting book, it is much too complex for most youngsters going to the ballet for the very first time.

THE NUTCRACKER: A STORY AND A BALLET   [822]

WRITTEN BY ELLEN SWITZER

Cloth: Atheneum
Published: 1985

Three stories in one: the author's version of E. T. A. Hoffmann's tale, a history of the ballet, and finally, the New York City Ballet version choreographed by George Balanchine, which is so well known to so many families. This fits rather neatly between the simple story book of the ballet and the Sendak version of the Hoffmann tale.

NUTTY FOR PRESIDENT [823]

WRITTEN BY DEAN HUGHES
ILLUSTRATED BY BLANCHE SIMS
Cloth: Atheneum
Paper: Bantam
Published: 1981

The first of the books about Nutty, a boy genius whose real name is
William Bilks. Here he generally disrupts a student council election.
Other titles in the popular series include *Nutty and the Case of the Master-
mind*, *Nutty and the Case of the Ski-Slope Spy*, and *Nutty Can't Miss*.

OLYMPIC GAMES IN
ANCIENT GREECE [824]

WRITTEN BY SHIRLEY GLUBOK AND ALFRED TAMARIN
Cloth: Harper
Paper: Harper
Published: 1976

This is a good introduction to the history of the Greek Olympics, full of
details about events such as chariot races, which have disappeared, as
well as running and jumping events, which are very evident in the
modern games.

ONE-EYED CAT [825]

WRITTEN BY PAULA FOX
Published: 1984
Cloth: Bradbury
Paper: Dell   PRIZES: NEWBERY HONOR BOOK

A powerful novel about maturation. Ned, a rather isolated boy, has an
invalid mother and a remote father. Ned believes he shot out the eye of
a wild cat and must come to terms with the guilt he cannot express.
The writing is simple and eloquent, which increases the impact of
the story.

ONION JOHN   [826]

WRITTEN BY JOSEPH KRUMGOLD
ILLUSTRATED BY SYMEON SHIMIN
Cloth: Crowell
Published: 1959   PRIZES: NEWBERY MEDAL

The story of a friendship between a twelve-year-old boy and an immigrant handyman that is misunderstood by well-intentioned townspeople. A didactic but well-written novel.

THE OXFORD BOOK OF POETRY FOR CHILDREN   [827]

COMPILED BY EDWARD BLISHEN
ILLUSTRATED BY BRIAN WILDSMITH
Cloth: Oxford
Paper: Bedrick
Published: 1963

A handsomely illustrated anthology of English poems for children, many of them—since there is a little of everything from Chaucer to Eliot—familiar to adults. Thoughtful introduction.

PADDLE-TO-THE-SEA   [828]

WRITTEN AND ILLUSTRATED BY HOLLING C. HOLLING
Cloth: Houghton Mifflin
Paper: Houghton Mifflin
Published: 1941

This book is both very old-fashioned to look at and thrillingly modern in its idea and organization. A boy living in the Great Lakes sets a toy Indian lad into a canoe and sends them downstream. The story follows the waterways to the ocean. Nearly half a century has passed since the story was written, and a great deal has changed—technology the least of it—and yet the book is wonderfully compelling.

PEEPING IN THE SHELL: A WHOOPING CRANE IS HATCHED [829]

WRITTEN BY FAITH McNULTY
ILLUSTRATED BY IRENE BRADY
Cloth: Harper
Published: 1986

At the center of this science book for middle-grade children is a thrilling description of the birth in captivity of a whooping crane. The larger text explains the plight of the whooping crane and the work of ornithologists, especially George Archibald, to help them survive.

THE PEOPLE COULD FLY: AMERICAN BLACK FOLKTALES [830]

WRITTEN BY VIRGINIA HAMILTON
ILLUSTRATED BY LEO AND DIANE DILLON
Cloth: Knopf
Published: 1985

A retelling of twenty-four black American folktales by a distinguished contemporary writer. There are animal stories, supernatural tales, and slave tales of freedom, all told in sharp, precise prose. The illustrations are mystical and affecting.

[830]

PETER PAN [831]

WRITTEN BY J. M. BARRIE
ILLUSTRATED BY JAN ORMEROD
Cloth: Viking
Paper: Puffin
Published: 1911

These are the well-known, albeit most from adaptation, adventures of the Darling children, the little lost boy Peter Pan, and the faithful fairy Tinkerbell. The language of the original, while formal, is not so difficult that it cannot be read at full length by a middle-grade reader. There is no need for abridged text editions, although there are some charming picture book versions available for younger children. Until the copyright expired, the only full-length edition available had illustrations by Nora Unwin. A number of others have been published recently. This one has striking full-color plates, and Tinkerbell decorates nearly every text page. Incidentally, Barrie based the novel on his own play; the various Disney versions take further liberties.

THE PHANTOM TOLLBOOTH [832]

WRITTEN BY NORTON JUSTER
ILLUSTRATED BY JULES FEIFFER
Cloth: Random House
Paper: Random House
Published: 1961

Milo drives his little car through what looks like a regular tollbooth, but it leads into enchanted lands of science, logic, and order, as well as mystery and threat, that surround the Mountains of Ignorance. A deserved classic. This brilliant story is suitably illustrated in Feiffer's distinctive and timeless style. Great for reading aloud with middle-grade listeners.

[832]

PHILIP HALL LIKES ME.
I RECKON MAYBE. [833]

WRITTEN BY BETTE GREENE
ILLUSTRATED BY CHARLES LILLY
Cloth: Dial
Paper: Dell
Published: 1974   PRIZES: NEWBERY HONOR BOOK

Beth is a bright, sassy, eleven-year-old black girl living in rural Arkansas. She is the smartest girl in the class, has a crush on the smartest boy in the class. The sequel is *Get On Out of Here, Philip Hall*.

THE PINBALLS [834]

WRITTEN BY BETSY BYARS
Cloth: Harper
Paper: Scholastic, Harper
Published: 1977

Three children, unwanted and unconnected—one battered, one maimed, one lost—meet and join forces in a warm and caring foster home. Sounds awful, but in the hands of such a careful writer it works and is actually rather inspiring.

PIPING DOWN THE VALLEYS WILD [835]

WRITTEN BY NANCY LARRICK
ILLUSTRATED BY ELLEN RASKIN
Cloth: Delacorte
Paper: Dell
Published: 1968

This is one of the most popular collections of poetry for children, and rightly so. The selections are varied and interesting and read aloud very well. The illustrations are apt.

POLLYANNA [836]

WRITTEN BY ELEANOR H. PORTER
Paper: Yearling Classic
Published: 1913

After years out of print, the story of the most relentlessly cheerful heroine in American literature, the inventor of the Glad Game, is back
in print. In fact, it is easy to see why, in simpler days, she was such a
popular heroine.

THE POWER OF LIGHT: EIGHT STORIES FOR HANUKKAH [837]

WRITTEN BY ISAAC BASHEVIS SINGER
ILLUSTRATED BY IRENE LIEBLICH
Cloth: Farrar, Straus
Published: 1980

A collection of eight stories by the Nobel Prize–winning author to mark
each night of Hanukkah. Set mostly in Poland in a time that seems very
long ago. Very good for reading aloud.

A PROUD TASTE FOR SCARLET AND MINIVER [838]

WRITTEN AND ILLUSTRATED BY E. L. KONIGSBURG
Cloth: Atheneum
Paper: Aladdin
Published: 1973

A very witty and imaginatively fictionalized biography of Eleanor of
Aquitaine. The queen and others, including her mother-in-law and
priest, are in heaven waiting for King Henry II to arrive.

THE PUSHCART WAR [839]

WRITTEN BY JEAN MERRILL
ILLUSTRATED BY RONNI SOLBERT
Cloth: Addison-Wesley
Paper: Dell
Published: 1964

This fictional account of a "war" between pushcart peddlers and truckers in New York City is told in a light and breezy way and raises serious political and social issues middle-and upper-grade students can address.

QUENTIN CORN [840]

WRITTEN BY MARY STOLZ
ILLUSTRATED BY PAMELA JOHNSON
Cloth: Godine
Published: 1985

A pig passes as a boy, with all manner of complications.

RABBIT HILL [841]

WRITTEN AND ILLUSTRATED BY ROBERT LAWSON
Cloth: Viking
Paper: Puffin
Published: 1941   PRIZES: NEWBERY MEDAL

Life among the creatures who live on Rabbit Hill is consistently entertaining. "New Folk" are coming to live in the Big House.

THE RED PONY [842]

WRITTEN BY JOHN STEINBECK
ILLUSTRATED BY WESLEY DENNIS
Cloth: Viking
Published: 1937

A boy and his horse. A classic. Is there more to say?

THE RELUCTANT DRAGON [843]

WRITTEN BY KENNETH GRAHAME
ILLUSTRATED BY ERNEST H. SHEPARD
Cloth: Holiday
Published: 1938

In this well-loved story with classic illustrations, a little boy makes friends with a very peaceful dragon. It's a good fantasy with implicit moral lessons. Other editions are available but are inadequate.

ROLL OF THUNDER, HEAR MY CRY [844]

WRITTEN BY MILDRED TAYLOR
Cloth: Dial
Paper: Bantam
Published: 1976   PRIZES: NEWBERY MEDAL

This bitter, memorable, and beautifully written story of a close-knit, poor black family in Mississippi during the Depression is drawn from stories from the author's family. The sequel is *Let the Circle Be Unbroken.*

RONIA, THE ROBBER'S DAUGHTER [845]

WRITTEN BY ASTRID LINDGREN
Cloth: Viking
Paper: Puffin
Published: 1983

Brave and adventurous Ronia is the only child of Matt the robber chief. They live deep in a forest. A rich and complex novel by the author of *Pippi Longstockings*, for older readers.

ROOTABAGA STORIES [846]

WRITTEN BY CARL SANDBURG
ILLUSTRATED BY MAUD AND MISKA PETERSHAM
Cloth: Harcourt Brace
Paper: Voyager/HBJ
Published: 1936

A glorious collection of nonsense and stories, with period illustrations. Easy to read, but better still to read aloud.

A RUSSIAN FAREWELL   [847]

WRITTEN AND ILLUSTRATED BY LEONARD EVERETT FISHER
Cloth: Four Winds
Published: 1980

It is 1905 and anti-Jewish attitudes are on the rise in Russia. In this compelling novel, based on a true story, the Shapiro family decides it is time to leave their village, Krolevets, and immigrate to the United States.

SAILING TO CYTHERA AND OTHER ANATOLE STORIES   [848]

WRITTEN BY NANCY WILLARD
ILLUSTRATED BY DAVID McPHAIL
Cloth: Harcourt Brace
Paper: Voyager/HBJ
Published: 1974   PRIZES: LEWIS CARROLL SHELF AWARD

The first volume of a fantasy trilogy by an award-winning poet and novelist. Anatole, the hero, is a boy with unusual friends, and their adventures include sailing to a mythical kingdom, searching for a rare herb, and rescuing the victims of the wizard Arcimboldo. The other titles are *The Island of the Grass King: The Further Adventures of Anatole* and *Uncle Terrible: More Adventures of Anatole.*

SARAH, PLAIN AND TALL   [849]

WRITTEN BY PATRICIA MacLACHLAN
Cloth: Harper
Paper: Harper
Published: 1985   PRIZES: NEWBERY MEDAL

In the sparest prose, Anna tells how her father placed an ad for a wife in an eastern newspaper, and Sarah replied. Their mother died when Caleb was born. The children want Sarah, who is "plain and tall" and comes from Maine with her cat, Seal, to stay with them, to accept the proposal. A flawless piece of storytelling that touches on many aspects of longing, self-esteem, and raw family needs. Wonderful to read aloud. Have tissues handy.

SCARY STORIES TO TELL IN THE DARK: COLLECTED FROM AMERICAN FOLKLORE [850]

WRITTEN BY ALVIN SCHWARTZ
ILLUSTRATED BY STEPHEN GAMMELL
Cloth: Lippincott
Paper: Harper
Published: 1981

Gather 'round and sit close by, here's a dandy collection—including ghosts, folktales, and some modern scary stories. Ideal for campfires and reading aloud. There's a second volume, *More Scary Stories to Tell in the Dark*, too.

SEASONS OF SPLENDOR [851]

WRITTEN BY MADHUR JAFFREY
ILLUSTRATED BY MICHAEL FOREMAN
Cloth: Atheneum
Paper: Puffin
Published: 1985

An exemplary collection of twenty Indian myths and legends tied to holidays and seasons. The author introduces each Hindu tale with recollections of her own childhood in a large and sophisticated extended family. The writing is inviting to Western readers, the stories enthralling, and the illustrations serve them well, capturing the spirit of Indian art without mimicking it. Good for reading aloud.

THE SECOND MRS. GIACONDA [852]

WRITTEN BY E. L. KONIGSBERG
Cloth: Atheneum
Paper: Aladdin
Published: 1975

A cleverly conceived and executed novel purporting to be the real story of the Mona Lisa, as told by Salai, Leonardo da Vinci's apprentice and valet. Illustrated with reproductions of work by da Vinci and others of the period.

THE SECRET GARDEN [853]

WRITTEN BY FRANCES HODGSON BURNETT
ILLUSTRATED BY TASHA TUDOR

Cloth: Lippincott
Paper: Harper
Published: 1912

One of the greatest novels ever written for children, and one of the greatest novels about gardening and health, this is the story of Mary Lennox, a spoiled orphan sent to live a solitary life on her guardian's estate on the Yorkshire moors. She encounters Dickon, a free-spirited country boy, Colin, the willful, ailing scion of the estate, and a secret walled garden. For many years this handsome edition was the only one available; however, the copyright on Burnett's work expired in 1987 and nearly a dozen illustrated editions appeared in both hard and soft cover. They all show essentially the same scenes in the same fashion. Choose whichever edition appeals, but do not choose an abridged text. Despite some bits of dialogue in dialect, the prose is not difficult; rather, it is quite splendid as it carries Mary from her sallow self-absorption to radiant physical and mental health. A thrilling book to read aloud.

THE SECRET LANGUAGE [854]

WRITTEN BY URSULA NORDSTROM

Cloth: Harper
Paper: Harper
Published: 1960

Vicky and Martha, both eight years old, are away at boarding school. As part of their sustaining friendship, they develop a secret language. Middle-grade girls still enjoy their special relationship.

[853]

SECRET OF THE ANDES [855]

WRITTEN BY ANN NOLAN CLARK
ILLUSTRATED BY JEAN CHARLOT
Cloth: Viking
Paper: Puffin
Published: 1952

This vivid story of Cusi, an Inca boy living in a hidden valley in the mountains of Peru with Chuto, a llama herder, is a perennial favorite. It is an exciting introduction to another culture.

SEVEN KISSES IN A ROW [856]

WRITTEN BY PATRICIA MacLACHLAN
ILLUSTRATED BY MARIA PIA MARRELLA
Cloth: Harper
Paper: Harper
Published: 1983

Uncle Elliot and Aunt Evelyn come to take care of Emma and her older brother while their parents are away at a professional conference. The children must train the adults to the rituals and responsibilities of family life. Warm and funny.

THE SHADOWMAKER [857]

WRITTEN BY RON HANSEN
ILLUSTRATED BY MARGOT TOMES
Cloth: Harper
Published: 1987

The Shadowmaker reaches town and convinces all the perfectly happy people that what they really need are new shadows. Drizzle and her brother, Soot, can't afford new shadows, but they learn the Shadowmaker's secret. There's great wit and style in both story and illustrations. Very good for reading aloud to younger children.

[857]

SING DOWN THE MOON [858]

WRITTEN BY SCOTT O'DELL
Cloth: Houghton Mifflin
Paper: Dell
Published: 1970

A historical novel about Bright Morning, a fifteen-year-old Navaho girl whose tribe has been evicted from their homes. She tells about the forced march and her capture by Spanish slavers.

SIRENS AND SPIES [859]

WRITTEN BY JANET TAYLOR LISLE
Cloth: Bradbury
Paper: Berkeley
Published: 1985

It turns out that Elsie's beloved French violin teacher, Miss Fitch, collaborated with the Germans during World War II, and Elsie doesn't want to hear any more about it. But, of course, Miss Fitch has her story to tell. A complex novel.

THE SLAVE DANCER [860]

WRITTEN BY PAULA FOX
Cloth: Bradbury
Paper: Dell
Published: 1973   PRIZES: NEWBERY MEDAL

A stunning novel about Jessie Bollier, in which he recalls the summer of 1840 when he was press-ganged aboard a slave ship bound for Africa and played his flute while the slaves were exercised.

SMALL POEMS [861]

WRITTEN BY VALERIE WORTH
ILLUSTRATED BY NATALIE BABBITT
Cloth: Farrar, Straus
Published: 1972

The first of a delightful series of small books of small poems, with small illustrations but great quantities of wit and style. The other titles include *More Small Poems*, *Still More Small Poems*, and *Small Poems Again*.

SOUNDER [862]

WRITTEN BY WILLIAM H. ARMSTRONG
ILLUSTRATED BY JAMES BARKLEY
Cloth: Harper
Paper: Harper
Published: 1969   PRIZES: NEWBERY MEDAL

This novel set in the rural South in the late nineteenth century tells about a poor black sharecropper's family. The father steals in order to feed his family and is arrested in front of them. His dog, Sounder, is wounded. Battered, the family does not fall. A related title, *Sour Land*, picks up the story when the son is an old man and helps three white children.

SOUP [863]

WRITTEN BY ROBERT NEWTON PECK
ILLUSTRATED BY CHARLES GEHM
Cloth: Knopf
Paper: Dell
Published: 1974

The first of a popular series of novels about the author's childhood pal Soup. The setting is rural Vermont in the 1920s; the style is terse and funny. Other titles include *Soup on Ice*, *Soup on Wheels*, *Soup's Goat*, and *Soup and Me*.

STORIES FOR CHILDREN [864]

WRITTEN BY ISAAC BASHEVIS SINGER
Cloth: Farrar, Straus
Paper: Farrar, Straus
Published: 1984

A splendid collection of short fiction, ostensibly for children but appropriate to all ages, some never previously published in book form. The tales allow every reader to have a Polish Jewish grandfather from whom to hear stories to think about in the night.

THE STORY OF KING ARTHUR AND HIS KNIGHTS   [865]

WRITTEN AND ILLUSTRATED BY HOWARD PYLE
Cloth: Scribners
Published: 1903

This is the first book of the classic four-volume retelling of the Arthurian legends in that fine, lushly illustrated large format that feels so secure in the hand. The other volumes include *The Story of Sir Lancelot & His Companions*, *The Story of the Champions of the Round Table*, and *The Story of the Grail and the Passing of Arthur.*

THE STORY OF ROCK 'N' ROLL   [866]

WRITTEN BY PETE FORNATALE
Cloth: Morrow
Paper: Morrow Jr.
Published: 1987

It's hard for some parents to grasp the idea that the story of rock and roll comes under the category of history. But to youngsters it does indeed. This breezy introduction puts the most popular music and performers of the last thirty years into some social context.

STRAWBERRY GIRL   [867]

WRITTEN AND ILLUSTRATED BY LOIS LENSKI
Cloth: Lippincott
Paper: Dell
Published: 1945   PRIZES: NEWBERY MEDAL

The story of Birdie Boyer, a so-called Cracker girl, who lives with her farming family in the rural Florida lake country half a century ago. The compelling and well-written novel tells of strawberry crops and neighborly strife.

[867]

A STRING IN THE HARP [868]

WRITTEN BY NANCY BOND
Cloth: McElderry
Paper: Puffin
Published: 1976   PRIZES: NEWBERY HONOR BOOK

A dandy fantasy novel about three American children living in Wales
and a harp tuning key that transports a boy back to the sixth century
and the life of the bard Taliesin.

STUART LITTLE [869]

WRITTEN BY E. B. WHITE
ILLUSTRATED BY GARTH WILLIAMS
Cloth: Harper
Paper: Harper
Published: 1945

The Little family were surprised when their second son appeared to be
a mouse. Stuart, a dignified chap who has splendid adventures growing up in New York City, eventually leaves his home and family to follow Margalo, a lovely wren who has flown north. This elegant fantasy
is a prized example of sophisticated writing for children that endures.

THE SUMMER OF THE SWANS [870]

WRITTEN BY BETSY BYARS
ILLUSTRATED BY TED COCONIS
Cloth: Viking
Paper: Puffin
Published: 1970   PRIZES: NEWBERY MEDAL

All on a summer's day, a fourteen-year-old deals with her conflicts
about herself, her beloved but retarded younger brother, who is lost,
and the attention of a boy who offers to help. And in the end she finds
her wings. This is a compelling and powerful story for older-grade
readers.

TALES OF A FOURTH GRADE NOTHING [871]

WRITTEN BY JUDY BLUME
ILLUSTRATED BY ROY DOTY
Cloth: Dutton
Paper: Dell
Published: 1972

One of the early and brighter titles in the Blume canon, accessible and user-friendly fiction for middle-class children. Peter Harcher, a nine-year-old, describes his life and problems with his little brother, Fudge. The sequels are *Fudge* and *Superfudge*.

[871]

THE TALES OF UNCLE REMUS: THE ADVENTURES OF BRER RABBIT [872]

WRITTEN BY JULIUS LESTER
ILLUSTRATED BY JERRY PINKNEY
Cloth: Dial
Published: 1987

A set of Brer Rabbit stories retold in a contemporary tone by a distinguished black writer. The appealing illustrations are very traditional and well done.

A TASTE OF BLACKBERRIES [873]

WRITTEN BY DORIS BUCHANAN SMITH
ILLUSTRATED BY CHARLES ROBINSON
Cloth: Crowell
Paper: Harper
Published: 1973

In this short, thoughtful novel, a young boy describes his friendship with Jamie and Jamie's sudden death.

THANK YOU, JACKIE ROBINSON   [874]

WRITTEN BY BARBARA COHEN
ILLUSTRATED BY RICHARD CUFFARI
Cloth: Lothrop
Published: 1974, reissued 1988

A poignant story about a fatherless young white boy and an old black man who are passionate fans of the Brooklyn Dodgers and especially Jackie Robinson. Good deeds are done before the old man dies.

THIMBLE SUMMER   [875]

WRITTEN BY ELIZABETH ENRIGHT
Cloth: Holt
Paper: Dell
Published: 1938

This story of a little girl growing up on a farm in Wisconsin and learning to appreciate and love it has period charm, particularly for avid girl readers, even half a century later.

THUNDER AND LIGHTNINGS   [876]

WRITTEN BY JAN MARK
ILLUSTRATED BY JIM RUSSELL
Cloth: Crowell
Published: 1979

An exciting British novel of self-discovery. The story is about RAF fighter planes and pilots. The author is particularly good with machine metaphors.

TITUBA OF SALEM VILLAGE   [877]

WRITTEN BY ANN PETRY
Cloth: Crowell
Published: 1964

A novel about Tituba, a slave from Barbados who with her husband is sold into the household of a Puritan minister and endures the hysteria of the Salem witchcraft trials. Vivid and frightening.

TO BE A SLAVE   [878]

WRITTEN BY JULIUS LESTER
ILLUSTRATED BY TOM FEELINGS
Cloth: Dial
Paper: Scholastic
Published: 1968

This landmark anthology of original material describing the experience of slavery is annotated with helpful commentary. An important and original book for older readers of all races.

TOM'S MIDNIGHT GARDEN   [879]

WRITTEN BY PHILIPPA PEARCE
ILLUSTRATED BY SUSAN EINZIG
Cloth: Lippincott
Paper: Dell
Published: 1958

A time-tripping novel, and a dandy one. In a magical garden, Tom can go back to meet a mysterious Victorian girl. This particular plot device works best when it combines realism with inherent, convincing fantasy, as it does here.

TREASURE ISLAND   [880]

WRITTEN BY ROBERT LOUIS STEVENSON
ILLUSTRATED BY N. C. WYETH
Cloth: Scribners
Published: 1911

This is a reissue of the handsome 1911 edition of that splendid adventure story dominated by Long John Silver, the pirate of all pirates. There are nearly a dozen other editions, some with illustrations, many abridged, but this one is peerless.

THE TRUMPETER OF KRAKOW   [881]

WRITTEN BY ERIC P. KELLY
ILLUSTRATED BY JANINA DOMANSKA
Cloth: Macmillan
Paper: Collier
Published: 1928   PRIZES: NEWBERY MEDAL

The exciting tale of a courageous boy and a precious jewel is set in Poland's most beautiful city in the fifteenth century. It was handsomely reillustrated in 1966.

THE TRUMPET OF THE SWAN   [882]

WRITTEN BY E. B. WHITE
ILLUSTRATED BY EDWARD FRASCINO
Cloth: Harper
Paper: Harper
Published: 1970

The third but not necessarily the least of E. B. White's books for children tells the story of Louis, a trumpeter swan born without a voice. The nature writing is matchless, the illustrations charming.

TUCK EVERLASTING   [883]

WRITTEN BY NATALIE BABBITT
Cloth: Farrar, Straus
Paper: Sunburst/Farrar, Straus
Published: 1975

The best children's books address the most serious questions in life in ways that make them manageable to readers. The title of this novel is a clue to its rich contents. The Tuck family drank from a magical spring and has been blessed (or is it cursed?) with eternal life. They try to live very inconspicuously, but ten-year-old Winnie Foster discovers their secret. An enthralling fantasy that is good to read aloud with early- and middle-grade listeners.

UNDERGROUND [884]

WRITTEN AND ILLUSTRATED BY DAVID MACAULAY
Cloth: Houghton Mifflin
Paper: Houghton Mifflin
Published: 1976

What you really want to know about what happens underneath the pavement of a city street, told in clear pen-and-ink illustrations and spare, precise text. A book to study endlessly and enjoyably.

UP FROM JERICHO TELL [885]

WRITTEN BY E. L. KONIGSBURG
Cloth: Atheneum
Paper: Dell
Published: 1986

Two ambitious latchkey children, Jeanmarie and Malcolm, encounter an old—and, it must be said, dead—actress named Tallulah under a small hill called Jericho Tell. In inimitable style and sassy prose, Tallulah gives them some pointed lessons in how to succeed. Tart and sophisticated. If parents don't read aloud, they might read along with older-grade children.

UPON THE HEAD OF A GOAT: A CHILDHOOD IN HUNGARY, 1939–1944 [886]

WRITTEN BY ARANKA SIEGAL
Cloth: Farrar, Straus
Published: 1981   PRIZES: NEWBERY HONOR BOOK

A remarkable, autobiographical novel in which the author, as Piri Davidowitz, describes her Jewish childhood and the destruction of her family in World War II. The sequel, *Grace in the Wilderness: After the Liberation, 1945–1948*, carries her from the Bergen-Belsen concentration camp through quarantine in Sweden on to embarkation for the United States. The pair are suitable companions to *Anne Frank*.

THE UPSTAIRS ROOM   [887]

WRITTEN BY JOHANNA REISS
Cloth: Crowell
Paper: Harper
Published: 1982

This is an autobiographical novel about a Dutch-Jewish family during World War II. The narrator, the youngest of three sisters, tells how a peasant family, the Oostervelds, hid her and one sister for more than two years. *The Journey Back* tells what happened after the war.

VOLCANO: THE ERUPTION AND HEALING OF MOUNT ST. HELENS   [888]

WRITTEN BY PATRICA LAUBER
Cloth: Bradbury
Published: 1986   PRIZES: NEWBERY HONOR BOOK

A fine photo-essay about the eruption of the Mount St. Helens volcano. The text and color photographs capture and explain with unusual clarity the healing abilities of nature in the years that followed.

WATERSHIP DOWN   [889]

WRITTEN BY RICHARD ADAMS
Cloth: Macmillan
Paper: Avon
Published: 1974

This maverick band of rabbits, with their rich culture and fully developed language, have become heroes to so many that this remarkable novel is considered a modern classic for both adults and children.

THE WESTING GAME   [890]

WRITTEN BY ELLEN RASKIN
Cloth: Dutton
Paper: Avon
Published: 1978   PRIZES: NEWBERY MEDAL

A very sophisticated mystery novel for older readers in which sixteen heirs of an eccentric millionaire are assembled, organized, and given clues that they believe will lead them to their inheritance.

WESTMARK [891]

WRITTEN BY LLOYD ALEXANDER
Cloth: Dutton
Published: 1981

This first volume of an exciting trilogy is about Theo, a printer's apprentice who flees when his master is killed by the king's chief minister. The other titles are *The Kestrel* and *The Beggar Queen*.

WHAT IF YOU COULDN'T...?
A BOOK ABOUT SPECIAL NEEDS [892]

WRITTEN BY FIGNE HANSON
Cloth: Scribners
Published: 1979

A book about humility—a series of simple experiments to let the reader understand specific problems of the handicapped.

WHAT I HEARD [893]

WRITTEN BY MARK GELLER
Cloth: Harper
Published: 1987

After receiving a telephone of his own for his twelfth birthday, Michael gets into the habit of eavesdropping on other people's conversations. Then one day he overhears his father in a compromising call. The short novel for upper-grade readers is well told and plausibly resolved.

WHERE THE LILIES BLOOM [894]

WRITTEN BY VERA AND BILL CLEAVER
ILLUSTRATED BY JIM SPANFELLER
Cloth: Lippincott
Paper: NAL
Published: 1969

Mary Call Luther, age fourteen, tells about her life in Appalachia and her efforts to keep her family together after the death of her father, a sharecropper. In *Trial Valley*, Mary Call's life is complicated by two suitors and an abandoned child.

WHERE THE RED FERN GROWS [895]

WRITTEN BY WILSON RAWLS

Cloth: Doubleday
Paper: Bantam
Published: 1961

A young boy in the Ozark Mountains during the Depression earns the money to buy, and then trains, a fine pair of coon hounds—Old Dan and Little Ann. A fine coming-of-age novel, with dreams and values tested and justified. The book's enduring popularity among middle-grade and older readers has been reinforced by a motion picture.

WHERE THE SIDEWALK ENDS: POEMS AND DRAWINGS [896]

WRITTEN AND ILLUSTRATED BY SHEL SILVERSTEIN

Cloth: Harper
Published: 1974

A wildly popular collection of poems and drawings for children and adults that ranges from silly to sad and back again.

THE WHIPPING BOY [897]

WRITTEN BY SID FLEISCHMAN
ILLUSTRATED BY PETER SIS

Cloth: Greenwillow
Paper: Troll
Published: 1986   PRIZES: NEWBERY MEDAL

The theme is like that of *The Prince and the Pauper,* done with a fine hand and light heart. Jemmy is the whipping boy to Prince Brat, who deserves his name. The prince runs away, taking Jemmy with him, and their adventures with a motley bunch of silly and unsavory sorts teach them both good lessons. The black-and-white illustrations are deft and witty. Good reading aloud.

[896]

THE WHITE STAG [898]

WRITTEN AND ILLUSTRATED BY KATE SEREDY
Cloth: Viking
Paper: Puffin
Published: 1938   PRIZES: NEWBERY MEDAL

The story of Atilla and the migration of the Huns and Magyars from
Asia to Europe. Bold and sweeping historical fiction of the timeless
variety.

WILLIE BEA AND THE TIME
THE MARTIANS LANDED [899]

WRITTEN BY VIRGINIA HAMILTON
Cloth: Greenwillow
Published: 1983

It is October 1938 in rural Ohio, and Willie Bea is getting ready for
Halloween. The radio makes it sound as though the world is coming to
an end. It is, of course, just Orson Welles's radio broadcast of *The War
of the Worlds*, a simple explanation the grown-ups understand sooner
than the child. The story is told sympathetically from the child's
perspective.

THE WIND IN THE WILLOWS [900]

WRITTEN BY KENNETH GRAHAME
ILLUSTRATED BY E. H. SHEPARD
Cloth: Scribners
Published: 1908

The riverbank adventures of those fine fellows, Rat, Mole, Toad, and
Badger. The stories celebrate a golden time just before the modern
world. (Was it ever really so golden?) Somehow the 1933 edition, with
Shepard's illustrations, captures the story so perfectly it seems pointless
to consider others. However, the language is difficult, so younger readers may prefer to hear it rather than read it to themselves, and there are
many abridged editions.

WINNIE-THE-POOH [901]

WRITTEN BY A. A. MILNE
ILLUSTRATED BY ERNEST H. SHEPARD
Cloth: Dutton
Paper: Dell
Published: 1926

Winnie-the-Pooh is the bear of little brain who belongs to Christopher Robin, a proper English boy hero of not so very long ago. Their adventures in and around Pooh Corner, with Eeyore, Piglet, Tigger, and the rest of their friends, continue in *The House at Pooh Corner*, and have been beloved for generations. They are small, whimsical adventures, but however charming the stories, some adults find the prose cloying. It is a fine early chapter book for reading aloud. The line drawings are enchanting.

THE WITCH OF FOURTH STREET AND OTHER STORIES [902]

WRITTEN BY MYRON LEVOY
ILLUSTRATED BY GABRIEL LISOWSKI
Cloth: Harper
Paper: Harper
Published: 1972

A collection of eight somewhat whimsical short stories that mix history, truth, magic, and European immigrant lore, all set on New York City's Lower East Side in the 1920s.

THE WONDERFUL WIZARD OF OZ [903]

WRITTEN BY L. FRANK BAUM
ILLUSTRATED BY W. W. DENSLOW
Cloth: Morrow
Paper: Dover
Published: 1900, reissued 1987

It is often called the original American fairy tale, and it certainly marked Kansas forever, because "there's no place like home." Because of the film it is hard to find a child who doesn't know this story, but as is often the case, the book is better. Much better. This 1987 volume is a facsimile of the handsome first edition. Most of the series—involving several writers and running to dozens of titles—is available in large-format paperback from Dover and small paperbacks from Ballantine. Start with Dorothy, Toto, and that first trip to Oz, but don't miss Ozma or the Patchwork Girl. Grand for reading aloud to middle-grade and younger children.

[901]

THE WRESTLING PRINCESS AND OTHER STORIES [904]

WRITTEN BY JUDY CORBALIS
ILLUSTRATED BY HELEN CRAIG
Cloth: Deutsch
Published: 1986

The title story is about Princess Ermyntrude, who is six feet tall, drives a forklift truck, and pilots a helicopter and is not about to let someone else choose her husband. A jolly collection that particularly pleases independent readers.

A WRINKLE IN TIME [905]

WRITTEN BY MADELINE L'ENGLE
Cloth: Farrar, Straus
Paper: Dell
Published: 1962   PRIZES: NEWBERY MEDAL

The first of the fine and very popular fantasy quartet of novels about the Murry family, especially Meg and Charles Wallace. In the first book, they go on a dangerous mission in search of their scientist father. The other titles include *A Wind in the Door* and *A Swiftly Tilting Planet* (these three are available in a boxed edition), and *Many Waters* follows the twins, Sandy and Dennys, back into biblical times.

THE YEARLING [906]

WRITTEN BY MARJORIE KINNAN RAWLINGS
ILLUSTRATED BY N. C. WYETH
Cloth: Scribners
Paper: Collier
Published: 1938   PRIZES: PULITZER PRIZE

The setting is the backwoods of Florida as the boy named Jody struggles to save the animals he loves, especially the yearling. The memorable N. C. Wyeth illustrations were rephotographed for a 1985 edition.

YOUNG FU OF THE UPPER YANGTZE [907]

WRITTEN BY ELIZABETH FOREMAN LEWIS
ILLUSTRATED BY ED YOUNG
Cloth: Holt
Published: 1932   PRIZES: NEWBERY MEDAL

A handsomely illustrated edition of the 1932 Newbery Medal book,
which is the story of life in prerevolutionary China as seen by a copper-
smith's apprentice, has some enduring fascination as historical fiction.

ZLATEH THE GOAT AND OTHER STORIES [908]

WRITTEN BY ISSAC BASHEVIS SINGER
ILLUSTRATED BY MAURICE SENDAK
Cloth: Harper
Paper: Harper
Published: 1966   PRIZES: NEW YORK TIMES BEST ILLUSTRATED BOOK

A fine collection of seven traditional Middle European folktales told
and illustrated by masters with unusual poignance. It appeals to children and adults, and is splendid to read aloud.

Young
Adult
Books

This is a small selection of titles written for adolescent readers and principally concerned with coming of age, self-awareness, role models and personal possibility. The serious sounding fare is leavened with humor.

THE AMERICAN REVOLUTIONARIES: A HISTORY IN THEIR OWN WORDS 1750–1800 [909]

WRITTEN BY MILTON MELTZER

Cloth: Harper

Published: 1987

This exemplary collection of selections from letters, diaries, journals, memoirs, and newspapers of the period gives a vivid sense of how the revolutionary era in this country felt to a wide range of people.

AND NOBODY KNEW THEY WERE THERE [910]

WRITTEN BY OTTO R. SALASSI

Cloth: Greenwillow

Published: 1984

Two teenage boy cousins are forced to spend the summer together and are not liking it. Then they accidentally discover the trail of a squad of marines who are on the move. The time is the 1950s; the action moves across the state of Louisiana.

ANNIE ON MY MIND [911]

WRITTEN BY NANCY GARDEN

Cloth: Farrar, Straus

Paper: Sunburst/Farrar, Straus

Published: 1982

An unusually strong and unsentimental novel that involves a lesbian relationship. Liza, the narrator, met Annie at the Metropolitan Museum of Art in New York City when they were in high school before she had any understanding of her own sexuality.

BAD MAN BALLAD   [912]

WRITTEN BY SCOTT R. SANDERS

Cloth: Bradbury
Published: 1986

An exciting novel of search and adventure set during the War of 1812, in which a seventeen-year-old boy and one companion, an adventurous Philadelphia lawyer, track a giantlike creature.

BEYOND THE DIVIDE   [913]

WRITTEN BY KATHRYN LASKY

Cloth: Macmillan
Paper: Dell
Published: 1983

This is a gripping pioneer story about Meribah and her father, who break with the Amish community and join a wagon train heading west for the gold rush.

CAPTIVES OF TIME   [914]

WRITTEN BY MALCOLM BOSSE

Cloth: Delacorte
Published: 1987

After the death of their parents, Anne Valens and her mute brother live with their Uncle Albrecht, who teaches Anne the valuable art and skill of clockmaking. It is an exciting although often violent story set in medieval Europe that touches on many themes, including social breakdown and change and the rise of cities.

THE CAT ATE MY GYMSUIT   [915]

WRITTEN BY PAULA DANZIGER

Cloth: Delacorte
Paper: Dell
Published: 1974

Marcy's view is that life is rotten: her social life, her weight, her parents —the usual. When she encounters a remarkable teacher, things begin to change fast. Inside the humor is a lesson about social protest.

THE CHANGEOVER: A SUPERNATURAL ROMANCE [916]

WRITTEN BY MARGARET MAHY

Cloth: McElderry
Paper: Scholastic
Published: 1984

A remarkably clever and stylishly written novel about witchcraft, family ties, and romance, by the inventive New Zealand writer. Laura's little brother becomes deathly ill, and she realizes that the cause is witchcraft and that her only chance to save him is to "change over" herself.

CHILD OF THE OWL [917]

WRITTEN BY LAURENCE YEP

Cloth: Harper
Published: 1977

This intriguing novel by the author of *Dragonwings* is also set in San Francisco's Chinatown, but it takes place in the 1960s, as teenage Casey searches for her roots and an understanding of her gambler father.

CHILDREN OF THE WOLF [918]

WRITTEN BY JANE YOLEN

Cloth: Viking
Published: 1984

A stunning novel based on actual documents that describe the treatment of feral, or wild, children found in India in the 1920s.

THE CHOCOLATE WAR [919]

WRITTEN BY ROBERT CORMIER

Cloth: Pantheon
Paper: Dell
Published: 1974

One of the finest contemporary young adult novels, this deals with power struggles and the misuse of power at a boys' boarding school in New England. The worthy sequel is *Beyond the Chocolate War.*

THE CONTENDER [920]

WRITTEN BY ROBERT LIPSYTE

Cloth: Harper
Paper: Harper
Published: 1967

This novel about Alfred, a seventeen-year-old boy in Harlem who almost accidentally begins training to be a professional fighter, does not seem dated; indeed it feels as fresh as when it was written. The issues—entrapment, education, escape, drugs—are, it seems, ever present in our society. Engrossing sports writing, too.

A DAY NO PIGS WOULD DIE [921]

WRITTEN BY ROBERT NEWTON PECK

Cloth: Knopf
Paper: Dell
Published: 1972

A thirteen-year-old Shaker boy living on a farm in Vermont is the central figure in this compelling novel as he takes on many of the responsibilities of an adult. Graphic scenes of farm life, beginning with the opening chapter, offer a view of rural reality that may shock urban teens. The author wrote the popular, and lighter, *Soup* series for younger readers.

DINKY HOCKER SHOOTS SMACK! [922]

WRITTEN BY M. E. KERR

Cloth: Harper
Paper: Dell
Published: 1972

Dinky doesn't use drugs, but she is fat, miserable and longs for attention. This novel from the wave of provocative young adult titles of the 1970s holds up very well; the adolescent issues are timeless, the dialogue remains sharp and funny.

DOGSONG [923]

WRITTEN BY GARY PAULSEN

Cloth: Bradbury
Paper: Puffin
Published: 1985   PRIZES: NEWBERY HONOR BOOK

An Eskimo boy sets out on a dogsled, turning his back on his modern village, and makes a journey of physical and spiritual self-discovery. Exciting reading for older-grade readers of both sexes.

DREAMS INTO DEEDS:
NINE WOMEN WHO DARED [924]

WRITTEN BY LINDA PEAVY AND URSULA SMITH

Cloth: Scribners
Published: 1985

A companion volume to *Women Who Changed Things*, this is a collection of brisk biographical sketches of Jane Addams, Marian Anderson, Rachel Carson, Alice Hamilton, Mother Jones, Juliette Gordon Low, Margaret Mead, Elizabeth Cady Stanton, and Babe Didrikson.

FOREVER [925]

WRITTEN BY JUDY BLUME

Cloth: Bradbury
Paper: Dell
Published: 1975

A first sexual relationship, entered into in good faith but outgrown in the course of ordinary events, is described by an author who has earned the trust and faith of her readers and serves them truthfully.

THE GIFT OF SARAH BARKER [926]

WRITTEN BY JANE YOLEN
Cloth: Viking
Paper: Scholastic
Published: 1981

A wonderfully romantic novel set in a nineteenth-century Shaker community, rich with detail, as it tells how Abel and Sarah are drawn to each other irresistibly in spite of the Shaker rules against sex or physical touching.

GOING BACKWARDS [927]

WRITTEN BY NORMA KLEIN
Cloth: Scholastic
Paper: Scholastic
Published: 1986

A thoughtful domestic problem novel in which Charles's beloved Grandmother Gustel has Alzheimer's disease. The ending is arbitrary; however, the plot development and the descriptions of how the disease affects everyone in the family are particularly well done, and may be helpful to readers encountering the problem.

GOOD-BYE AND KEEP COLD [928]

WRITTEN BY JENNY DAVIS
Cloth: Orchard
Published: 1987

Edda, the heroine and narrator of this particularly well written first novel set in the mountains of Kentucky, reconstructs her family life before and mostly after her father's death in a strip-mining accident that happened when Edda was eight years old.

GRAVEN IMAGES: 3 STORIES [929]

WRITTEN BY PAUL FLEISCHMAN
ILLUSTRATED BY ANDREW GLASS
Cloth: Harper
Paper: Harper
Published: 1982   PRIZES: NEWBERY HONOR BOOK

Three haunting stories about graven images—a sailor figure from a
death ship, a weather vane figure of St. Crispin, and a statue commis-
sioned by a ghost.

THE HAUNTING [930]

WRITTEN BY MARGARET MAHY
Cloth: McElderry
Paper: Scholastic
Published: 1982   PRIZES: CARNEGIE

The contemporary New Zealand novelist is such a masterful storyteller
that around the world people who actively dislike ghost stories read her
books. Barney, a boy who is afraid to tell about the messages he receives
from a dead relative, is the center of this prize-winning tale.

A HERO AIN'T NOTHIN' BUT A SANDWICH [931]

WRITTEN BY ALICE CHILDRESS
Cloth: Coward-McCann
Paper: Avon
Published: 1973

This harrowing novel about Benjie, a thirteen-year-old black boy who
is using heroin, is told from the perspectives of many of the people who
know him. The ending is problematic but holds promise. Recognized
at once, it remains one of the best of the socially aware young adult
novels of the 1970s.

HOME BEFORE DARK   [932]

WRITTEN BY SUE ELLEN BRIDGERS

Cloth: Knopf

Paper: Bantam

Published: 1976

In broad outline, this is the story of a migrant worker family settling down. The central character is Stella Mae Willis, fourteen years old as the novel begins. Her father brings the family to live and work on the tobbaco farm his younger brother has inherited.

I AM THE CHEESE   [933]

WRITTEN BY ROBERT CORMIER

Cloth: Pantheon

Paper: Dell

Published: 1977

This is a complex and suspenseful novel of psychological exploration. Adam Farmer describes his bicycle trip to see his father in Vermont, deals with a psychiatric interview, and confronts some memories. Very well written.

IN SUMMER LIGHT   [934]

WRITTEN BY ZIBBY ONEAL

Cloth: Viking

Paper: Bantam

Published: 1985

Kate Brewer's seventeenth summer is described in this insightful and romantic novel. Her father, an older, world-famous painter, dominates the family, which lives on a coastal island. Kate's unfinished paper on *The Tempest* helps carry the theme of Prospero through the novel.

I WILL CALL IT GEORGIE'S BLUES   [935]

WRITTEN BY SUZANNE NEWTON

Cloth: Viking
Paper: Dell
Published: 1983

Despite the facade, the relationships inside the preacher's family are strained to the breaking point by the father's demand of perfection. The breaking point is reached.

JACOB HAVE I LOVED   [936]

WRITTEN BY KATHERINE PATERSON

Cloth: Crowell
Paper: Avon
Published: 1980   PRIZES: NEWBERY MEDAL

Sara Louise, her relationship to her twin sister, adolescence, and, incidentally, the Chesapeake Bay area, are the heroine and the themes of this well-written and thought-provoking novel.

KILLING MR. GRIFFIN   [937]

WRITTEN BY LOIS DUNCAN

Cloth: Little, Brown
Paper: Dell
Published: 1982

This gripping story takes a turn on the idea of best-laid plans going awry. The plan is to scare the teacher, but he dies suddenly of a heart attack.

KIM/KIMI   [938]

WRITTEN BY HADLEY IRWIN

Cloth: McElderry
Paper: Puffin
Published: 1987

Kim is both Irish American (mother's side) and Japanese American (father's side), and to answer some questions about herself she travels

317

from Iowa (where she has grown up) to the California Japanese-American community her father came from. Absorbing.

LILLIAN WALD OF HENRY STREET [939]

WRITTEN BY BEATRICE SIEGAL

Cloth: Macmillan

Published: 1983

A clearly written biography of the founder of New York City's Henry Street Settlement in the late ninteenth century. The story of Miss Wald's life incorporates social history, the emergent notion of community service, and issues of suffrage, and is clearly for older readers.

THE LORD OF THE RINGS TRILOGY [940]

WRITTEN BY J. R. R. TOLKIEN

Cloth: Houghton Mifflin

Paper: Houghton Mifflin

Published: 1954

The trilogy— *The Fellowship of the Ring*, *The Two Towers*, and *The Return of the King*—is a saga of good and evil, cast as the War of the Ring and set in a mysterious Middle Earth. The writing is lush and fast paced. There are many imitations of this formula and style, none as riveting.

THE MAGICAL ADVENTURES OF THE PRETTY PEARL [941]

WRITTEN BY VIRGINIA HAMILTON

Cloth: Harper

Paper: Harper

Published: 1983   PRIZES: NEWBERY MEDAL

An allegorical blending of folklore, fantasy, and history, the story of a girl, Pretty Pearl, who travels on a slave ship from Africa to the New World with her older brother, John de Conquer. She reemerges during the Reconstruction and, finally, with a group of blacks and Cherokees who eventually set off for Ohio. There is both magic and history. The language is lush, difficult, exciting. This is rich and provocative fiction.

THE MOONLIGHT MAN [942]

WRITTEN BY PAULA FOX

Cloth: Bradbury

Published: 1986

Catherine spends part of her summer vacation with her father, the first time she has really been with him since her parents' divorce when she was very young. Despite his charm and wit he is, she realizes, an alcoholic. This is a beautifully written and haunting novel of self-discovery and maturation.

MOTOWN AND DIDI: A LOVE STORY [943]

WRITTEN BY WALTER DEAN MYERS

Cloth: Viking

Paper: Dell

Published: 1984

A convincing novel about two teenagers in Harlem, coping with life and getting on with it. There is a strong, implicit antidrug message.

THE MOVES MAKE THE MAN [944]

WRITTEN BY BRUCE BROOKS

Cloth: Harper

Paper: Harper

Published: 1984   PRIZES: NEWBERY HONOR BOOK

This fine story of growing up and friendship is also a very good novel about basketball, as both a game and as a metaphor. Jerome Foxworthy is the first black at his high school; Bix is the best white athlete he's ever seen.

NIGHT KITES [945]

WRITTEN BY M. E. KERR

Cloth: Harper

Paper: Harper

Published: 1986

Erick Rudd has a difficult, provocative girl friend, a rather pompous father, and a kind older brother who, it turns out, has AIDS. The novel deals with the problem of AIDS within a family, acknowledging the sexual preference and history of an adult child with skill and tact as the background to Erick's own maturation.

ONE FAT SUMMER [946]

WRITTEN BY ROBERT LIPSYTE
Cloth: Harper
Published: 1977

The first of three books about Bobby Marks, who starts out, at four-teen, in the 1950s, fat and insecure. This book tells about his first job. He deals with first love in *Summer Rules* and, when he is eighteen, hazardous working conditions in a laundry where he works in *The Summerboy.*

THE OUTSIDERS [947]

WRITTEN BY S. E. HINTON
Cloth: Viking
Paper: Dell
Published: 1967

Perhaps the classic gang novel—writ large and compelling—the story details the relationships of the city gang members to each other and their remove from social conventions, filled with suspense and action. Successive generations of high school readers have been discovering it with stunned delight for more than twenty years. The companion tales are *Rumble Fish*, *Tex* and *That Was Then, This Is Now.*

PAGEANT [948]

WRITTEN BY KATHRYN LASKY
Cloth: Four Winds
Paper: Dell
Published: 1986

A Jewish girl attending a mostly Christian private school in Indianapolis, Indiana, comes of age during the Kennedy years. Funny and touching at the same time. It doesn't feel like historical fiction.

THE RETURN [949]

WRITTEN BY SONIA LEVITIN

Cloth: Atheneum
Paper: Fawcett
Published: 1987

A novel about the Falasha, the Ethiopian Jews, and the so-called Operation Moses, the airlift that took a small number of them to Israel via the Sudan. The heroine is a brave girl named Desta. Full of fascinating anthropological detail.

THE SUMMER OF
MY GERMAN SOLDIER [950]

WRITTEN BY BETTE GREENE

Cloth: Dial
Paper: Bantam
Published: 1973

A Jewish storekeeper's young daughter living in Arkansas during World War II befriends an escaped German prisoner-of-war. It is a poignant coming-of-age story in which Patty confronts a number of subtle issues.

SWEET WHISPERS, BROTHER RUSH [951]

WRITTEN BY VIRGINIA HAMILTON

Cloth: Philomel
Paper: Avon
Published: 1982

Tree, a fourteen-year-old girl, is alone most of the time and in charge of her older, retarded brother. In this well-written novel, Tree comes to terms with her family's tragic history and with her memories and fantasies of a dead uncle. For older readers.

TO ALL GENTLENESS: WILLIAM CARLOS WILLIAMS, THE DOCTOR-POET [952]

WRITTEN BY NEIL BALDWIN
Cloth: Macmillan
Published: 1984

A thoughtful biography of the twentieth-century American poet, who was also a practicing doctor and found joy in the noises of daily life. He put poetry together with "as much painstaking care as he took in the delivery of a baby," and his life may be of particular interest to teenage poets.

THE TRICKSTERS [953]

WRITTEN BY MARGARET MAHY
Cloth: McElderry
Paper: Scholastic
Published: 1987

Perhaps the most sophisticated of the imaginative New Zealand novelist's efforts yet, this is the story of a family Christmas holiday at the beach and the arrival of three handsome strangers. Harry, the seventeen-year-old who is secretly writing a novel, has a special sense of who the strangers are and their powers.

WOMEN WHO CHANGED THINGS [954]

WRITTEN BY LINDA PEAVY AND URSULA SMITH
Cloth: Scribners
Published: 1983

A bouquet of biographical studies of unheralded but splendid women—including a reformer, an astronomer, an educator, and a psychologist—that will intrigue readers trying to imagine adult careers.

THE YEAR IT RAINED   [955]

WRITTEN BY CRESCENT DRAGONWAGON

Cloth: Macmillan

Paper: Pocket

Published: 1985

A fine, upsetting, first-person novel about seventeen-year-old Elizabeth and her mother—"the mother everyone wants"—who loves her perhaps too much. Elizabeth has had a breakdown and is trying to piece her life together. The prose is unflinching as Elizabeth moves from an area of emotional darkness toward the light of everyday frustrations.

THE YEAR WITHOUT MICHAEL   [956]

WRITTEN BY SUSAN BETH PFEFFER

Cloth: Bantam

Paper: Bantam

Published: 1987

What happens to a family when one child disappears. This novel gives episodic glimpses of the stresses and strains in Jody's family—herself, her kid sister, and her parents—over the year after her brother, Michael, leaves the house and never gets to softball practice.

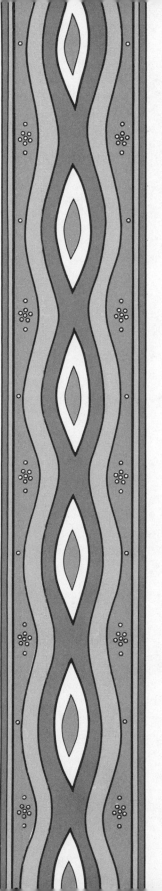

INDEXES

The thirty-four indexes that follow are all based on the principle that the books listed in this guide are numbered consecutively, and the permanent record number remains consistent. Every reference to a book carries that record number, so you can go back into the main entries and check the description. The first indexes are traditional—they include *all* titles mentioned in the guide, all authors and all illustrators. The others are unique. One addresses age appropriateness, another listening levels—since young children can understand much they cannot read alone—and one lists books that specially lend themselves to reading aloud. There are also several dozen special subject indexes, which allow you to look for books in as many ways as you choose.

INDEX TO ALL TITLES

* Related titles or editions are discussed in the text

[675]

SWORDFISH

[354]

334

[145]

337

[896]

341

[612]

[513]

[555]

AUTHORS

Aardema, Verna [46, 557]

Abells, Chana Byers [312]

Adams, Richard [889]

Ahlberg, Janet and Allan [64]

Alcott, Louisa May [794]

Aleichem, Sholom [744]

Alexander, Lloyd [655, 891]

Alexander, Martha [32, 250]

Aliki [75, 432, 449, 539, 580, 582]

Allard, Harry [439, 518]

Allen, Pamela [261]

Andersen, Hans Christian [68, 280, 454, 541, 558]

Andrews, Jan [544]

Anno, Mitsumasa [3, 4, 5, 36, 637]

Archambault, John [556]

Ardizzone, Edward [419]

Arkin, Alan [789]

Armstrong, William H. [862]

Asch, Frank [97, 105]

Atwater, Richard and Florence [602]

Azarian, Mary [73]

Babbitt, Natalie [507, 701, 713, 783, 883]

Bagnold, Enid [814]

Baker, Olaf [555]

Baldwin, Neil [952]

Bang, Molly [11, 60, 226]

Banks, Lynn Reid [760]

Barklem, Jill [302]

Barrett, Judi [34, 35, 53, 504]

Barrie, J. M. [831]

Barth, Edna [536]

Bate, Lucy [415]

Bauer, Caroline Feller [170]

Baum, L. Frank [903]

Bawden, Nina [714]

Bayer, Jane E. [567]

Bayley, Nicola [40]

Baylor, Byrd [340, 372, 550, 296, 329, 386]

Bellairs, John [748]

Bemelmans, Ludwig [145]

Benét, Rosemary and Stephen Vincent [660]

Benchley, Nathaniel [611]

Benjamin, Carol Lea [816]

Berenstain, Stan and Jan [43, 294]

Berger, Barbara Helen [100]

Bierhorst, John [509]

Blake, Quentin [515]

Blegvad, Erik [230]

Blegvad, Lenore [277]

Blishen, Edward [827]

Blos, Joan [152, 459, 666, 724]

Blumberg, Rhoda [688]

Blume, Judy [638, 871, 925]

Blyton, Enid [715]

Bodecker, N. M., translator [129]

Bond, Michael [571]

Bond, Nancy [868]

Boorstin, Daniel J. [785]

Bornstein, Ruth [141]

Bosse, Malcolm [914]

Boynton, Sandra [112]

Brandenberg, Franz [284]

Brett, Jan [279]

Bridgers, Sue Ellen [932]

Briggs, Raymond [8, 19]

Bright, Robert [171]

Brinckloe, Julie [344]

Brink, Carol Ryrie [668]

Brooks, Bruce [944]

Brooks, Walter R. [721]

Brown, M. K. [135]

Brown, Marc [77, 282, 332]

Brown, Marc, and Laurene Krasny [299, 333]

Brown, Marcia [180, 217]

Brown, Margaret Wise [99, 139, 140, 206, 317]

Brown, Ruth [59]

Browne, Anthony [194]

Bryan, Ashley [325, 467, 549]

Bulla, Clyde Robert [576]

Bunting, Eve [427, 593]

Burgess, Thornton W. [606]

Burnett, Frances Hodgson [793, 853]

Burnford, Sheila   [758]
Burningham, John   [102, 164]
Burton, Virginia Lee   [414, 435]
Byars, Betsy   [690, 834, 870, 820]
Calhoun, Mary   [777]
Cameron, Ann   [614]
Cameron, Eleanor   [771]
Carey, Ernestine   [676]
Carey, Valerie Scho   [330]
Carle, Eric   [161, 242, 243]
Carlson, Nancy   [143]
Carlstrom, Nancy White   [133]
Carrick, Carol   [268, 472]
Catling, Patrick Skene   [681]
Caudill, Rebecca   [579]
Cauley, Lorinda Bryan   [535]
Cendrars, Blaise   [499]
Chaikin, Miriam   [640, 754, 762]
Charlip, Remy   [369]
Childress, Alice   [931]
Chorao, Kay   [41]
Christopher, Matt   [703, 719]
Ciardi, John   [564]
Clark, Ann Nolan   [855]
Cleary, Beverly   [103, 609, 699, 808]
Cleaver, Elizabeth   [23, 69]
Cleaver, Vera and Bill   [738, 791, 894]
Clifton, Lucille   [339]
Coatsworth, Elizabeth   [672]
Cohen, Barbara   [441, 874]
Cohen, Miriam   [559]
Cohn, Janice   [387]
Cole, Brock   [560]
Cole, Joanna   [342, 385, 426]
Cole, Sheila   [251]
Collier, Christopher   [811]
Collier, James Lincoln   [811]
Collodi, Carlo   [627]
Colum, Padraic   [677]
Cone, Molly   [804]
Cooney, Barbara   [440]
Cooper, James Fenimore   [787]
Cooper, Susan   [498, 697]
Corbalis, Judy   [904]
Cormier, Robert   [919, 933]

Craft, Ruth   [264]
Cresswell, Helen   [643]
Crews, Donald   [89]
D'Aulaire, Ingri and Edgar Parin   [326, 327]
Dahl, Roald   [297, 338, 662, 674, 766]
Daly, Niki   [177]
Daniel, Mark   [314]
Danziger, Paula   [915]
Davis, Jenny   [928]
de Brunhoff, Jean   [513]
de Regniers, Beatrice Schenk   [156]
DeClements, Barthe   [819]
Delton, Judy   [126, 782]
de Paola, Tomie   [172, 234, 320, 348, 433, 517, 532]
de Trevino, Elizabeth Borton   [756]
Dickens, Charles   [682]
Dickinson, Peter   [396, 673]
Disch, Thomas M.   [663]
Dragonwagon, Crescent   [271, 955]
Drescher, Henrik   [20]
Dr. Seuss   [182, 380, 383, 563, 574, 587, 590]
du Bois, William Pène   [538]
Duke, Kate   [104]
Duncan, Lois   [937]
Dunn, Judy   [137]
Duvoisin, Roger   [193]
Eager, Edward   [735]
Eastman, P. D.   [569]
Edelman, Elaine   [125]
Eichenberg, Fritz   [37, 57]
Elliott , Dan   [588]
Elwell, Peter   [408]
Emberley, Barbara   [63]
Engvick, William   [422]
Enright, Elizabeth   [875]
Estes, Eleanor   [755, 806]
Farjeon, Eleanor   [412]
Farley, Walter   [657, 797]
Feelings, Muriel   [131]
Ferguson, Alane   [527]
Field, Rachel   [742]
Fisher, Leonard Everett   [368, 847]
Fitzgerald, John   [733]
Fitzhugh, Louise   [737, 817]
Flack, Marjorie   [512]

Fleischman, Paul   [929]
Fleischman, Sid   [897]
Florian, Douglas   [1]
Flournoy, Valerie   [471]
Forbes, Esther   [769]
Foreman, Michael   [50]
Fornatale, Pete   [866]
Fosburgh, Lisa   [809]
Fox, Paula   [658, 825, 860, 942]
Frank, Anne   [635]
Freedman, Russell   [689, 759]
Freeman, Don   [54]
Freudberg, Judy   [520]
Friedman, Ina   [382]
Fritz, Jean   [364, 568, 745]
Gackenbach, Dick   [107, 197]
Gag, Wanda   [159]
Galdone, Paul   [52, 225, 228]
Gammell, Stephen   [245]
Gannett, Ruth Stiles   [603]
Gantos, Jack   [205]
Garden, Nancy   [911]
Gardner, Beau   [371]
Garfield, Leon   [406]
Gates, Doris   [659]
Gauch, Patricia Lee   [316]
Geisert, Arthur   [470, 479]
Geiss, Tony   [520]
Geller, Mark   [893]
George, Jean   [813]
George, Jean Craighead   [772]
Gerez, Toni de   [420]
Gerrard, Roy   [502]
Gerstein, Mordicai   [281, 446, 492, 523]
Gibbons, Gail   [158, 241, 349]
Giblin, James Cross   [679]
Giff, Patricia Reilly   [531, 583]
Gilbreth, Frank B.   [676]
Ginsburg, Mirra   [86, 98, 254, 384]
Gish, Lillian   [626]
Glubok, Shirley   [824]
Goble, Paul   [305, 355, 358]
Godden, Rumer   [706, 718]
Goffstein, M. B.   [39, 211, 363]
Goodall, John S.   [16]

Graham, Bob   [79]
Grahame, Kenneth   [843, 900]
Graves, Robert   [298]
Greaves, Margaret   [413]
Greenaway, Kate   [22]
Greene, Bette   [833, 950]
Greene, Constance C.   [729]
Greenfield, Eloise   [115]
Greenwald, Sheila   [586]
Gretz, Suzanna   [224]
Griego, Margot C.   [235]
Grifalconi, Ann   [545]
Griffith, Helen   [353]
Grimes, Nikki   [506]
Grimm Brothers   [417, 775]
Gryski, Camilla   [575]
Guthrie, Donna   [561]
Haas, Irene   [146]
Hague, Kathleen   [29, 150]
Hague, Michael   [150, 445]
Hale, Mary Josepha   [153]
Haley, Gail E.   [218]
Hall, Donald   [466]
Hamilton, Virginia   [747, 800, 830, 899, 941, 951]
Hansen, Ron   [857]
Hanson, Figne   [892]
Harrison, David L.   [621]
Hartley, Deborah   [542]
Hass, E. A.   [757]
Hautzig, Deborah   [516, 547, 546, 598]
Haywood, Carolyn   [573]
Hearn, Michael Patrick   [483]
Hedderwick, Mairi   [405]
Heide, Florence Parry   [612]
Heine, Helme   [90, 192, 195, 461]
Hendershot, Judith   [393]
Herzig, Alison Cragin   [458]
Hest, Amy   [321, 485]
Hewett, Joan   [493]
Hill, Eric   [256]
Hill, Susan   [362]
Hines, Anna Grossnickle   [25]
Hinton, S. E.   [947]
Hirsh, Marilyn   [403]
Hoban, Lillian   [570]

Hoban, Russell   [293]
Hoban, Tana   [13]
Hodges, Margaret   [511]
Hoff, Syd   [578]
Hoffmann, E. T. A.   [821]
Hogrogian, Nonny   [175, 181, 331, 360]
Holabird, Katharine   [33]
Holling, Holling C.   [803, 828]
Hooks, William H.   [444]
Hopkins, Lee Bennett   [210, 616]
Houston, James   [617]
Howard, Katherine   [450]
Howe, Deborah   [667]
Howe, James   [667, 746]
Howker, Janni   [642]
Hughes, Dean   [823]
Hughes, Shirley   [144, 270]
Hurd, Thacher   [148]
Hutchins, Pat   [9, 184, 204]
Hutton, Warwick   [402, 455]
Hyman, Trina Schart   [503]
Irwin, Hadley   [938]
Jaffrey, Madhur   [851]
Jakes, John   [521]
Jarrell, Randall   [356, 634, 645]
Jeffers, Susan   [229, 475]
Johnson, Crockett   [106]
Johnston, Tony   [80]
Jonas, Ann   [114, 252]
Jones, Malcolm   [773]
Joslin, Sesyle   [248]
Joyce, William   [92]
Jukes, Mavis   [411, 605]
Juster, Norton   [832]
Keats, Ezra Jack   [212]
Keller, Holly   [93]
Kellogg, Steven   [48, 481, 295, 473]
Kelly, Eric P.   [881]
Kennedy, Richard   [610, 630]
Kennedy, X. J.   [303]
Kerr, M. E.   [922, 945]
Khalsa, Dayal Kaur   [522]
Kipling, Rudyard   [774, 776]
Kitamura, Satoshi   [249]

Kitchen, Bert   [2]
Kjelgaard, Jim   [652]
Klein, Norma   [807, 927]
Knight, Eric   [786]
Kohn, Bernice   [290]
Komaiko, Leah   [389]
Konigsburg, E. L.   [722, 838, 852, 885]
Korczak, Janusz   [780]
Kraus, Robert   [253]
Krauss, Ruth   [113]
Krementz, Jill   [620, 749, 750, 751]
Krensky, Stephen   [332]
Krumgold, Joseph   [632, 826]
Kunhardt, Dorothy   [190]
Kurelek, William   [484]
Kuskin, Karla   [401, 478, 613]
L'Engle, Madeline   [905]
Laird , Elizabeth
   (with Abba Aregawi Wolde Gabriel)   [437]
Lakin, Patricia   [62]
Lalicki, Barbara   [122]
Lamorisse, Albert   [488]
Landis, J. D.   [695]
Lang, Andrew   [686]
Langstaff, John   [91, 179]
Langton, Jane   [716]
Larrick, Nancy   [553, 835]
Lasker, Joe   [335, 434]
Lasky, Kathryn   [286, 615, 622, 815, 913, 948]
Lauber, Patrica   [702, 888]
Law, Felicia   [698]
Lawson, Robert   [648, 841]
Leaf, Margaret   [71]
Leaf, Munro   [219]
Lee, Dennis   [400]
Lee, Jeanne M.   [288]
Lenski, Lois   [209, 867]
LeShan, Eda   [788]
Lessac, Frané   [451]
Lesser, Rika   [370]
Lester, Helen   [196]
Lester, Julius   [409, 872, 878]
Levinson, Riki   [123, 236, 581]
Levitan, Sonia   [770, 949]

[857]

Muller, Jorg [310]
Munro, Roxie [127]
Murphy, Jill [81]
Murphy, Shirley Rousseau [223]
Musgrove, Margaret [283]
Myers, Walter Dean [943]
Nash, Ogden [693]
Neville, Emily Cheney [649, 764]
Newton, Laura P. [263]
Newton, Suzanne [935]
Nhuong, Quang Nhuong [784]
Nic Leodhas, Sorche [272]
Nilsson, Lennart [753]
Noble, Trinka Hakes [328]
Nordstrom, Ursula [854]
Norton, Mary [661]
O'Brien, Robert C. [810]
O'Dell, Scott [656, 763, 781, 858]
O'Donnell, Elizabeth Lee [425]
O'Kelley, Mattie Lou [350]
Oakley, Graham [318]
Olson, Arielle North [119]
Oneal, Zibby [934]
Orgel, Doris [700]
Ormerod, Jan [14, 183]
Oxenbury, Helen [72, 101, 373]
Parish, Peggy [566]
Parker, Nancy Winslow [306]
Parks, Van Dyke [773]
Parrish, Peggy [604]
Paterson, Katherine [664, 687, 734, 799, 936]
Paulsen, Gary [923]
Pearce, Philippa [879]
Pearson, Tracey Campbell [21]
Peavy, Linda [924, 954]
Peck, Robert Newton [863, 921]
Peek, Merle [154]
Peet, Bill [468]
Perez, Carla [267]
Perrault, Charles [319]
Peters, David [354]
Petry, Ann [877]
Pfeffer, Susan Beth [956]
Phelps, Ethel Johnston [796]

Phillips, Mildred [501]
Piper, Watty [138]
Politi, Leo [214]
Polushkin, Maria [149, 162]
Pomerantz, Charlotte [257]
Porter, Eleanor H. [836]
Potter, Beatrix [222]
Prelutsky, Jack [200, 487]
Prokofiev, Sergei [476]
Provensen, Alice and Martin
    [187, 237, 265, 361, 474, 500]
Pyle, Howard [865]
Rabe, Bernice [287]
Raffi [199]
Ransome, Arthur [346]
Raskin, Ellen [176, 215, 890]
Rawlings, Marjorie Kinnan [906]
Rawls, Wilson [895]
Rayner, Mary [163, 323]
Regniers, Beatrice Schenk de [128, 244, 418]
Reiss, Johanna [887]
Rettich, Margret [519]
Rey, H. A. [56]
Richler, Mordecai [765]
Risom, Ole [121]
Robinson, Barbara [650]
Robinson, Deborah [267]
Rockwell, Anne [528]
Rockwell, Harlow [67]
Rockwell, Thomas [752]
Rodowsky, Colby [725]
Roennfelt, Robert [10]
Rogers, Fred [95]
Rogers, Jean [407]
Rogers, Mary [720]
Rogers, Paul [85]
Roop, Peter and Connie [594]
Root, Phyllis [443]
Rounds, Glen [246, 460]
Ryan, Cheli Duran [378]
Rylant, Cynthia [202, 712]
Sachs, Marilyn [646]
Saint Exupery, Antoine de [792]
Salassi, Otto R. [910]

Sandburg, Carl   [247, 846]
Sanders, Scott R.   [740, 912]
Scarry, Richard   [203, 489, 490]
Schlee, Ann   [641]
Schwartz, Alvin   [591, 850]
Schwartz, Amy   [289, 375, 447]
Schwartz, David M.   [381]
Seeger, Pete   [24, 83]
Seeger, Charles   [83]
Seeger, Ruth Crawford   [275]
Segal, Lore   [514, 525]
Selden, Bernice   [802]
Selden, George   [691, 726]
Sendak, Maurice   [110, 178, 259, 394, 463, 505]
Seredy, Kate   [898]
Seuss, Dr.   [182, 380, 383, 563, 574, 587, 590]
Sewall, Marcia   [480]
Sewell, Anna   [654]
Sewell, Anna (adapted by Robin McKinley)   [653]
Sharmat, Marjorie Weinman   [94, 160, 392, 728]
Shaw, Nancy   [208]
Shreve, Susan   [717]
Shub, Elizabeth   [623, 625]
Shulevitz, Uri   [61, 185]
Shyer, Marlene Fanta   [111]
Siegal, Aranka   [886]
Siegal, Beatrice   [939]
Silverstein, Shel   [359, 790, 896]
Simon, Seymour   [276, 710, 795]
Singer, Isaac Bashevis   [431, 837, 864, 908]
Skofield, James   [27]
Slobodkina, Esphyr   [49]
Small, David   [469]
Smart, Christopher   [347]
Smith, Doris Buchanan   [873]
Smith, Janice Lee   [595]
Smith, Robert Kimmel   [680, 768]
Smith, Ursula   [924, 954]
Snyder, Carol   [801]
Snyder, Zilpha Keately   [709, 739]
Sobol, Donald J.   [711]
Sommer-Bodenburg, Angela   [812]
Speare, Elizabeth George   [665]
Sperry, Armstrong   [669]

[116]

Spier, Peter   [17, 55, 456]
Stadler, John   [116]
Stanley, Diane   [477]
Steig, William
   [30, 266, 274, 304, 307, 334, 365, 494, 624, 707]
Steinbeck, John   [842]
Stepto, Michele   [213]
Steptoe, John   [220, 448, 510]
Stevenson, James   [377, 562]
Stevenson, Robert Louis   [313, 779, 880]
Stiles, Norman   [391]
Stolz, Mary   [704, 818, 840]
Streatfeild, Noel   [644]
Swift, Hildegarde Hoyt   [416]
Switzer, Ellen   [822]
Tafuri, Nancy   [109]
Tamarin, Alfred   [824]
Taylor, Mark   [374]
Taylor, Mildred   [731, 844]
Taylor, Sydney   [629]
Tejima,   [87]
Tesnohlidek, Rudolf   [692]
Thaler, Mike   [189, 592]
Thomas, Dylan   [678]

Thompson, Kay   [337]
Thurber, James   [429]
Todd, Leonard   [651]
Tolkein, J. R. R.   [743, 940]
Townsend, John Rowe   [696]
Travers, P. L.   [798]
Tripp, Wallace   [367, 430]
Tunis, John R.   [778]
Turk, Hanne   [12]
Turkle, Brinton   [232]
Turner, Ann   [324]
Tusa, Tricia   [410]
Uchida, Yoshiko   [767]
Udry, Janice May   [238]
Ungerer, Tomi   [231, 291, 442]
Van Allsburg, Chris   [351, 404, 452, 482]
van de Wetering, Janwillem   [589]
Van Leeuwen, Jean   [565]
Vincent, Gabrielle   [70]
Viorst, Judith   [269, 390, 526]
Vipont, Elfrida   [66]
Voak, Chatlotte   [464]
Waber, Bernard   [395, 424]
Wachter, Oralee   [457]
Waddell, Martin   [366, 618]
Wahl, Jan   [118]
Walker, Mildred Pitts   [169]
Walsh, Jill Paton   [723]
Walter, Mildred Pitts   [540]
Wasson, Valentine P.   [315]
Watanabe, Shiego   [117]
Watson, Clyde   [38, 51, 74]

Webster, Jean   [694]
Weiss, Ellen   [524]
Wells, Rosemary   [136, 155, 191]
Wescott, Nadine Bernard   [124]
Wheeler, Cindy   [151]
White, E. B.   [675, 869, 882]
Wilde, Oscar   [497]
Wilder, Laura Ingalls   [597]
Willard, Nancy   [548, 848]
Williams, Barbara   [305]
Williams, Jay   [341]
Williams, Margery   [543]
Williams, Vera B.   [309, 529]
Winter, Jeanette   [120]
Winter, Paula   [6]
Winthrop, Elizabeth   [311, 534]
Wiseman, Bernard   [600]
Wolde, Gunilla   [227]
Wood, Audrey   [173]
Worth, Valerie   [861]
Wright, Blanche Fisher   [201]
Wright, Joan Richards   [306]
Yagawa , Sumiko   [322]
Yep, Laurence   [708, 917]
Yolen, Jane   [357, 423, 465, 577, 730, 918, 926]
Yorinks, Arthur   [376, 399, 421]
Young, Ed   [15]
Zelinsky, Paul O.   [495]
Zemach, Harve   [336]
Zemach, Margot   [398]
Ziefert, Harriet   [130, 453]
Zolotow, Charlotte   [44, 108, 165, 168, 188, 262, 388]

ILLUSTRATORS

Aaron, Jane [457]
Ahlberg, Janet and Allan   [64]
Akaba, Suekichi [322]
Alexander, Martha   [32, 44, 250]
Aliki   [75, 284, 342, 432, 449, 539, 580, 582]
Allen, Pamela   [261]
Allen, Thomas B.   [393, 576]
Ancona, George   [369]
Anno, Mitsumasa   [3, 4, 5, 36, 637]
Apple, Margot   [208, 681]
Ardizzone, Edward   [280, 412, 419]
Aruego, Jose   [160, 253, 254, 384]
Asch, Frank   [97, 105]
Babbitt, Natalie   [507, 701, 783, 861]
Bacon, Paul   [521]
Bang, Molly   [11, 60, 226]
Barklem, Jill   [302, 862]
Barkley, James   [862]
Barrett, Ron   [34, 35, 53]
Barth, Edna   [536]
Barton, Byron   [94, 98, 257, 729]
Baruffi, Andrea   [130]
Bassett, Jeni   [47]
Bayley, Nicola   [40]
Baynes, Pauline   [396, 683, 718]
Bemelmans, Ludwig   [145]
Benson, Patrick   [618]
Berenstain, Stan and Jan   [43, 294]
Berger, Barbara Helen   [100]
Bernstein, Zena   [810]
Berridge, Celia   [85]
Blake, Quentin   [297, 338, 515, 693]
Blegvad, Eric   [526, 230, 264, 277]
Bloom, Lloyd   [411, 605, 639, 796]
Bodecker, N. M.   [129, 735]
Bomzer, Barry   [703]
Bond, Felicia   [149]
Booth, Graham   [374]
Bornstein, Ruth   [141]
Boynton, Sandra   [112]
Brady, Irene   [829]

Bragg, Michael   [406]
Brett, Jan   [240, 279, 795]
Brewster, Patience   [62]
Briggs, Raymond   [8, 19, 66]
Bright, Robert   [171]
Brinkloe, Julie   [344, 599]
Brook, Judy   [650, 698]
Brown, M. K.   [135]
Brown, Marc   [77, 200, 282, 299, 332, 333, 598]
Brown, Marcia   [180, 217, 319, 499]
Brown, Richard   [96]
Brown, Ruth   [59]
Browne, Anthony   [194]
Bryan, Ashley   [325, 467, 549]
Bryant, Samuel   [781]
Burger, Carl   [758]
Burkert, Nancy Ekholm   [766]
Burningham, John   [102, 164]
Burton, Virginia Lee   [414, 435]
Cady, Harrison   [606]
Carle, Eric   [161, 242, 243]
Carlson, Nancy   [143]
Carrick, Donald   [111, 268, 444, 472, 493, 496]
Cauley, Lorinda Bryan   [535]
Chamberlin, Margaret   [428]
Chambliss, Maxie   [592]
Charlot, Jean   [632, 855]
Chartier, Norman   [588]
Child, Charles   [660]
Chorao, Kay   [41, 392]
Cleaver, Elizabeth   [23, 69]
Coalson, Glo   [315]
Cober, Alan   [697]
Coconis, Ted   [870]
Cogancherry, Helen   [581]
Cole, Brock   [560, 723, 760]
Cooney, Barbara
   [139, 235, 275, 317, 420, 440, 466, 509]
Craig, Helen   [33, 904]
Crespi, Francesca   [413]
Crews, Donald   [89]

Cruz, Ray [269]
Cuffari, Richard [633, 874]
Cummings, Pat [169]
d'Aulaire, Ingri and Edgar Parin [326, 327]
Dabcovich, Lydia [119, 542]
Daly, Niki [177]
Daniel, Alan [667]
Darling, Louis [808]
Dawson, Diane [162]
de Brunhoff, Jean [513]
de Groat, Diane [276, 415, 631, 717]
Degan, Bruce [133, 426, 577]
Dennis, Wesley [842]
Denslow, W. W. [903]
de Paola, Tomie
    [153, 172, 223, 234, 320, 348, 364, 433, 532]
Deraney, Michael J. [441]
Dewey, Ariene [160, 253, 254, 384]
Diamond, Donna [664]
di Grazia, Thomas [744]
Dillon, Diane and Leo [115, 283, 483, 557, 830]
Domanska, Janina [881]
Doty, Roy [871]
Downing, Julie [809]

Drescher, Henrik [20]
Dr. Seuss [182, 380, 383, 563, 574, 587]
du Bois, William Pène [168, 262, 538]
Duke, Kate [104]
Dunn, Phoebe [137]
Dupasquier, Philippe [366]
Duvoisin, Roger [193]
Eastman, P. D. [569]
Egielski, Richard [376, 399, 421, 630, 762]
Eichenberg, Fritz [37, 57]
Einzig, Susan [879]
Elwell, Peter [408]
Emberley, Ed [63]
Eyolfson, Norman [765]
Feelings, Tom [131, 506, 878]
Feiffer, Jules [832]
Fiammenghi, Gioia [680]
Fisher, Leonard Everett [308, 368, 847]
Fitzhugh, Louise [737, 817]
Florian, Douglas [1]
Foreman, Michael [50, 774, 776, 851]
Fortnum, Peggy [571]
Frame, Paul [777]
Frampton, David [401]
Frascino, Edward [882]
Freeman, Don [54]
Friedman, Marvin [640]
Gackenbach, Dick [107, 197, 595]
Gag, Wanda [159]
Galdone, Paul [52, 128, 225, 228, 705]
Gammell, Stephen [202, 245, 459, 555, 850]
Gannett, Ruth Chrisman [603]
Gardner, Beau [371]
Gehm, Charles [863]
Geisert, Arthur [470, 479]
George, Jean [813]
Gerrard, Roy [502]
Gerstein, Mordicai [281, 446, 492, 523]
Giavanopoulos, Paul [788]
Gibbons, Gail [158, 241, 349]
Glanzman, Louis S. [608, 818]
Glass, Andrew [929]
Glienke, Amelie [812]
Goble, Paul [305, 355, 358]

[494]

Goembel, Ponder   [740]

Goffstein, M. B.   [39, 211, 363]

Goodall, John S.   [16]

Goode, Diane   [123, 516]

Gorey, Edward   [564, 612, 748]

Graham, Bob   [79]

Grebu, Devis   [403]

Greenaway, Kate   [22]

Greenwald, Sheila   [586]

Gretz, Suzanna   [224]

Grifalconi, Ann   [339, 545]

Grossman, Nancy   [579]

Haas, Irene   [146]

Hague, Michael   [29, 150, 445, 743]

Haley, Gail E.   [218]

Hanson, Peter E.   [594]

Hauman, George and Doris   [138]

Hays, Michael   [24, 731]

Haywood, Carolyn   [573]

Hedderwick, Mairi   [405]

Heine, Helme   [90, 192, 195, 461]

Hill, Eric   [256]

Himler, Ronald   [296, 324]

Himmelman, John   [213]

Hines, Anna Grossnickle   [25]

Hoban, Lillian   [126, 287, 534, 559, 570]

Hoban, Tana   [13]

Hoff, Syd   [578]

Hogrogian, Nonny   [175, 181, 272, 331, 360, 625]

Holling, Holling C.   [803, 828]

Houston, James   [617]

Hughes, Shirley   [144, 270]

Hurd, Clement   [99, 206]

Hurd, Thacher   [148]

Hutchins, Pat   [9, 184, 204]

Hutton, Warwick   [402, 455, 498]

Hyman, Trina Schart
   [417, 503, 511, 668, 678, 682, 815]

Isadora, Rachel   [345, 623]

Jagr, Miroslav   [83]

Jeffers, Susan   [229, 558, 653]

Jeschke, Susan   [475]

John, Helen   [629]

Johnson, Crockett   [106]

Johnson, Larry   [719]

Johnson, Lonni Sue   [504]

Johnson, Pamela   [840]

Jonas, Ann   [114, 252]

Jones, Bob   [768]

Joyce, William   [92, 118]

Judkis, Jim   [95]

Julian-Ottie, Vanessa   [362]

Keats, Ezra Jack   [212]

Keller, Holly   [93]

Kelley, True   [236]

Kellogg, Steven   [48, 295, 301, 328, 381, 473, 481, 567]

Khalsa, Dayal Kaur   [522]

Kitamura, Satoshi   [249]

Kitchen, Bert   [2]

Knight, Christopher G.   [286, 622, 615]

Knight, Hilary   [166, 337, 524]

Konigsburg, E. L.   [722, 838]

Krementz, Jill   [620, 749, 750, 751]

Krush, Beth and Joe   [661]

Kuhn, Bob   [652]

Kunhardt, Dorothy   [190]

Kurelek, William   [484]

Kuskin, Karla   [613]

Lamorisse, Albert   [488]

Lantz, Paul   [659]

Laroche, Giles   [209]

Larrea , Victoria de   [244]

Lasker, Joe   [335, 434]

Lathrop, Dorothy P.   [742]

Lawson, Robert   [219, 602, 648, 841]

Le Cain, Errol   [537]

Lee, Jeanne M.   [288]

Lee, Jody   [636]

Lemieux, Michele   [273]

Lenski, Lois   [572, 867]

Lent, Blair   [233]

Lessac, Frané   [451]

Lewin, Ted   [814]

Lieblich, Irene   [837]

Lilly, Charles   [833]

Lincoln, Patricia Henderson   [626]

Linden, Madelaine Gill   [26]

Lionni, Leo   [88, 221]

Lisowski, Gabriel   [902]
Lloyd, Megan   [616]
Lobel, Anita   [174, 186, 198, 453]
Lobel, Arnold   [260, 300, 330, 343, 378, 390, 436, 486, 487, 585, 601, 607, 611, 619]
Locker, Thomas   [258]
Lorenz, Lee   [551]
Low, Joseph   [157]
Macaulay, David   [671, 684, 884]
MacDonald, Suse   [28]
Madden, Don   [757]
Maestro, Betsy and Giulio   [255]
Mai, Vo-Dinh   [784]
Mariana   [438]
Maris, Ron   [167]
Marrella, Maria Pia   [856]
Marshall, James   [132, 352, 439, 508, 518, 584]
Marstall, Bob   [134]
Martin, Charles   [397]
Maruki, Toshi   [379]
Mathers, Petra   [754]
Mathieu, Joe   [391, 520, 546, 547]
Mayer, Mercer   [7, 292, 341, 733]
McCarthy, Patricia   [207]
McCloskey, Robert   [45, 147]
McCully, Emily Arnold   [18, 347, 752, 805]
McDermott, Gerald   [31, 58, 216, 627]
McPhail, David   [42, 78, 82, 848]
Mikolaycak, Charles   [285, 311, 423, 427]
Milhous, Katherine   [65]
Montaufier, Poupa   [462]
Montresor, Beni   [156]
Mordvinoff, Will and Nicholas   [76]
Moser, Barry   [773]
Most, Bernard   [552]
Muñoz, Rie   [407]
Muller, Jorg   [476]
Munro, Roxie   [127]
Munsinger, Lynn   [196, 589]
Murphy, Jill   [81]
Natti, Susanna   [531]
Nicholson, William   [543]
O'Kelley, Mattie Lou   [350]
Oakley, Graham   [318]

Ohtomo, Yasuo   [117]
Ormerod, Jan   [14, 183, 831]
Owens, Gail   [387, 771]
Oxenbury, Helen   [72, 101, 373]
Palladini, David   [730]
Parker, Nancy Winslow   [170, 179, 306]
Parnall, Peter   [278, 329, 340, 372, 386, 550]
Pearson, Tracey Campbell   [21]
Peek, Merle   [154]
Peet, Bill   [468]
Peters, David   [354]
Petersham, Maud and Miska   [846]
Pincus, Harriet   [247, 525]
Pinkney, Jerry   [471, 872]
Pinto, Ralph   [409]
Pogany, Willy   [677]
Politi, Leo   [214]
Potter, Beatrix   [222]
Primavera, Elsie   [316]
Provensen, Alice and Martin
   [187, 237, 265, 361, 474, 500, 548]
Pyle, Howard   [865]
Raible, Alton   [709, 739]
Rand, Ted   [556]
Raskin, Ellen   [176, 215, 835]
Ray, Deborah   [530]
Rayner, Mary   [163, 323]
Rettich, Margret   [519]
Rey, H. A.   [56]
Robinson, Charles   [770, 873]
Robinson, Deborah   [267]
Rockwell, Anne   [68, 528]
Rockwell, Harlow   [67]
Roennfelt, Robert   [10]
Rogers, Jacqueline   [263]
Rojankovsky, Feodor   [91]
Rounds, Glen   [246, 460]
Rubel, Nicole   [205]
Russell, Jim   [876]
Ryan, DyAnne DiSalvo   [103]
Saint Exupery, Antoine de   [792]
Sandin, Joan   [789]
Sankey, Tom   [575]
Say, Allan   [382]

[830]

[146]

360

AGE-APPROPRIATE INDEXES

Preschoolers

[574]

[247]

The Two of Them   (Story Book)   [539]

Ty's One-Man Band   (Story Book)   [540]

The Ugly Duckling   (Story Book)   [541]

Uncle Elephant   (Early Reading Book)   [619]

Up Goes the Skyscraper   (Picture Book)   [241]

The Very Busy Spider   (Picture Book)   [242]

The Very Hungry Caterpillar   (Picture Book)   [243]

A Visit to the Sesame Street Hospital   (Story Book)   [546]

A Visit to the Sesame Street Library   (Story Book)   [547]

Wake Up, Bear ...It's Christmas   (Picture Book)   [245]

Wake Up, Sun   (Early Reading Book)   [621]

The Wedding Procession of the Rag Doll and the Broom
   Handle and Who Was in It   (Picture Book)   [247]

A Weekend in the Country   (Story Book)   [551]

Whatever Happened to the Dinosaurs?   (Story Book)   [552]

What's Inside? The Alphabet Book   (Picture Book)   [249]

When the Dark Comes Dancing: A Bedtime Poetry Book
   (Story Book)   [553]

When the New Baby Comes I'm Moving Out
   (Picture Book)   [250]

When the Tide Is Low   (Picture Book)   [251]

When We Were Very Young   (Story Book)   [554]

When You Were a Baby   (Picture Book)   [252]

Where Are You Going, Little Mouse?
   (Picture Book)   [253]

Where Does The Sun Go at Night?   (Picture Book)   [254]

Where Is My Friend? A Word Concept Book
   (Picture Book)   [255]

Where's Spot?   (Picture Book)   [256]

Where's the Bear?   (Picture Book)   [257]

Where the Wild Things Are   (Picture Book)   [259]

Whiskers & Rhymes   (Picture Book)   [260]

The White Stallion   (Early Reading Book)   [623]

Who Sank the Boat?   (Picture Book)   [261]

Why Mosquitos Buzz in People's Ears: A West African
   Tale   (Story Book)   [557]

William's Doll   (Picture Book)   [262]

William the Vehicle King   (Picture Book)   [263]

Will I Have a Friend?   (Story Book)   [559]

Winnie-the-Pooh   (Middle Reading Book)   [901]

The Winter Bear   (Picture Book)   [264]

The Winter Wren   (Story Book)   [560]

The Witch Who Lives down the Hall   (Story Book)   [561]

Worse Than Willy!   (Story Book)   [562]

The Year at Maple Hill Farm   (Picture Book)   [265]

The Yellow Umbrella   (Wordless Book)   [20]

Yertle the Turtle and Other Stories   (Story Book)   [563]

Your Turn, Doctor   (Picture Book)   [267]

Early Grades

A Apple Pie   (Picture Book)   [21]

A-Apple Pie   (Picture Book)   [22]

Abiyoyo   (Picture Book)   [24]

The Accident   (Story Book)   [268]

Airplane Ride   (Wordless Book)   [1]

Alexander and the Terrible, Horrible, No Good, Very Bad
   Day   (Story Book)   [269]

All Small   (Picture Book)   [26]

All Wet! All Wet!   (Picture Book)   [27]

Alphabatics   (Picture Book)   [28]

Alphabears: An ABC Book   (Picture Book)   [29]

Always, Always   (Story Book)   [271]

Always Room for One More   (Story Book)   [272]

Amahl and the Night Visitors   (Story Book)   [273]

Amanda Pig and Her Big Brother Oliver
   (Early Reading Book)   [565]

Amelia Bedelia   (Early Reading Book)   [566]

American Folk Songs for Children   (Story Book)   [275]

Amos & Boris   (Picture Book)   [30]

A, My Name Is Alice   (Early Reading Book)   [567]

Anansi the Spider: A Tale from the Ashanti
   (Picture Book)   [31]

And My Mean Old Mother Will Be Sorry, Blackboard Bear
   (Picture Book)   [32]

Angelina Ballerina   (Picture Book)   [33]

Animal Alphabet   (Wordless Book)   [2]

The Animal Family   (Middle Reading Book)   [634]

Animals Should Definitely NOT Act Like People
   (Picture Book)   [34]

Animals Should Definitely NOT Wear Clothing
   (Picture Book)   [35]

Anna Banana and Me   (Story Book)   [277]

Annie and the Old One   (Story Book)   [278]

Annie and the Wild Animals   (Story Book)   [279]

Anno's Alphabet: An Adventure in Imagination
   (Picture Book)   [36]

Anno's Counting Book   (Wordless Book)   [3]

No More Secrets for Me   (Story Book)   [457]

No More Monsters for Me   (Early Reading Book)   [604]

Nothing Ever Happens on My Block
   (Picture Book)   [176]

Not So Fast, Songololo   (Picture Book)   [177]

The Nutcracker   (Middle Reading Book)   [821]

Oh, A-Hunting We Will Go   (Picture Book)   [179]

Old Henry   (Story Book)   [459]

Old Mother West Wind   (Early Reading Book)   [606]

One Day in Paradise   (Story Book)   [461]

One Fine Day   (Picture Book)   [181]

One Fish, Two Fish, Red Fish, Blue Fish
   (Picture Book)   [182]

101 Things to Do with a Baby   (Picture Book)   [183]

1 Hunter   (Picture Book)   [184]

One Monday Morning   (Picture Book)   [185]

One Summer at Grandmother's House   (Story Book)   [462]

The Other Bone   (Wordless Book)   [15]

Our Animal Friends at Maple Hill Farm
   (Picture Book)   [187]

Outside Over There   (Story Book)   [463]

Over and Over   (Picture Book)   [188]

Owl at Home   (Early Reading Book)   [607]

Ox-Cart Man   (Story Book)   [466]

The Ox of the Wonderful Horns and Other African Folktales
   (Story Book)   [467]

Paddy's Evening Out   (Wordless Book)   [16]

Pamela Camel   (Story Book)   [468]

Paper John   (Story Book)   [469]

The Patchwork Quilt   (Story Book)   [471]

Patrick's Dinosaurs   (Story Book)   [472]

Paul Bunyan   (Story Book)   [473]

A Peaceable Kingdom: The Shaker Abecedarius
   (Story Book)   [474]

The Pearl   (Picture Book)   [192]

Perfect the Pig   (Story Book)   [475]

Peter and the Wolf   (Story Book)   [476]

Peter Spier's Rain   (Wordless Book)   [17]

Peter the Great   (Story Book)   [477]

The Philharmonic Gets Dressed   (Story Book)   [478]

Piggybook   (Picture Book)   [194]

Pigs from A to Z   (Story Book)   [479]

The Pigs' Wedding   (Picture Book)   [195]

Pinkerton, Behave   (Story Book)   [481]

Piping Down the Valleys Wild
   (Middle Reading Book)   [835]

Pippi Longstocking   (Early Reading Book)   [608]

The Polar Express   (Story Book)   [482]

Pookins Gets Her Way   (Picture Book)   [196]

The Porcelain Cat   (Story Book)   [483]

Potatoes, Potatoes   (Picture Book)   [198]

A Prairie Boy's Winter   (Story Book)   [484]

The Purple Coat   (Story Book)   [485]

The Random House Book of Mother Goose
   (Story Book)   [486]

The Random House Book of Poetry for Children
   (Story Book)   [487]

Read-Aloud Rhymes for the Very Young
   (Picture Book)   [200]

The Red Balloon   (Story Book)   [488]

The Relatives Came   (Picture Book)   [202]

Richard Kennedy: Collected Stories
   (Early Reading Book)   [610]

Richard Scarry's What Do People Do All Day?
   (Story Book)   [490]

The Ridiculous Story of Gammer Gurton's Needle
   (Story Book)   [491]

The Room   (Story Book)   [492]

Rootabaga Stories   (Middle Reading Book)   [846]

Rosalie   (Story Book)   [493]

Rotten Island   (Story Book)   [494]

Rotten Ralph   (Picture Book)   [205]

Rumpelstiltskin   (Story Book)   [495]

Saint George and the Dragon   (Story Book)   [511]

Sam the Minuteman   (Early Reading Book)   [611]

Sarah, Plain and Tall   (Middle Reading Book)   [849]

Secrets of a Small Brother   (Story Book)   [496]

The Selfish Giant   (Story Book)   [497]

The Selkie Girl   (Story Book)   [498]

17 Kings and 42 Elephants   (Picture Book)   [207]

Shadow   (Story Book)   [499]

Shaker Lane   (Story Book)   [500]

The Sign in Mendel's Window   (Story Book)   [501]

Sir Cedric   (Story Book)   [502]

The Sky Is Full of Song   (Picture Book)   [210]

The Sleeping Beauty   (Story Book)   [503]

Sleepy People   (Picture Book)   [211]

A Snake Is Totally Tail   (Story Book)   [504]

[522]

Middle Grades

[164]

READ-ALOUD BOOKS

[182]

HUMMINGBIRD, Weasel, Pickerel, Moose,

[490]

mixing trough

[146]

SPECIAL SUBJECT INDEXES

Alphabet

Animals

[282]

[532]

Watership Down (Middle Reading Book) [889]

Whatever Happened to the Dinosaurs? (Story Book) [552]

Where Does The Sun Go at Night? (Picture Book) [254]

Where Is My Friend? A Word Concept Book
(Picture Book) [255]

Where's Spot? (Picture Book) [256]

Where's the Bear? (Picture Book) [257]

Where the Red Fern Grows
(Middle Reading Book) [895]

White Dynamite and Curly Kidd (Story Book) [556]

Who Sank the Boat? (Picture Book) [261]

The Wind in the Willows (Middle Reading Book) [900]

Winnie-the-Pooh (Middle Reading Book) [901]

The Winter Bear (Picture Book) [264]

The Year at Maple Hill Farm (Picture Book) [265]

Yertle the Turtle and Other Stories (Story Book) [563]

Anthologies

American Folk Songs for Children (Story Book) [275]

The Helen Oxenbury Nursery Story Book
(Story Book) [373]

James Marshall's Mother Goose (Picture Book) [132]

The Random House Book of Poetry for Children
(Story Book) [487]

Read-Aloud Rhymes for the Very Young
(Picture Book) [200]

Tomie de Paola's Favorite Nursery Tales
(Story Book) [532]

Tomie de Paola's Mother Goose (Picture Book) [234]

When the Dark Comes Dancing: A Bedtime Poetry Book
(Story Book) [553]

Bedtime

The Baby's Bedtime Book (Picture Book) [41]

Catch Me & Kiss Me & Say It Again
(Picture Book) [51]

D'Aulaire's Norse Gods and Giants (Story Book) [327]

Each Peach Pear Plum: An "I Spy" Story
(Picture Book) [64]

Fables (Story Book) [343]

Family (Picture Book) [72]

Four Brave Sailors (Picture Book) [86]

George Shrinks (Picture Book) [92]

Goldie the Dollmaker (Story Book) [363]

Goodbye House (Picture Book) [97]

Goodnight Moon (Picture Book) [99]

Grandfather Twilight (Picture Book) [100]

Harold and the Purple Crayon (Picture Book) [106]

Hector Protector and As I Went over the Water:
Two Nursery Rhymes (Picture Book) [110]

Hildilid's Night (Story Book) [378]

Horton Hatches the Egg (Story Book) [380]

Humphrey's Bear (Picture Book) [118]

Hush Little Baby (Picture Book) [120]

I Am a Bunny (Picture Book) [121]

In the Night Kitchen (Story Book) [394]

I Won't Go to Bed! (Picture Book) [130]

Jesse Bear, What Will You Wear? (Picture Book) [133]

The Jungle Book (Middle Reading Book) [774]

Just So Stories (Middle Reading Book) [776]

Little Bear (Early Reading Book) [596]

The Little Fur Family (Picture Book) [140]

Little Gorilla (Picture Book) [141]

Lucy & Tom's 1 2 3 (Picture Book) [144]

The Lullaby Songbook (Story Book) [423]

The Maggie B (Picture Book) [146]

Many Moons (Story Book) [429]

Moonlight (Wordless Book) [14]

Moon Tiger (Story Book) [443]

Mother, Mother, I Want Another (Picture Book) [162]

Mr. and Mrs. Pig's Evening Out (Picture Book) [163]

Mr. Rabbit and the Lovely Present (Picture Book) [165]

The Napping House (Picture Book) [173]

One Fish, Two Fish, Red Fish, Blue Fish
(Picture Book) [182]

Owly (Picture Book) [189]

The Philharmonic Gets Dressed (Story Book) [478]

The Porcelain Cat (Story Book) [483]

The Real Mother Goose (Picture Book) [201]

Richard Scarry's Best Word Book Ever
(Picture Book) [203]

The Runaway Bunny (Picture Book) [206]

Sleepy People (Picture Book) [211]

Snuggle Piggy and the Magic Blanket
(Picture Book) [213]

The Something (Story Book) [507]

Behavior Problems

Biography/Autobiography

Boys

[603]

SCOLOSAURUS
20 feet long
6,000 pounds

[582]

Seven Kisses in a Row   (Middle Reading Book)   [856]
Some Swell Pup or Are You Sure You Want a Dog?
   (Story Book)   [505]
Sounder   (Middle Reading Book)   [862]
Stevie   (Story Book)   [510]
The Stories Julian Tells   (Early Reading Book)   [614]
Stories for Children   (Middle Reading Book)   [864]
The Story of Babar   (Story Book)   [513]
The Story of Mrs. Lovewright and Purrless Her Cat
   (Story Book)   [514]
Susan and Gordon Adopt a Baby   (Story Book)   [520]
Tales of a Fourth Grade Nothing
   (Middle Reading Book)   [871]
Tales of a Gambling Grandma   (Story Book)   [522]
Teddy Bears Cure a Cold   (Picture Book)   [224]
Telephone Time: A First Book of Telephone Do's and
   Don't's   (Story Book)   [524]
Ten, Nine, Eight   (Picture Book)   [226]
Three Days on a River in a Red Canoe
   (Story Book)   [529]
A Trip to the Doctor   (Picture Book)   [239]
Up Goes the Skyscraper   (Picture Book)   [241]
Very Last First Time   (Story Book)   [544]
A Visit to the Sesame Street Library   (Story Book)   [547]
Waiting for Mama   (Picture Book)   [244]
When the New Baby Comes I'm Moving Out
   (Picture Book)   [250]
When You Were a Baby   (Picture Book)   [252]
Where Are You Going, Little Mouse?
   (Picture Book)   [253]
Where the Lilies Bloom   (Middle Reading Book)   [894]
Willie Bea and the Time the Martians Landed
   (Middle Reading Book)   [899]
Worse Than Willy!   (Story Book)   [562]

Fantasy

Abel's Island   (Middle Reading Book)   [624]
The Adventures of Pinocchio
   (Middle Reading Book)   [627]
Amy's Eyes   (Middle Reading Book)   [630]
The Animal Family   (Middle Reading Book)   [634]
Arnold of the Ducks   (Story Book)   [281]
A Bear Called Paddington   (Early Reading Book)   [571]

The BFG   (Story Book)   [297]
The Big Green Book   (Story Book)   [298]
The Black Cauldron   (Middle Reading Book)   [655]
The Borrowers   (Middle Reading Book)   [661]
Brave Irene   (Story Book)   [304]
The Brave Little Toaster   (Middle Reading Book)   [663]
The Changeover: A Supernatural Romance
   (Young Adult)   [916]
Charlie and the Chocolate Factory
   (Middle Reading Book)   [674]
Charlotte's Web   (Middle Reading Book)   [675]
The Chocolate Touch   (Middle Reading Book)   [681]
The Chronicles of Narnia   (Middle Reading Book)   [683]
The Church Mouse   (Story Book)   [318]
The Cricket in Times Square
   (Middle Reading Book)   [691]
The Dark Is Rising   (Middle Reading Book)   [697]
The Doll's House   (Middle Reading Book)   [706]
Dominic   (Middle Reading Book)   [707]
The Fledgling   (Middle Reading Book)   [716]
Four Dolls: Impunity Jane, the Fairy Doll, Holly, Candy
   Floss   (Middle Reading Book)   [718]
The Garden of Abdul Gasazi   (Story Book)   [351]
The Genie of Sutton Place   (Middle Reading Book)   [726]
George Shrinks   (Picture Book)   [92]
Half Magic   (Middle Reading Book)   [735]
The Haunting   (Young Adult)   [930]
The Hero and the Crown   (Middle Reading Book)   [741]
The Hobbit   (Middle Reading Book)   [743]
The Indian in the Cupboard
   (Middle Reading Book)   [760]
In the Night Kitchen   (Story Book)   [394]
Jacob Two-Two and the Dinosaur
   (Middle Reading Book)   [765]
James and the Giant Peach
   (Middle Reading Book)   [766]
Jumanji   (Story Book)   [404]
King Matt the First   (Middle Reading Book)   [780]
The King of the Pipers   (Story Book)   [408]
Kneeknock Rise   (Middle Reading Book)   [783]
Louis the Fish   (Story Book)   [421]
The Man Who Could Call Down Owls
   (Story Book)   [427]
Mary Poppins   (Middle Reading Book)   [798]
Moon Man   (Story Book)   [442]

The Mouse and the Motorcycle
   (Middle Reading Book)   [808]
Mrs. Frisby and the Rats of NIMH
   (Middle Reading Book)   [810]
My Father's Dragon   (Early Reading Book)   [603]
The Mysteries of Harris Burdick   (Story Book)   [452]
The Nutcracker   (Middle Reading Book)   [821]
One Monday Morning   (Picture Book)   [185]
Outside Over There   (Story Book)   [463]
Patrick's Dinosaurs   (Story Book)   [472]
Peter Pan   (Middle Reading Book)   [831]
The Phantom Tollbooth   (Middle Reading Book)   [832]
Quentin Corn   (Middle Reading Book)   [840]
The Red Balloon   (Story Book)   [488]
The Reluctant Dragon   (Middle Reading Book)   [843]
Rotten Island   (Story Book)   [494]
Sailing to Cythera and Other Anatole Stories
   (Middle Reading Book)   [848]
The Shadowmaker   (Middle Reading Book)   [857]
A String in the Harp   (Middle Reading Book)   [868]
Stuart Little   (Middle Reading Book)   [869]

[185]

Tom's Midnight Garden   (Middle Reading Book)   [879]
The Tricksters   (Young Adult)   [953]
The Trumpet of the Swan   (Middle Reading Book)   [882]
Tuck Everlasting   (Middle Reading Book)   [883]
Up from Jericho Tell   (Middle Reading Book)   [885]
Watership Down   (Middle Reading Book)   [889]
Where the Wild Things Are   (Picture Book)   [259]
The Wind in the Willows   (Middle Reading Book)   [900]
The Wonderful Wizard of Oz
   (Middle Reading Book)   [903]
A Wrinkle in Time   (Middle Reading Book)   [905]
Yellow and Pink   (Picture Book)   [266]

Fear

Geraldine's Blanket   (Picture Book)   [93]
Gila Monsters Meet You at the Airport
   (Picture Book)   [94]
Go Away, Bad Dreams!   (Story Book)   [362]
Goodbye House   (Picture Book)   [97]
Harry and the Terrible Whatzit   (Picture Book)   [107]
Hiroshima No Pika   (Story Book)   [379]
Holes and Peeks   (Picture Book)   [114]
The Hospital Book   (Middle Reading Book)   [746]
Humphrey's Bear   (Picture Book)   [118]
*I Had a Friend Named Peter: Talking to Children About the
   Death of a Friend*   (Story Book)   [387]
Learning to Say Good-By: When a Parent Dies
   (Middle Reading Book)   [788]
Let's Go Swimming with Mr. Sillypants
   (Picture Book)   [135]
Libby's New Glasses   (Story Book)   [410]
Little Rabbit's Loose Tooth   (Story Book)   [415]
Maggie Doesn't Want to Move   (Story Book)   [425]
Mitchell Is Moving   (Picture Book)   [160]
My Mom Travels a Lot   (Picture Book)   [170]
Night Kites   (Young Adult)   [945]
No More Secrets for Me   (Story Book)   [457]
One-Eyed Cat   (Middle Reading Book)   [825]
Outside Over There   (Story Book)   [463]
Snuggle Piggy and the Magic Blanket
   (Picture Book)   [213]
The Something   (Story Book)   [507]
Spectacles   (Picture Book)   [215]

A Trip to the Doctor   (Picture Book)   [239]
Uncle Elephant   (Early Reading Book)   [619]
Your Turn, Doctor   (Picture Book)   [267]

Folk Tales

Abiyoyo   (Picture Book)   [24]
About Wise Men and Simpletons: Twelve Tales from
   Grimm   (Middle Reading Book)   [625]
Always Room for One More   (Story Book)   [272]
American Folk Songs for Children   (Story Book)   [275]
Anansi the Spider: A Tale from the Ashanti
   (Picture Book)   [31]
Babushka: An Old Russian Folktale   (Story Book)   [285]
Bringing the Rain to Kapiti Plain: A Nandi Tale
   (Picture Book)   [46]
Buffalo Woman   (Story Book)   [305]
The Children's Homer: The Adventures of Odysseus and the
   Tale of Troy   (Middle Reading Book)   [677]
Clever Gretchen and Other Forgotten Folk Tales
   (Middle Reading Book)   [685]
Colour Fairy Books   (Middle Reading Book)   [686]
The Crane Wife   (Story Book)   [322]
The Dancing Granny   (Story Book)   [325]
Daniel O'Rourke   (Picture Book)   [58]
D'Aulaire's Book of Greek Myths   (Story Book)   [326]
Dawn   (Picture Book)   [60]
The Devil and Mother Crump   (Story Book)   [330]
Duffy and the Devil   (Story Book)   [336]
The Emperor's New Clothes   (Picture Book)   [68]
The Enchanted Caribou   (Picture Book)   [69]
Everyone Knows What a Dragon Looks Like
   (Story Book)   [341]
Eyes of the Dragon   (Picture Book)   [71]
Flossie & the Fox   (Story Book)   [345]
Foolish Rabbit's Big Mistake   (Picture Book)   [84]
The Fool of the World and the Flying Ship
   (Story Book)   [346]
The Gift of the Sacred Dog   (Story Book)   [355]
The Girl Who Cried Flowers and Other Tales
   (Middle Reading Book)   [730]
The Girl Who Loved Wild Horses   (Story Book)   [358]
The Good Giants and the Bad Pukwudgies
   (Story Book)   [364]

Hear the Wind Blow: American Folk Songs Retold
   (Middle Reading Book)   [740]
The Helen Oxenbury Nursery Story Book
   (Story Book)   [373]
How the Sun Was Brought Back to the Sky
   (Story Book)   [384]
It Could Always Be Worse: A Yiddish Folk Tale
   (Story Book)   [398]
Jump! The Adventures of Brer Rabbit
   (Middle Reading Book)   [773]
The Juniper Tree   (Middle Reading Book)   [775]
The Knee-High Man and Other Tales   (Story Book)   [409]
Little Red Riding Hood   (Story Book)   [417]
Louhi, Witch of North Farm   (Story Book)   [420]
The Maid of the North: Feminist Folk Tales From Around the
   World   (Middle Reading Book)   [796]
The Man Who Kept House   (Picture Book)   [150]
Mazel and Shlimazel: Or the Milk of a Lioness
   (Story Book)   [431]
Millions of Cats   (Picture Book)   [159]
Mufaro's Beautiful Daughters: An African Tale
   (Story Book)   [448]
Ol' Paul, the Mighty Logger   (Story Book)   [460]
One Fine Day   (Picture Book)   [181]
The Ox of the Wonderful Horns and Other African Folktales
   (Story Book)   [467]
Paul Bunyan   (Story Book)   [473]
The People Could Fly: American Black Folktales
   (Middle Reading Book)   [830]
Potatoes, Potatoes   (Picture Book)   [198]
Scary Stories to Tell in the Dark: Collected from American
   Folklore   (Middle Reading Book)   [850]
Seasons of Splendor   (Middle Reading Book)   [851]
The Selkie Girl   (Story Book)   [498]
Shadow   (Story Book)   [499]
The Sign in Mendel's Window   (Story Book)   [501]
The Stonecutter: A Japanese Folktale   (Picture Book)   [216]
Stone Soup   (Picture Book)   [217]
A Story, a Story   (Picture Book)   [218]
The Story of Jumping Mouse   (Picture Book)   [220]
Tales of Pan   (Story Book)   [523]
The Teeny-Tiny Woman   (Picture Book)   [225]
The Three Bears & Fifteen Other Stories
   (Story Book)   [528]

[15]

Grandparents

Growing Up

[293]

[853]

Health

History

Holidays

[49]

Humor

[176]

Perfect the Pig   (Story Book)   [475]
The Pigs Wedding   (Picture Book)   [195]
Quentin Corn   (Middle Reading Book)   [840]
The Three Little Pigs   (Picture Book)   [230]

Poetry and Verse
A Apple Pie   (Picture Book)   [21]
All Small   (Picture Book)   [26]
A, My Name Is Alice   (Early Reading Book)   [567]
As I Was Going Up and Down   (Picture Book)   [40]
The Baby's Bedtime Book   (Picture Book)   [41]
A Book of Americans   (Middle Reading Book)   [660]
The Book of Pigericks: Pig Limericks   (Story Book)   [300]
Brats   (Story Book)   [303]
Catch Me & Kiss Me & Say It Again
   (Picture Book)   [51]
The Cat in the Hat   (Early Reading Book)   [574]
Celebrations   (Story Book)   [308]
A Child's Garden of Verses   (Story Book)   [313]

My pj's with feet
And face on the seat

[133]

A Child's Treasury of Poems   (Story Book)   [314]
Custard and Company   (Middle Reading Book)   [693]
Dawn   (Picture Book)   [61]
Everett Anderson's Goodbye   (Story Book)   [339]
Father Fox's Pennyrhymes   (Picture Book)   [74]
Finger Rhymes   (Picture Book)   [77]
For I Will Consider My Cat Jeoffry   (Story Book)   [347]
A Great Big Ugly Man Came Up and Tied His Horse to Me   (Story Book)   [367]
Green Eggs and Ham   (Early Reading Book)   [587]
Hector Protector and As I Went over the Water: Two Nursery Rhymes   (Picture Book)   [110]
Honey, I Love and Other Love Poems
   (Picture Book)   [115]
Horton Hatches the Egg   (Story Book)   [380]
How the Grinch Stole Christmas   (Story Book)   [383]
It Does Not Say Meow and Other Animal Riddle Rhymes
   (Picture Book)   [128]
It's Raining Said John Twaining: Danish Nursery Rhymes
   (Picture Book)   [129]
James Marshall's Mother Goose   (Picture Book)   [132]
Jelly Belly   (Story Book)   [400]
Jesse Bear, What Will You Wear?   (Picture Book)   [133]
The Light in the Attic   (Middle Reading Book)   [790]
Marguerite, Go Wash Your Feet!   (Story Book)   [430]
Mother Goose: A Collection of Classic Nursery Rhymes
   (Story Book)   [445]
The Night Before Christmas   (Picture Book)   [174]
One Fish, Two Fish, Red Fish, Blue Fish
   (Picture Book)   [182]
Over the Moon: A Book of Nursery Rhymes
   (Story Book)   [464]
The Oxford Book of Poetry for Children
   (Middle Reading Book)   [827]
Piping Down the Valleys Wild
   (Middle Reading Book)   [835]
The Random House Book of Mother Goose
   (Story Book)   [486]
The Random House Book of Poetry for Children
   (Story Book)   [487]
Read-Aloud Rhymes for the Very Young
   (Picture Book)   [200]
The Real Mother Goose   (Picture Book)   [201]
Secrets of a Small Brother   (Story Book)   [496]

Rabbits

[222]

Reference Books

Religion

Science

Siblings

I Love My Baby Sister (Most of the Time)
(Picture Book) [125]
A Lion for Lewis (Picture Book) [136]
Little Rabbit's Loose Tooth (Story Book) [415]
The Maggie B (Picture Book) [146]
Max's First Word (Picture Book) [155]
Mr. and Mrs. Pig's Evening Out (Picture Book) [163]
My Mama Needs Me (Picture Book) [169]
Oh, Boy! Babies! (Story Book) [458]
101 Things to Do with a Baby (Picture Book) [183]
Outside Over There (Story Book) [463]
Rotten Island (Story Book) [494]
Secrets of a Small Brother (Story Book) [496]
Stevie (Story Book) [510]
That New Pet! (Story Book) [527]
This Is Betsy (Picture Book) [227]
Thy Friend Obadiah (Picture Book) [232]
When the New Baby Comes I'm Moving Out
(Picture Book) [250]
Where the Lilies Bloom (Middle Reading Book) [894]
Worse Than Willy! (Story Book) [562]

Sports

The Contender (Young Adult) [920]
Dirt Bike Racer (Middle Reading Book) [703]
The Fox Steals Home (Middle Reading Book) [719]
Hooray for Snail (Picture Book) [116]
The Kid from Tomkinsville
(Middle Reading Book) [778]
The Moves Make the Man (Young Adult) [944]

Series Books

The Accident (Story Book) [268]
Alfie Gives a Hand (Story Book) [270]
Amanda Pig and Her Big Brother Oliver
(Early Reading Book) [565]
Amelia Bedelia (Early Reading Book) [566]
Anastasia Krupnik (Middle Reading Book) [631]
And My Mean Old Mother Will Be Sorry, Blackboard Bear
(Picture Book) [32]
Angelina Ballerina (Picture Book) [33]
Anne of Green Gables (Middle Reading Book) [636]

Anno's Counting House (Middle Reading Book) [637]
Anno's Journey (Wordless Book) [5]
Arthur's Honey Bear (Early Reading Book) [570]
Arthur's Nose (Story Book) [282]
The Baby's Bedtime Book (Picture Book) [41]
The Bagthorpe Saga (Middle Reading Book) [643]
Ballet Shoes (Middle Reading Book) [644]
A Bear Called Paddington (Early Reading Book) [571]
Bedtime for Frances (Story Book) [293]
The Berenstain Bears' Trouble with Money
(Story Book) [294]
Betsy Tacy (Early Reading Book) [572]
Big Red (Middle Reading Book) [652]
"B" Is for Betsy (Early Reading Book) [573]
The Black Cauldron (Middle Reading Book) [655]
The Black Stallion (Middle Reading Book) [657]
The Borrowers (Middle Reading Book) [661]
A Boy, a Dog and a Frog (Wordless Book) [7]
The Brambly Hedge Books (Story Book) [302]
Building the Snowman (Wordless Book) [8]
Bunnicula: A Rabbit Tale of Mystery
(Middle Reading Book) [667]
A Chair for My Mother (Story Book) [309]
The Chalk Box Kid (Early Reading Book) [576]
The Changes (Middle Reading Book) [673]
The Chronicles of Narnia (Middle Reading Book) [683]
The Church Mouse (Story Book) [318]
Colour Fairy Books (Middle Reading Book) [686]
Commander Toad in Space (Early Reading Book) [577]
The Cricket in Times Square
(Middle Reading Book) [691]
Curious George (Picture Book) [56]
The Dark Is Rising (Middle Reading Book) [697]
A Dog on Barkham Street (Middle Reading Book) [704]
Einstein Anderson, Science Sleuth
(Middle Reading Book) [710]
Encyclopedia Brown, Boy Detective
(Middle Reading Book) [711]
Ernest and Celestine (Picture Book) [70]
Everett Anderson's Goodbye (Story Book) [339]
Family (Picture Book) [72]
Fish Face (Early Reading Book) [583]
Five Fall into Adventure (Middle Reading Book) [715]
Fix-It (Picture Book) [82]

[754]

Mitzi's Honeymoon with Nana Potts
  (Middle Reading Book)   [805]
The Moffats   (Middle Reading Book)   [806]
Morris and Boris: Three Stories
  (Early Reading Book)   [600]
The Mouse and the Motorcycle
  (Middle Reading Book)   [808]
Mrs. Piggle-Wiggle   (Early Reading Book)   [166]
My Book   (Picture Book)   [167]
My Father's Dragon   (Early Reading Book)   [603]
My Friend the Vampire   (Middle Reading Book)   [812]
The Not-Just-Anybody Family
  (Middle Reading Book)   [820]
Nutty for President   (Middle Reading Book)   [823]
One Fat Summer   (Young Adult)   [946]
Paddy's Evening Out   (Wordless Book)   [16]
Pinkerton, Behave   (Story Book)   [481]
Pippi Longstocking   (Early Reading Book)   [608]
Ramona   (Early Reading Book)   [609]
Rotten Ralph   (Picture Book)   [205]
Sailing to Cythera and Other Anatole Stories
  (Middle Reading Book)   [848]
The Shrinking of Treehorn   (Early Reading Book)   [612]
Small Poems   (Middle Reading Book)   [861]
Soup   (Middle Reading Book)   [863]
Space Case   (Story Book)   [508]
The Story of Babar   (Story Book)   [513]
The Story of King Arthur and His Knights
  (Middle Reading Book)   [865]
The Stupids Have a Ball   (Story Book)   [518]
This Is Betsy   (Picture Book)   [227]
Today Was a Terrible Day   (Story Book)   [531]
The Tomten and the Fox   (Story Book)   [533]
A Very Young Dancer   (Early Reading Book)   [620]
Westmark   (Middle Reading Book)   [891]
Where Is My Friend? A Word Concept Book
  (Picture Book)   [255]
Where's Spot?   (Picture Book)   [256]
The Wild Swans   (Story Book)   [558]
Will I Have a Friend?   (Story Book)   [559]
Winnie-the-Pooh   (Middle Reading Book)   [901]
The Wonderful Wizard of Oz
  (Middle Reading Book)   [903]
Worse Than Willy!   (Story Book)   [562]
A Wrinkle in Time   (Middle Reading Book)   [905]

Books in Other Recommended Editions

A Child's Christmas in Wales
  (Middle Reading Book)   [678]
A Christmas Carol   (Middle Reading Book)   [682]
Cinderella   (Story Book)   [319]
The Emperor's New Clothes   (Picture Book)   [68]
Hansel and Gretel   (Story Book)   [370]
Kidnapped: Being the Memoirs of the Adventures of David
  Balfour in the Year 1751
  (Middle Reading Book)   [779]
A Little Princess   (Middle Reading Book)   [793]
Little Red Riding Hood   (Story Book)   [417]
The Nightingale   (Story Book)   [454]
Ol' Paul, the Mighty Logger   (Story Book)   [460]
Peter and the Wolf   (Story Book)   [476]
Rumpelstiltskin   (Story Book)   [495]
The Secret Garden   (Middle Reading Book)   [853]
The Sleeping Beauty   (Story Book)   [503]
The Teeny-Tiny Woman   (Picture Book)   [225]
The Three Little Pigs   (Picture Book)   [230]
Treasure Island   (Middle Reading Book)   [880]
The Twelve Days of Christmas   (Picture Book)   [240]
The Ugly Duckling   (Story Book)   [541]
The Velveteen Rabbit   (Story Book)   [543]
The Wild Swans   (Story Book)   [558]

Reading Rainbow Titles

Abiyoyo   (Picture Book)   [24]
Alexander and the Terrible, Horrible, No Good, Very Bad
  Day   (Story Book)   [269]
The Amazing Bone   (Story Book)   [274]
Anno's Journey   (Wordless Book)   [5]
Bea and Mr. Jones   (Story Book)   [289]
Best Friends   (Story Book)   [295]
The Bionic Bunny Show   (Story Book)   [299]
Bringing the Rain to Kapiti Plain: A Nandi Tale
  (Picture Book)   [46]
Caps for Sale   (Picture Book)   [49]
A Chair for My Mother   (Story Book)   [309]
Dakota Dugout   (Story Book)   [324]
The Day Jimmy's Boa Ate the Wash   (Story Book)   [328]
Digging Up Dinosaurs   (Early Reading Book)   [580]

[166]

BIBLIOGRAPHY

There are a great many books about children's books and reading as they relate to child development. This core list will lead you to many other titles.

American Picturebooks from Noah's Ark to The Beast Within by Barbara Bader. New York: Macmillan, 1976.

Choosing Books for Children: A Commonsense Guide by Betsy Hearne. New York: Delacorte, 1981.

Choosing Books for Kids: Choosing the Right Book for the Right Child at the Right Time by Joanne F. Oppenheim, Barbara Brenner, Betty D. Boegehold. New York: Ballantine Books, 1986.

A Parent's Guide to Children's Reading by Nancy Larrick. New York: Bantam, 1982.

The Read Aloud Handbook by Jim Trelease. New York: Penguin, 1979.

Reading for the Love of It. Best Books for Young Readers by Michele Landsberg. New York: Prentice-Hall, 1987.

The RIF Guide to Encouraging Young Readers, edited by Ruth Graves. New York: Doubleday, 1987.

The Uses of Enchantment by Bruno Bettelheim. New York: Knopf. 1976.

CONTINUATION OF THE PERMISSIONS/ACKNOWLEDGMENTS

Clarion Books: Illustration from *Harry and the Terrible Whatzit* by Dick Gackenbach. Copyright © 1977 by Dick Gackenbach; illustration from *Little Sister and the Month Brothers* by Beatrice Schenk de Regniers. Text copyright © 1976 by Beatrice Schenk de Regniers. Pictures Copyright © 1976 by Margo Tomes. Reprinted by permission of Clarion Books/Ticknor & Fields, a Houghton Mifflin Company.

Coward-McCann, Inc.: Illustrations by Wanda Gag from *Millions of Cats* by Wanda Gag, copyright 1928 by Coward-McCann, Inc., copyright renewed 1956 by Robert Janssen. Reprinted by permission of Coward-McCann, Inc.

Dial Books for Young Readers: Illustration from *Your Turn, Doctor* by Deborah Robinson and Carla Perez, M.D., pictures by Deborah Robinson. Pictures copyright © 1982 by Deborah Robinson; illustration from *A Boy, a Dog and a Frog* by Mercer Mayer. Copyright © 1976 by Mercer Mayer; illustration from *Flossie and the Fox* by Patricia C. McKissack, pictures by Rachel Isadora. Pictures copyright © 1986 by Rachel Isadora; illustration from *Amanda Pig and Her Big Brother Oliver* by Jean Van Leeuwen, pictures by Ann Schweninger. Pictures copyright © 1982 by Ann Schweninger; illustration from *The Boy Who Was Followed Home* by Margaret Mahy, pictures by Steven Kellogg. Pictures copyright © 1975 by Steven Kellogg; illustration from *Max's First Word* by Rosemary Wells. Copyright © 1979 by Rosemary Wells. Reprinted by permission of the publisher, Dial Books for Young Readers.

Doubleday & Co.: Illustrations from *D'Aulaires' Book of Greek Myths* by Ingri and Edgar Parin D'Aulaire. Copyright © 1962 by Ingri and Edgar Parin d'Aulaire; illustration from *Noah's Ark* by Peter Spier. Copyright © 1977 by Peter Spier. Reprinted by permission of Doubleday, a division of Bantam, Doubleday, Dell Publishing Group, Inc.

E.P. Dutton: Illustration from *The Balancing Girl* by Bernice Rabe, illustrated by Lillian Hoban. Illustrations copyright © 1981 by Lillian Hoban; illustration from *The Guinea Pig ABC* by Kate Duke. Copyright © 1983 by Kate Duke; illustration from *Rumpelstiltskin* by Paul O. Zelinsky. Copyright © 1986 by Paul O. Zelinsky; illustration from *Tales of a Fourth Grade Nothing* by Judy Blume, illustrated by Roy Doty. Illustrations copyright © 1972 by E.P. Dutton; illustration from *Winnie-the-Pooh* by A.A. Milne, illustrated by Ernest H. Shepard. Copyright 1926 by E.P. Dutton, renewed 1954 by A.A. Milne. Rights in the U.S. administered by E.P. Dutton. Rights in Canada administered by McClelland & Steward Ltd. Reprinted by permission of the publishers, E.P. Dutton, a division of NAL Penguin Inc. and the Canadian publisher, McClelland and Stewart, Toronto.

Farrar, Straus, Giroux: Illustration from *The Winter Wren* by Brock Cole. Copyright © 1984 by Brock Cole; illustration from

Louis the Fish by Arthur Yorinks, illustrated by Richard Egielski. Copyright © 1980 by Arthur Yorinks and Richard Egielski; illustration from *Goldie the Dollmaker* by M.B. Goffstein. Copyright © 1969 by M.B. Goffstein; illustration from *Amos and Boris* by William Steig. Copyright © 1971 by William Steig; illustration from *Duffy and the Devil* by Harve and Margot Zemach. Copyright © 1973 by Farrar, Straus and Giroux, Inc. Reprinted by permission of Farrar, Straus and Giroux, Inc.

Four Winds Press: Illustration from *Everyone Knows What a Dragon Looks Like* by Jay Williams, illustrated by Mercer Mayer. Illustration Copyright © 1976 by Mercer Mayer; illustrations from *Up Goes the Skyscraper* by Gail Gibbons. Copyright © 1986 by Gail Gibbons. Reprinted with permission of Four Winds Press, an Imprint of Macmillan Publishing Company.

David R. Godine, Publisher.: Illustrations from *Rotten Island* by William Steig. Copyright © 1969, 1984 by William Steig. Reprinted by permission of David R. Godine, Publisher.

Greenwillow Books: Illustration from *A Chair for My Mother* by Vera Williams. Copyright © 1982 by Vera Williams; illustration from *Ernest and Celestine* by Duculot Paris-Gembloux. Copyright © 1981 by Duculot Paris-Gembloux; illustration from *Freight Train* by Donald Crews. Copyright © 1978 by Donald Crews; illustration from *Ten, Nine, Eight* by Molly Bang. Copyright © 1983 by Molly Garrett Bang; illustration from *Have You Seen My Duckling?* by Nancy Tafuri. Copyright © 1984 by Nancy Tafuri. Reprinted by permission of Greenwillow Books, a division of William Morrow & Co., New York.

Harcourt Brace Jovanovich, Inc.: Illustration from *Jump: The Adventures of Brer Rabbit* by Joel Chandler Harris, adapted by Van Dyke Parks. Illustration by Barry Most, copyright © 1986 by Pennyroyal Press, Inc.; illustration from *The Man Who Kept House* by Michael Hague and Kathleen Hague. Illustration copyright © 1981 by Michael Hague; illustration from *Many Moons* by James Thurber, illustrated by Louis Slobodkin, copyright 1943 by James Thurber, renewed 1971 by Helen Thurber; illustrations from *A Visit to William Blake's Inn* by Nancy Willard. Illustration copyright © 1981 by Alice Provensen and Martin Provensen; illustration from *The Wedding Procession of the Rag Doll and the Broom Handle and Who Was In It* by Carl Sandburg. Illustration copyright © 1967 by Harriet Pincus; illustration from *The Borrowers* by Mary Norton. Illustration copyright © 1981 by Beth Krush and Joe Krush; illustration from *Mary Poppins,* Revised edition, by P.L. Travers. Illustration by Mary Shepard. Copyright 1934, © 1962 by P.L. Travers. Illustration from *Merry Christmas, Strega Nona* by Tomie de Paola. Illustrations copyright © 1986 by Tomie de Paola. Reprinted by permission of Harcourt Brace Jovanovich, Inc.

Harper & Row, Publishers, Inc.: Illustration from *Bedtime for Frances* by Russell C. Hoban, pictures by Garth Williams. Pictures copyright © 1960 by Garth Williams; illustration from *Betsy-Tacy* by Maud Hart Lovelace/(Thomas Y. Crowell). Illustrations by Lois

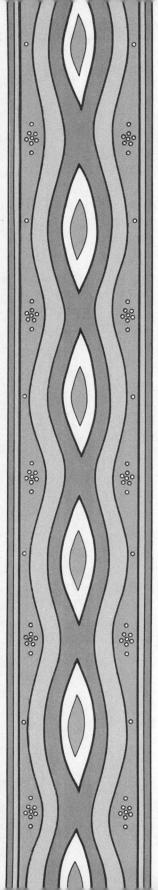

NOTES